IMAGES
of America

Boricuas in the Magic City

Puerto Ricans in Miami

On the Cover: Revelers enjoy the Fiesta San Juan Bautista while performers from Puerto Rico play in this annual event in 1980. These events were usually held either at the Waikiki Hotel or the Marco Polo Hotel in North Miami Beach. Attendees would dance into the night, and then many would walk down to the beach to perform the ritual of jumping into the water backward near midnight. (Courtesy of Gil Garcia.)

IMAGES
of America

Boricuas in the Magic City

Puerto Ricans in Miami

Dr. Victor Vazquez-Hernandez

ARCADIA
PUBLISHING

ISBN 978-1-4671-0648-1

Published by Arcadia Publishing
Charleston, South Carolina

Printed in the United States of America

Library of Congress Control Number: 2021934615

For all general information, please contact Arcadia Publishing:
Telephone 843-853-2070
Fax 843-853-0044
E-mail sales@arcadiapublishing.com
For customer service and orders:
Toll-Free 1-888-313-2665

Visit us on the Internet at www.arcadiapublishing.com

I want to dedicate this book to the Puerto Rican Community in Miami and especially to the hundreds and thousands of Boricuas who have made the trek to the land of the Tequesta to carve out space, especially in Wynwood, for the past 100 years. I also dedicate this book to my family and my parents, who moved here half a century ago and made Miami an ancestral home for the Vazquez-Hernandez clan.

Contents

Acknowledgments

I started documenting the history of Puerto Ricans in Miami in 2005. I met several people when I first moved here who helped me navigate the community and met the leaders, who welcomed me. A key figure in this process was the late Raul A. Martinez, who was the CEO of ASPIRA, one of the organizations featured in this book. Through his contacts, I was able to interview some important people in this community. Some, like Raul, are no longer with us. So, as I undertook the task of producing this book, I had to identify not only key individuals, but because this book relies on photographs to tell the story, I had to also identify important archival sources. Then, as I was about to begin collecting photographs, COVID-19 hit, and all the archives closed; in fact, as of the printing of this book, they remain closed. I lost a super important source of photographs. In addition, many individuals who had photographs and archives in their homes understandably did not feel comfortable letting strangers in.

Fortunately, some really special folks came through, and I was able to gather enough photographs to make a decent attempt. I am indebted to Carmen Pedrogo and her daughter. Carmen and her husband, Jose, came to Miami in 1956, and have been here since. As she is a founding member of the National Conference of Puerto Rican Women–Miami Chapter (NACOPRW) and is the archivist of the group, she put the collection at my disposal. Her daughter, also named Carmen, provided family photographs that also helped to tell the story. Dr. Paul George, a great friend and historian, was a blessing because of his knowledge of the history of South Florida. Paul read a draft of the manuscript and provided a critical eye, and put me in touch with Dave Martinez, a Puerto Rican whose family moved to Miami in the 1940s. Paul also connected me to Casey Piket and Larry Wiggins, great documentarians who provided photographs and articles. On the community side, Luis DeRosa, president of the Puerto Rican Chamber of Commerce, shared his collection of photographs with me, as did Miream Sierra, CEO of ASPIRA, who provided me access to their photos. Paul Velez, CEO of Borinquen Clinics, was very helpful in understanding this important institution and for providing some materials as well. Hector Diaz, a founding member of the Puerto Rican Professional Association (PROFESA), connected me to Raul Duany, the first president of the group, who provided photographs and context. Jose Luis Rodriguez of the Puerto Rican Cultural Center helped with photographs of the group. Leticia Baro provided access to her family photographs. Norah Venegas of NACOPRW was very helpful in bettering my understanding of the organization. My wife's family connected me to Deacon Gregorio Velez's daughters, who also provided photographs. My wife Mayra, daughter Sofia, and son Victor also pitched in and took a few photographs I needed as well.

However, there is always that one indispensable person without whom I would have been sunk, and that is Gil Garcia Andino. Gil was my lifesaver because not only is he an accomplished chemist, he is also a professional photographer with his own studio. The photographs in this book were all prepared by him in order to be published. I could not have done that, period. In addition, Gil has been photographing and documenting this community for almost 40 years. There would not have been a book without Gil. Thank you all!

INTRODUCTION

Puerto Ricans began making their trek to Miami before 1920. In 1917, after 20 years of US colonial control of the island, Puerto Ricans became US citizens. Unencumbered by immigration restrictions, they left the island for all points north. At first, the bulk of Puerto Ricans headed for large cigar manufacturing cities like New York, Philadelphia, Key West, and Tampa. But as Miami began to flourish in the 1920s, some Puerto Ricans began to give the city a look. When Pan American Airways began direct flights between Miami and San Juan in 1929, the fuse was lit. Mechanics, entertainers, hotel workers, bankers, and farmers, among others, began to trickle in, and later, a steady stream of travelers arrived in the Magic City. Others who had ventured north decided to follow another stream that headed south from New York and other places. They converged on places like Wynwood and the beginnings of a garment manufacturing hub.

World War II put Miami on the map for all the soldiers, sailors, and airmen who were trained here. Of those who came through during the war, some returned to try their luck in the postwar boom. A handful of Puerto Rican industrialists and bankers concerned about political developments on the island decided to bring some of their capital and invest in South Florida. So, by the early 1950s, a Puerto Rican Barrio became evident in Wynwood that would expand and grow over the next decades.

Puerto Ricans in Miami, like all other groups before and after, established organizations, businesses, and religious groups and worked hard, sometimes for little money. But they established roots and character.

This photographic essay attempts to provide the reader with a visual overview of that movement and its transformation over a 100-year period.

One

Citizenship and the Search for a Better Life

The 1920s and 1930s proved to be an important decade for the arrival of Puerto Ricans in Miami. The advent of commercial aviation, led by the rise of Pan American Airways, created travel opportunities for islanders and, as it turned out, employment possibilities for arriving Puerto Ricans. By 1920, they began arriving in Miami in a small but steady stream to work in the growing tourism, manufacturing, and agricultural sectors. A few of the first Puerto Ricans arrived to work as either farmworkers or domestics, and they settled in the area of the Redlands, in Homestead.

In January 1929, Pan Am began direct flights between San Juan and Miami, establishing a direct line of migration to the city. Not all Puerto Ricans came directly from the island. Most of the steady flow of migrants came by rail or automobile from places like New York, where a larger Puerto Rican community already existed. By the mid-1930s, as the economic situation deteriorated on the island amid the Great Depression, the exodus of Puerto Ricans to the United States, which had slowed in the late 1920s, resumed. Florida appeared primed to welcome and encourage Puerto Ricans to move there. An important reason for this development stemmed from Pres. Franklin D. Roosevelt's appointment in 1933 of Robert H. Gore, a part-time Floridian, as governor of Puerto Rico. Gore was a wealthy newspaperman from the Midwest who spent his winters in Fort Lauderdale. From the beginning of his tenure in Puerto Rico, Governor Gore touted Florida as an excellent place to send unemployed Puerto Rican laborers. Indeed, there was a need at the time for workers in the Sunshine State, especially in agriculture.

When World War II broke out, Miami and its vicinity became a hub for training soldiers and sailors. Tens of thousands of service members passed through, a few of them Puerto Ricans. As a result of having been in the city, some remained here or returned permanently after the war. Others came for the business opportunities and remained in the city as well.

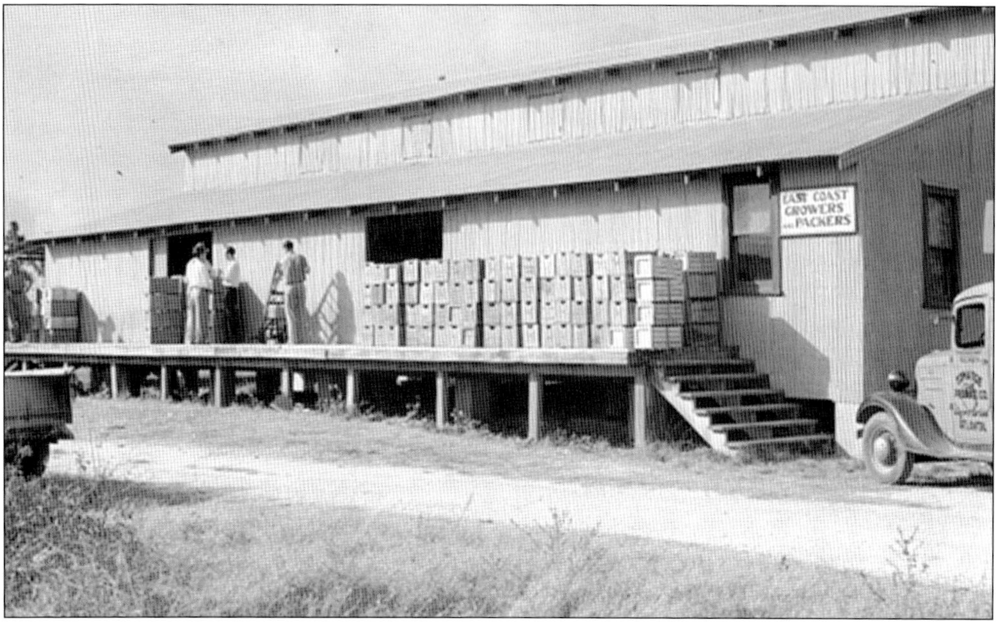

The 1920 US Census found a handful of Puerto Ricans living in Miami–Dade County. Some, like Francisca Landron and her son Angel Lopez, lived in the agricultural community of the Redlands, near Homestead in South Miami. Both Landron and her son were listed as "Black," and she worked as a servant with a private family while Angel worked in a fruit store similar to the one pictured here in 1930. (Courtesy of National Archives.)

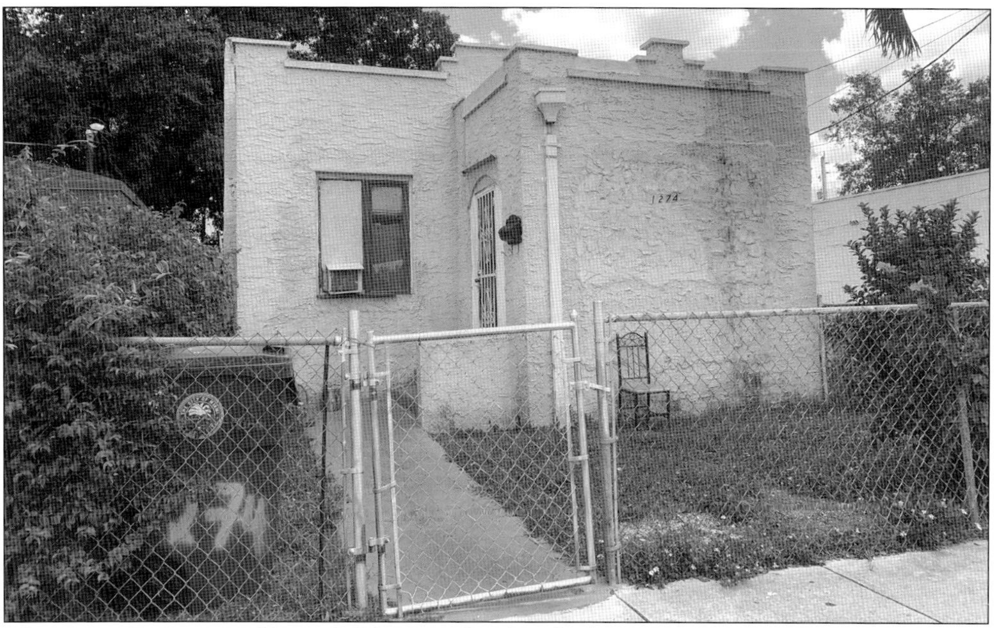

J. Lawrence Gutierrez and his wife, Margaret, lived in this house at 1274 NW Thirty-Ninth Street in 1930. He was part of a smattering of Puerto Ricans living in Miami at the time, having arrived in 1923. J. Lawrence worked for Pan American Airways at the municipal airport as a shipping clerk. His brother Benito joined him in 1931 and worked as a commercial artist in downtown Miami. (Courtesy of Luz. S. Vazquez-Hernandez.)

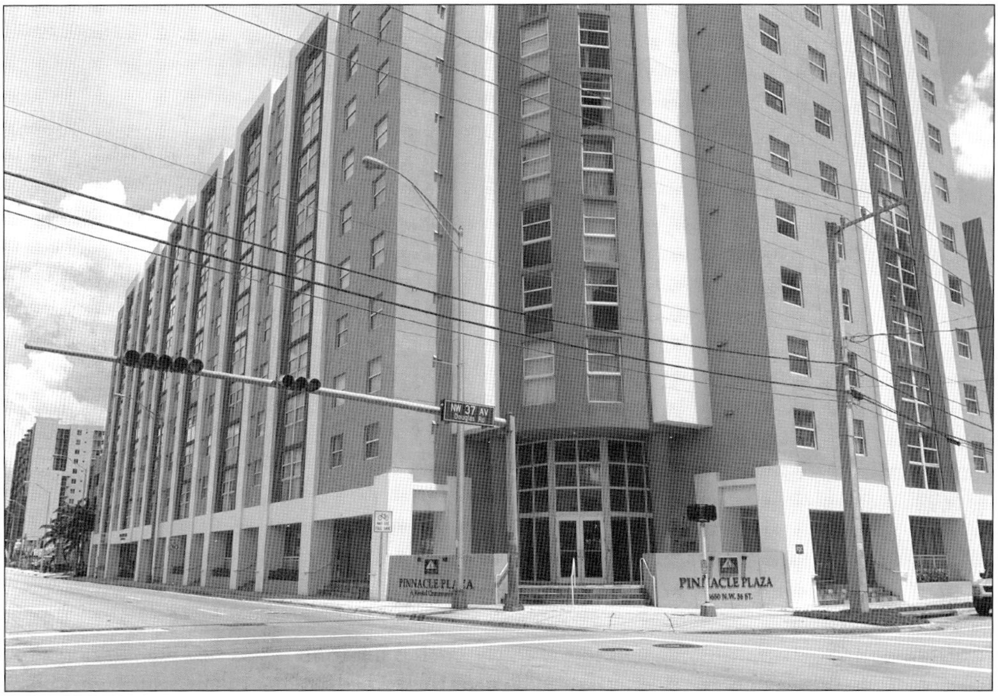

Pictured here is the current intersection of NW Thirty-Sixth Street and NW Thirty-Seventh Avenue. In 1940, Andre Marin and his wife, both Puerto Ricans, managed a barbecue stand at this location on the southeast corner, adjacent to eastbound traffic toward downtown. They were among the several hundred Puerto Ricans who lived in Miami at the time. The stand was an ideal location for those heading to the city from the airport. (Courtesy of Mayra L. Hernandez.)

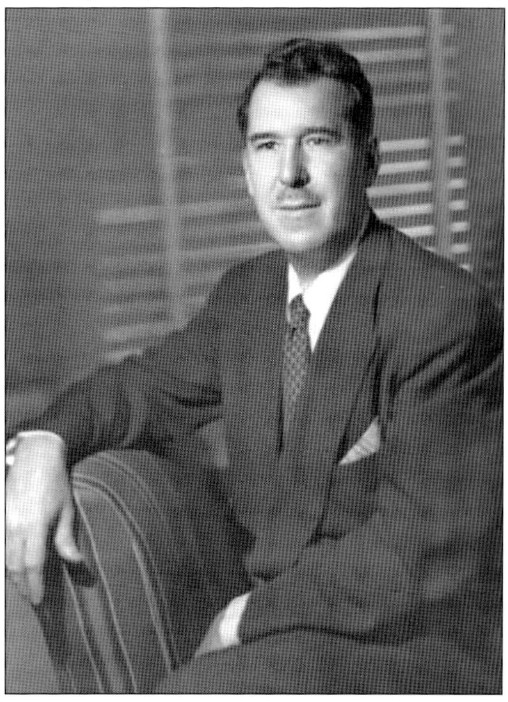

Jose A. Ferre, an industrialist and landowner in Puerto Rico, pictured here in 1940, moved his family, including seven-year-old son Maurice, to Miami in 1942. He settled in the Brickell area along with other prominent families from the island. They opened businesses and helped to develop office spaces downtown. In addition, some of them bought large tracts of land to develop into sugar-producing plantations. (Courtesy of Meme Ferre.)

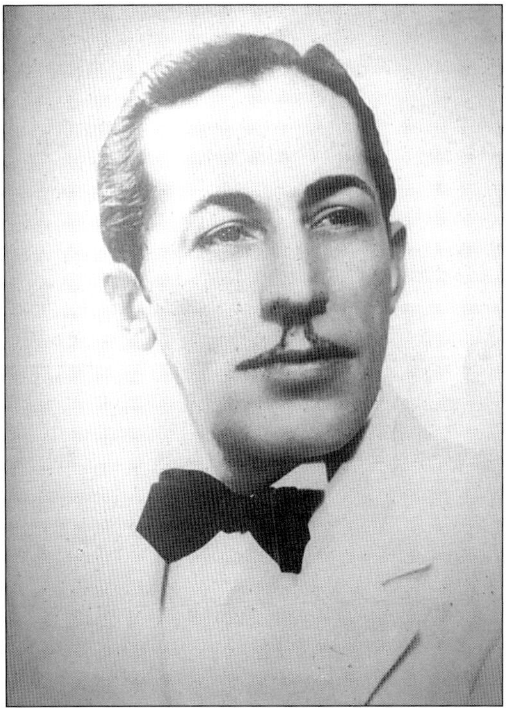

During World War II, Miami became a major hub for training US Navy and Army Air Corps personnel. This included Puerto Ricans like Rudy Israel Velez, pictured here in the late 1930s. Velez, born in Puerto Rico but raised in New York City, joined the US Army when war broke out. He was sent to Miami to train as a photographer. After the war, he returned to Miami and became a police officer. (Courtesy of Paul Velez.)

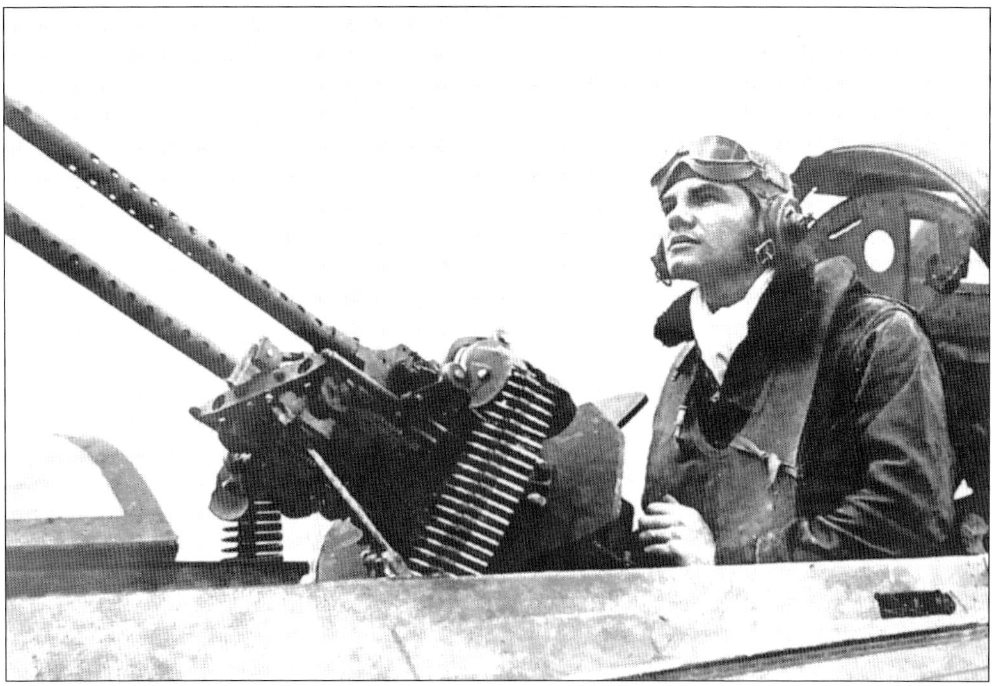

William "Marty" Martinez Jr., a gunner in a Curtis Helldiver, pictured here in 1945, was born in Puerto Rico. During the Great Depression, his father, William Sr., moved the family to New York City. When the war began, William Jr. joined the Navy. In 1943, when he was stationed at the Key West Naval Station, his father moved the whole family to Florida. (Courtesy of David Martinez-Morales.)

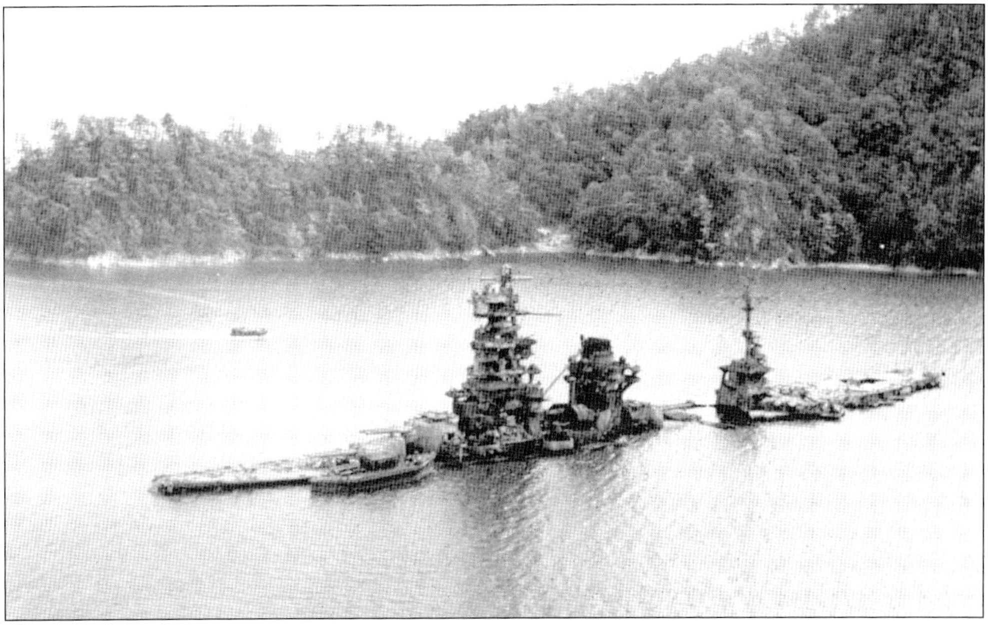

On July 24, 1945, Martinez and fellow airman William John Thompson of Air Group 87 of the USS *Ticonderoga* scored a hit with a 1,000-pound bomb on the Japanese battleship–aircraft carrier Hyuga. The ship, pictured here, was sunk, and the two airmen received a commendation from James Forrestal, secretary of the Navy. (Courtesy of David Martinez-Morales.)

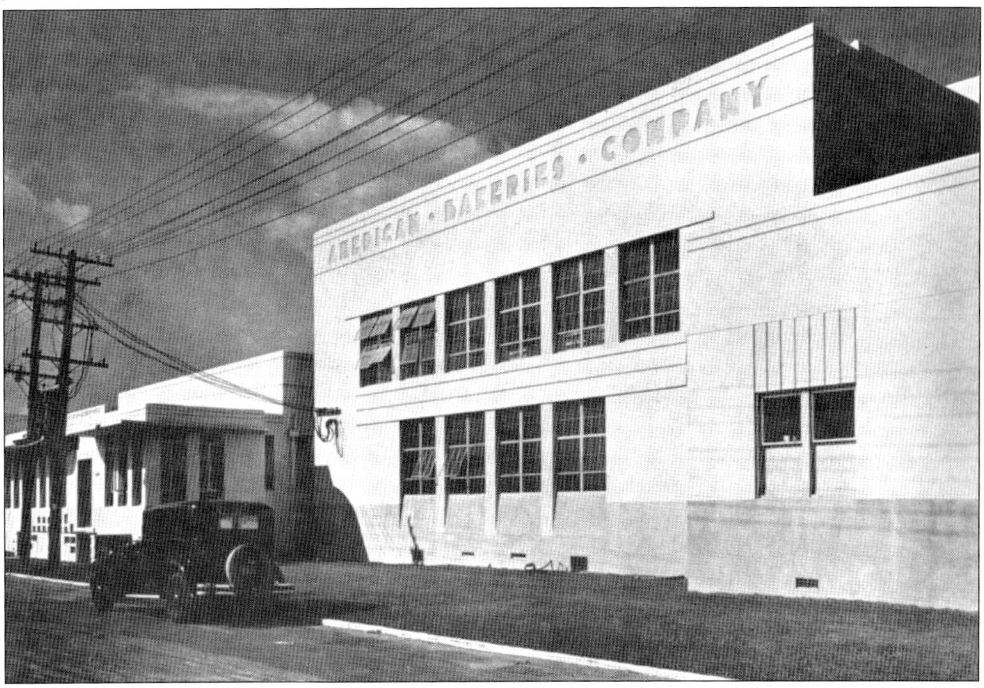

The American Bakeries Company, at 561 NW Thirty-Second Street in Wynwood, was famous for its Merita bread. Puerto Ricans like the Martinez family, who lived near there, remember the strong aroma of baked goods in the mornings. A much smaller version still exists in Wynwood. This photograph is from 1930. (Courtesy of Casey Piket.)

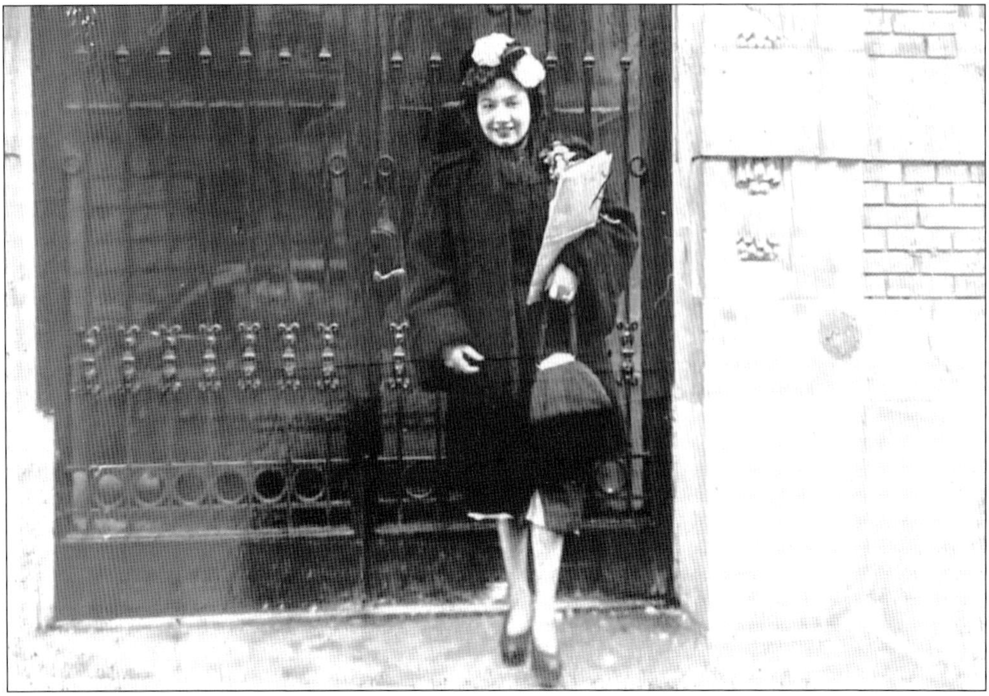

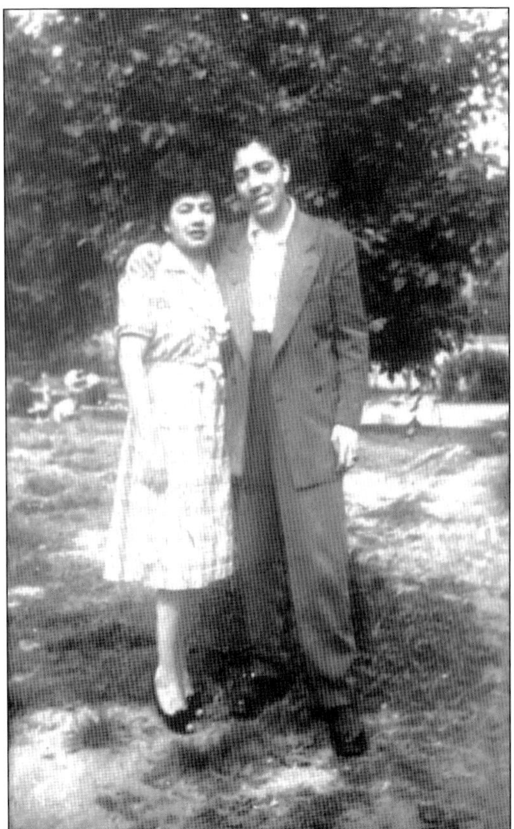

Many Puerto Ricans who move to Miami, then and now, often do not come directly from the island. Alicia (Santos) Baro was one of them; she was born on the island, but at a young age, her family moved to New York City, settling in an expanding Puerto Rican settlement in the Bronx. Young Alicia dedicated herself to study and graduated from high school in the 1930s. (Courtesy of Leticia Baro.)

Alicia is pictured with her brother around 1940 in New York. This photograph was probably taken in Crotona Park in the Bronx. Following a trend in the 1930s and 1940s, Puerto Ricans living in Manhattan began migrating to the Bronx. Soon, a large settlement began to grow there. Around this time, Alicia completed a degree in linguistics from Hunter College. (Courtesy of Leticia Baro.)

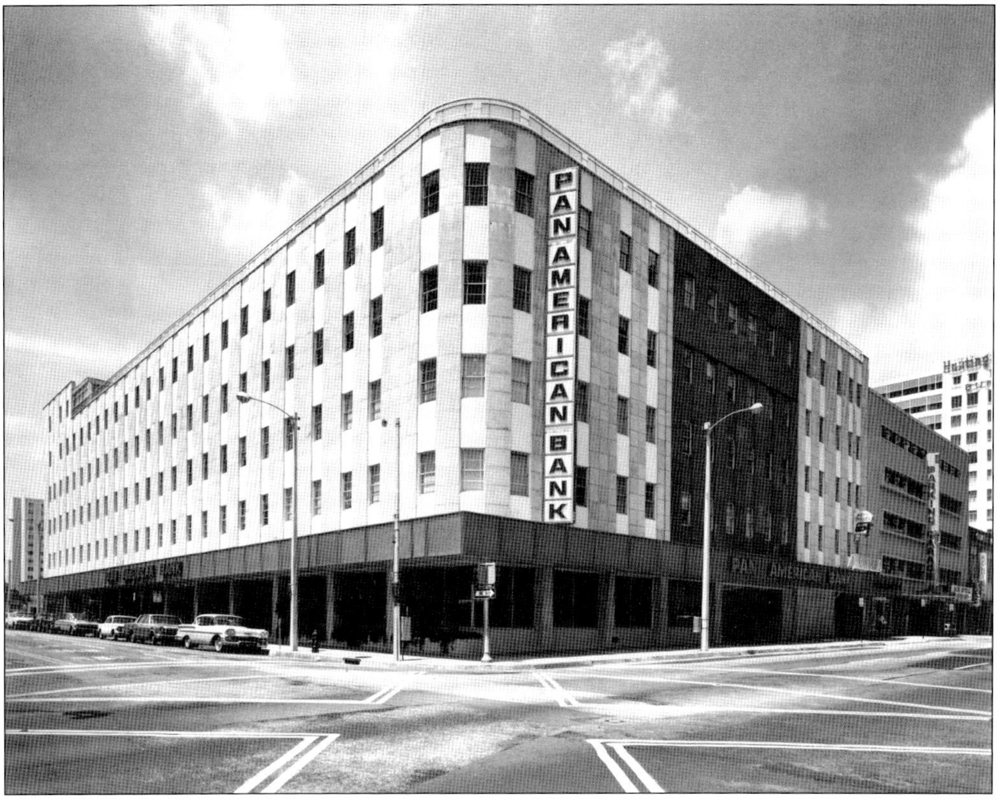

The Pan American Bank of Miami, at 250 SE First Street downtown, was founded in 1945 by Puerto Rican businessman Pedro J. Serralles. A member of the wealthy family of producers of Don Q rum and owners of thousands of acres of sugar-producing lands on the island, Serralles had begun investing in South Florida during World War II. (Courtesy of Casey Piket.)

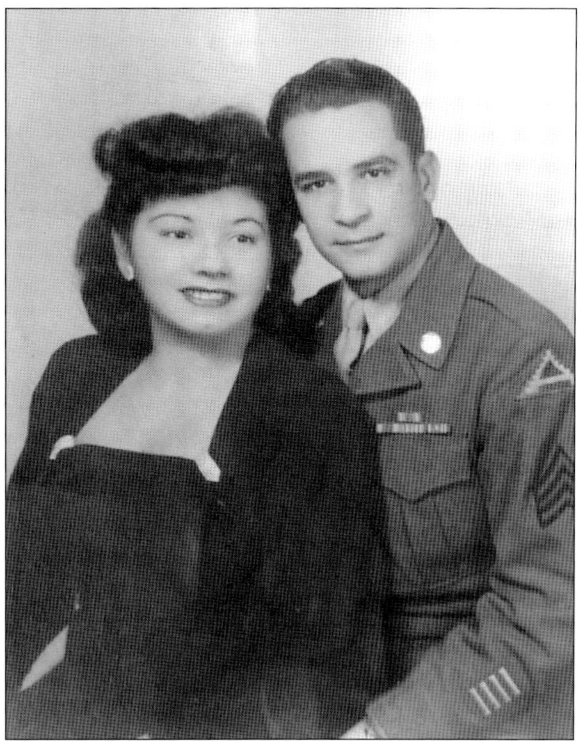

Alicia Santiago-Baro is pictured here with her husband, Sgt. Jose Baro, in 1945, when he returned from the war. Sergeant Baro had fought in many parts of Europe, including the Battle of the Bulge. Alicia and Jose moved to Miami in the early 1950s. She became an advocate of Puerto Ricans, founding numerous groups. (Courtesy of Leticia Baro.)

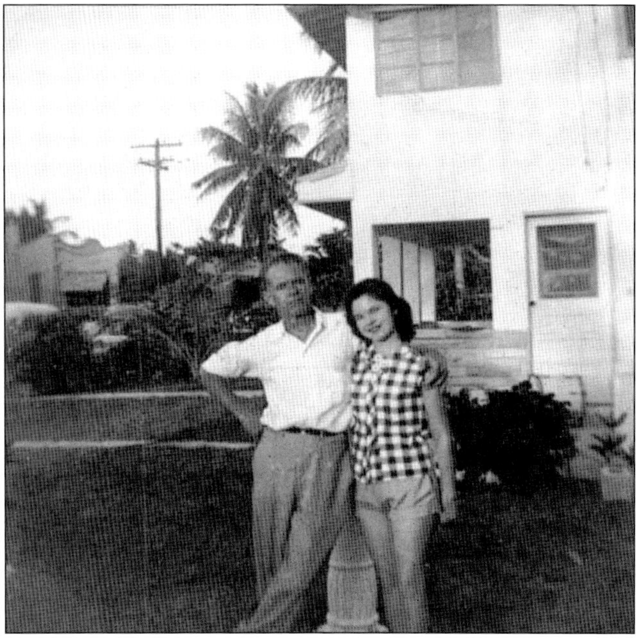

In 1945, Guillermo "William" Martinez Sr. moved his family from Key West to Wynwood. They were one of the first Puerto Rican families in the neighborhood. In this early-1950s photograph is Martinez Sr. and his daughter Yolanda. Their home is behind them, at NW Thirty-Three Street and NW Third Avenue. William did all the masonry work himself to convert the two-story/two-family home into a one-family house. (Courtesy of David Martinez-Morales.)

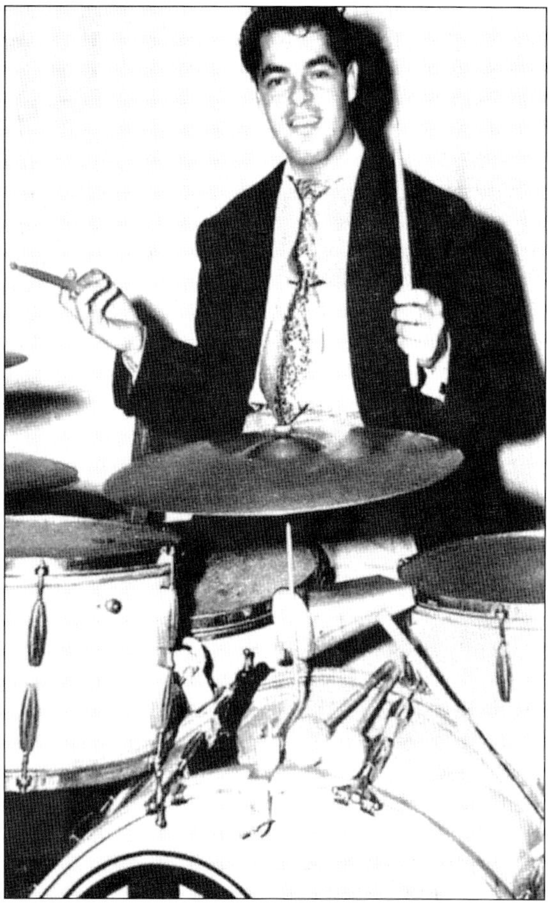

Hector Martinez is pictured in 1945 drumming at the La Concha Hotel, a Key West nightclub. He inherited his father's musical talents. William Martinez Sr. had played in an Army band in Puerto Rico and also played a church organ. Hector learned to play the drums in high school in New York. He made his debut as a professional drummer at the age of 16. (Courtesy of David Martinez-Morales.)

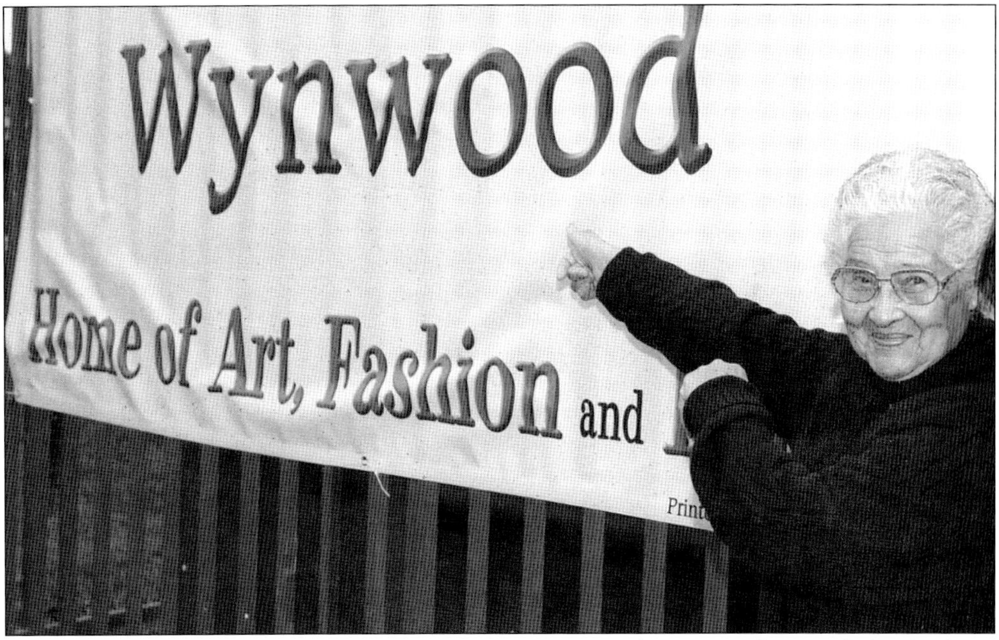

Dorothy "Dottie" Quintana moved to Miami from New York in 1951, along with her husband and daughter. Quintana established herself in Wynwood, then a budding Puerto Rican enclave, and became a community icon helping her brethren as they established themselves in the 1950s and 1960s. After her death at the age of 101, the Wynwood Community Center was named after her. (Courtesy of Luis De Rosa.)

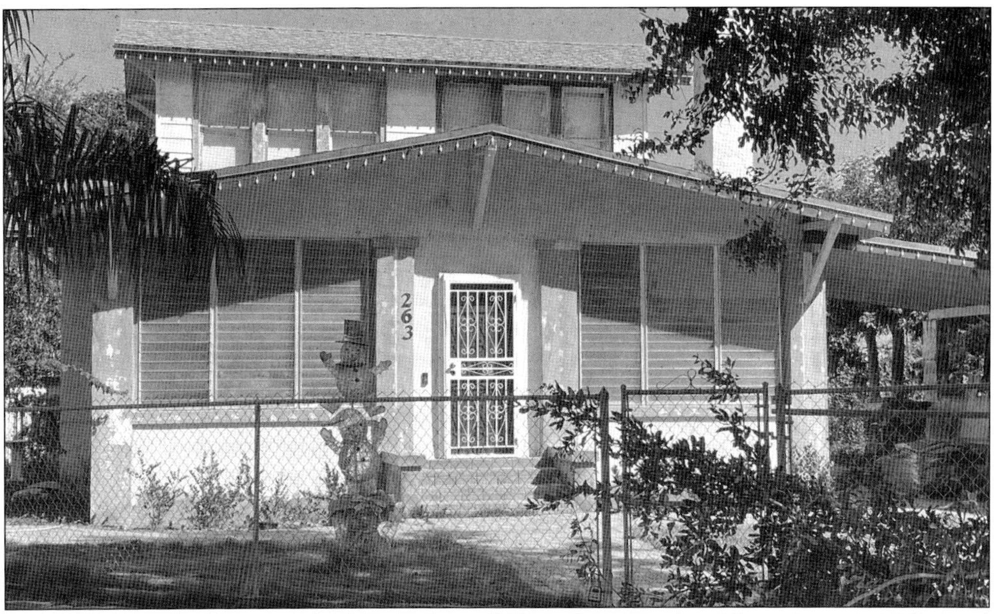

Pictured here is the home in which Dorothy and Efrain Quintana lived from the early 1950s until Dorothy passed away in 2011. For more than half a century, Dorothy was a force to be reckoned with. She was a blue-collar worker and organized her community to defend and improve itself. She was part of many groups and was a formidable leader. Many a politician who ran for office came to consult with her here. (Author photograph.)

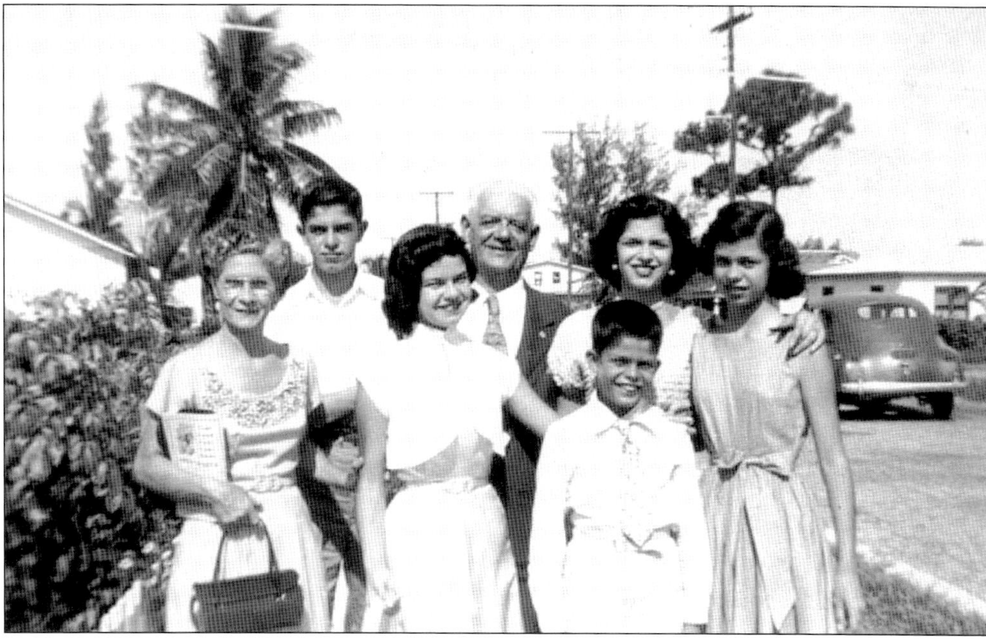

In this 1952 photograph is part of the Martinez family in Wynwood accompanied by the Rev. Dr. Manuel Alfaro, in back wearing a tie and jacket. Alfaro, who had come to Miami from New York, was the founding pastor of the Spanish American Methodist Church at 1200 North Miami Court. The building was razed to make room for Interstate 95. (Courtesy of David Martinez-Morales.)

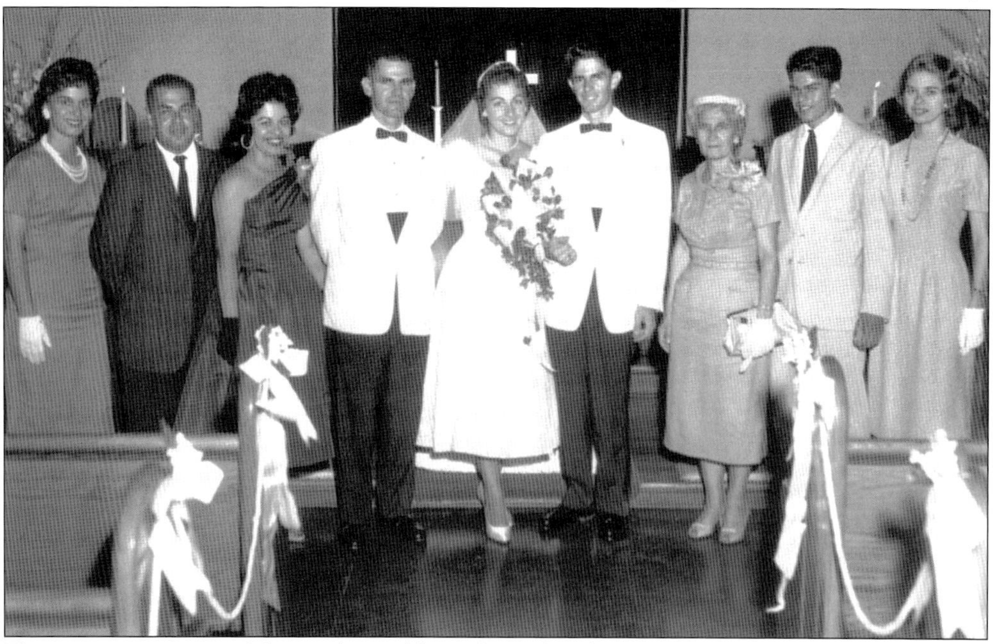

This image was captured during the wedding of David and Dorothy Martinez on August 29, 1958, at the Spanish American Methodist Church, where the Martinez family worshipped and where their family friend, Pastor Alfaro, officiated. From left to right are Heidy (sister), Hector (brother), Mayra (sister), Bill (brother), Dorothy, Dave, Manuela (mother), Edward (brother), and Ivonne (sister). (Courtesy of David Martinez-Morales.)

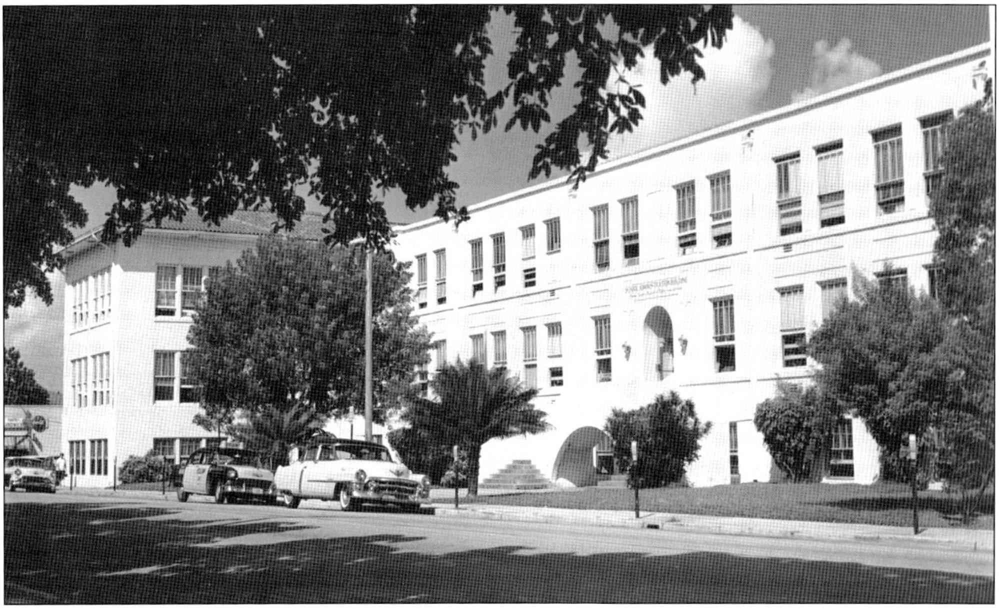

The Buena Vista Elementary School in Wynwood, where the Martinez-Morales children attended in the 1950s, is seen here. Many other Puerto Rican children attended this school as well in the 1960s and 1970s. It was at 3001 NW Second Avenue, in the heart of the Puerto Ricans enclave. It is now the Young Men's Preparatory Academy. (Courtesy of David Martinez-Morales.)

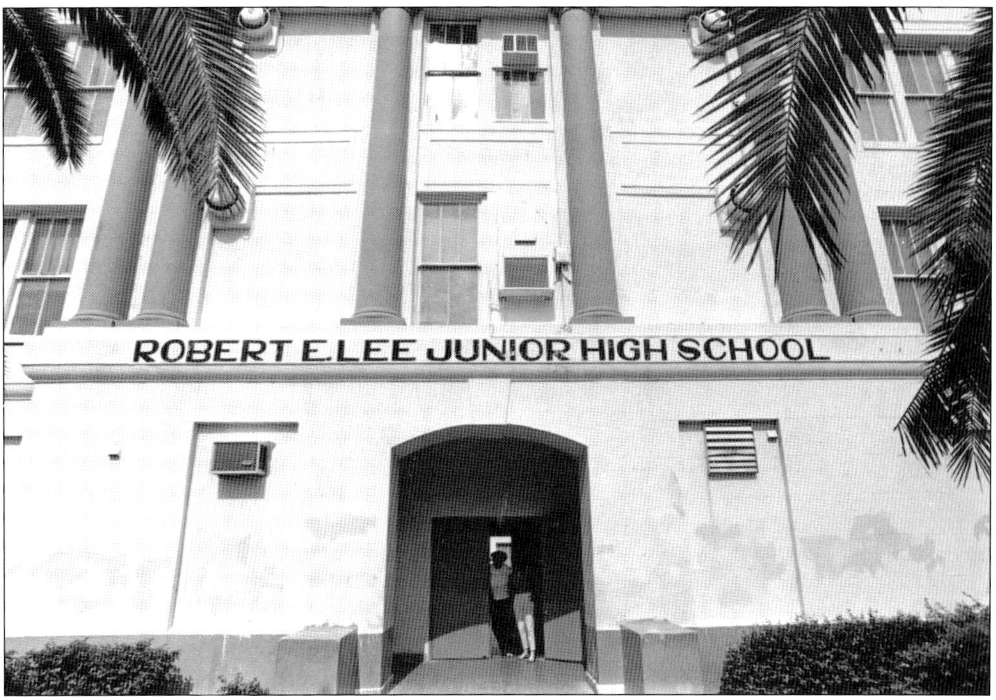

Robert E. Lee Junior High School in Wynwood is where the Martinez-Morales children and other Puerto Rican children attended in the late 1940s and early 1950s. It was demolished in the 1960s, and a new school was built named after a Puerto Rican political figure from the island, Jose De Diego. (Courtesy of David Martinez-Morales.)

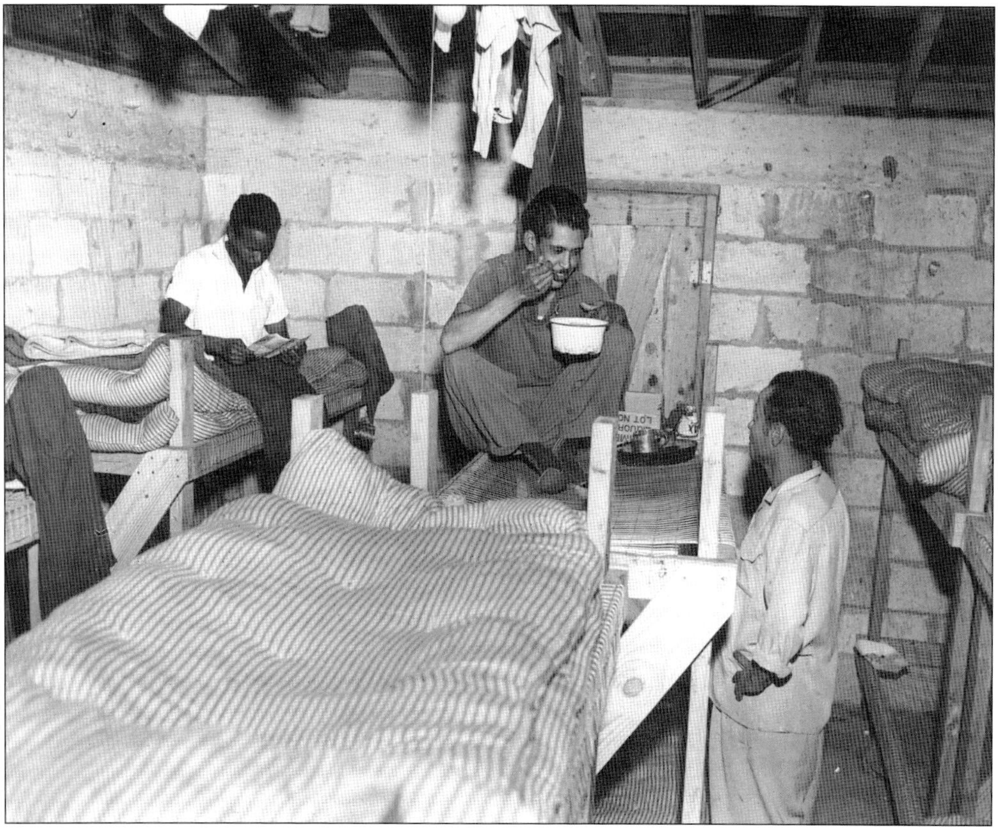

In the early 1950s, Puerto Rican farmworkers began arriving in Homestead in South Miami. Many came without contracts and, upon arrival, found dire conditions, like those seen in this 1954 photograph. In that same year, a group of Puerto Ricans protested against these conditions. One owner placed dozens of workers in a truck and dropped them off in front of the Christ Fellowship Church in downtown Miami and abandoned them there. (Courtesy of History Miami Museum.)

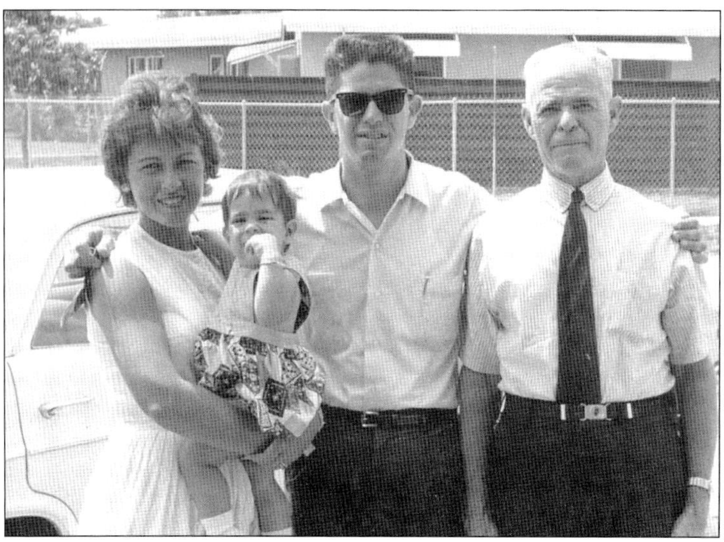

In this 1965 photograph are William Martinez Sr. (right) with his son Dave, daughter-in-law Dot, and granddaughter Patty. William Sr. was living with his son's family at their home on SW Ninety-Third Avenue and SW Eighth Street. Dave was working with the Kodak Film Company, where he worked for more than 30 years. (Courtesy of David Martinez-Morales.)

On June 2, 1945, Jose Ramon Pedrogo, 22 years old, from the town of Catano, and Carmen Maria Alvarez, from Bayamon, 16 years old, were married. Due to her age, Carmen's father only gave his permission for the marriage after being assured that Carmen would stay in school and graduate from high school. She graduated the next year and then went on to take two years of secretarial studies. (Courtesy of Carmen Pedrogo.)

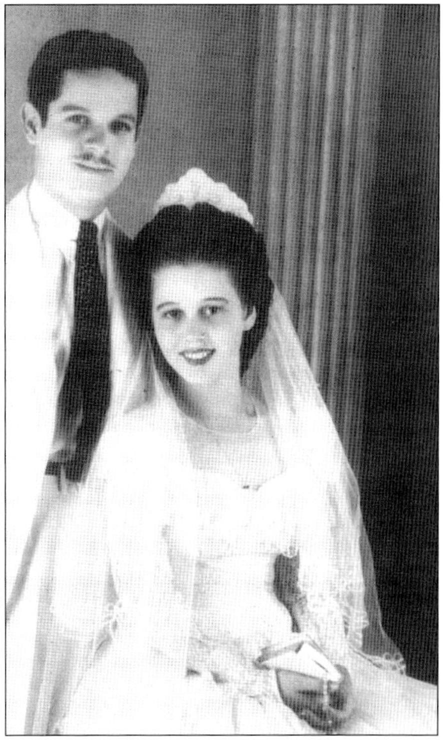

Pictured here is a family get-together on a rooftop in Old San Juan in 1949. From left to right are Jose and Carmen Pedrogo, Jose's sister Irma, his mother Rose Cordero Pedrogo, his other sister Rose Pedrogo Farley, and her husband Artic Dale Farley. The building is in front of Christopher Columbus Plaza. (Courtesy of Carmen Pedrogo.)

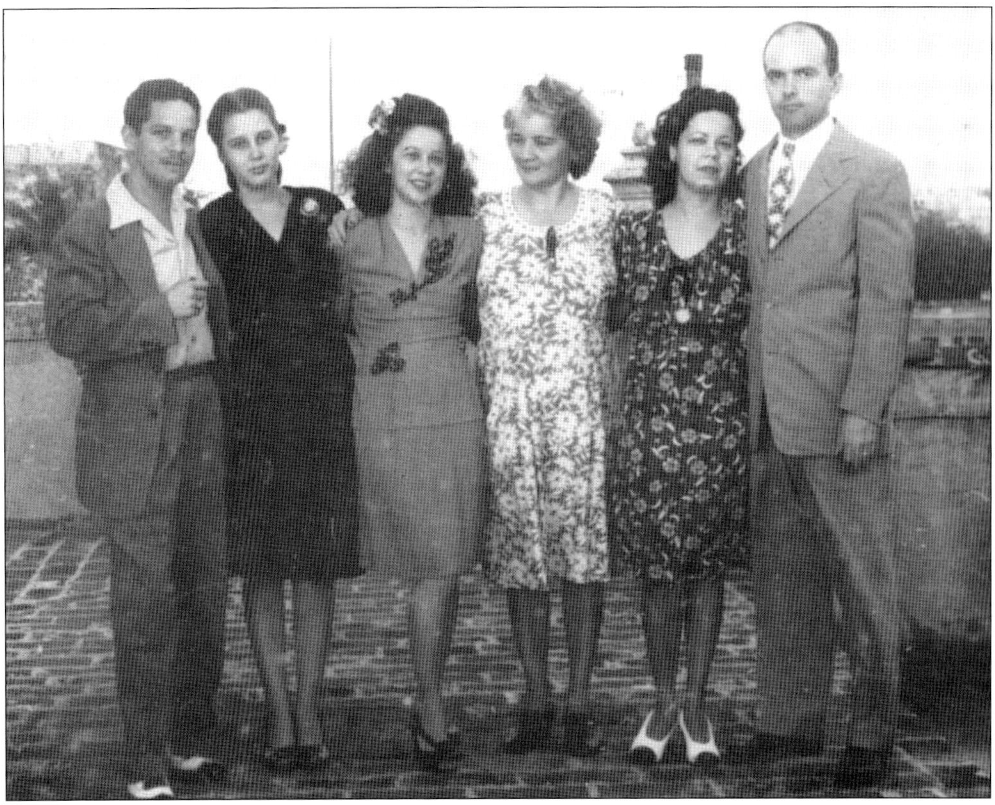

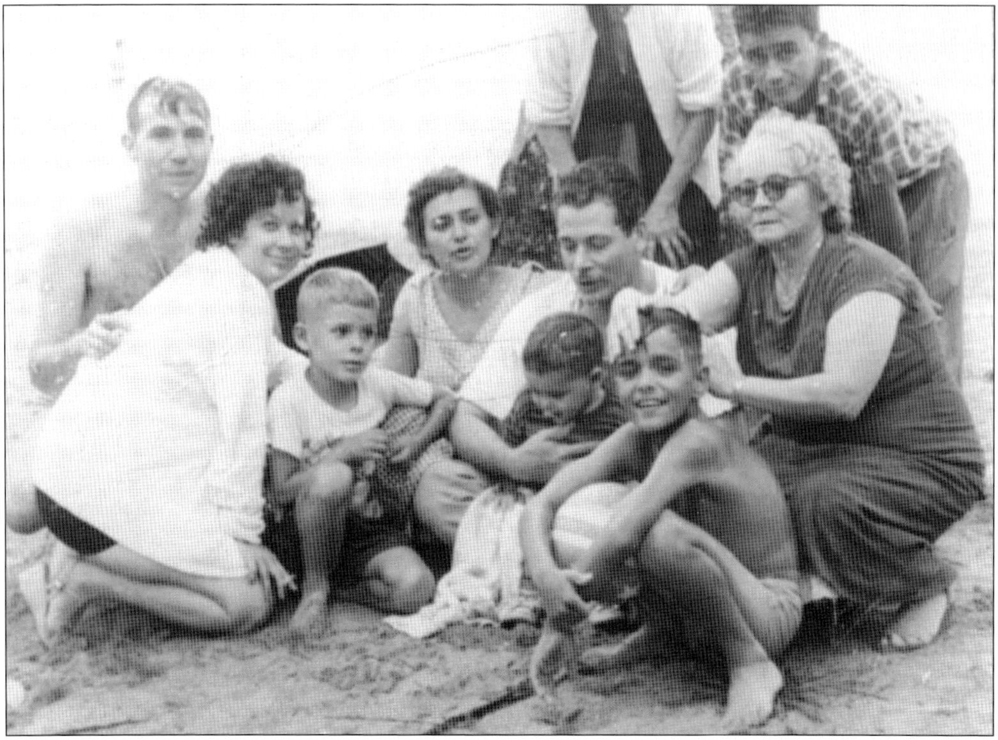

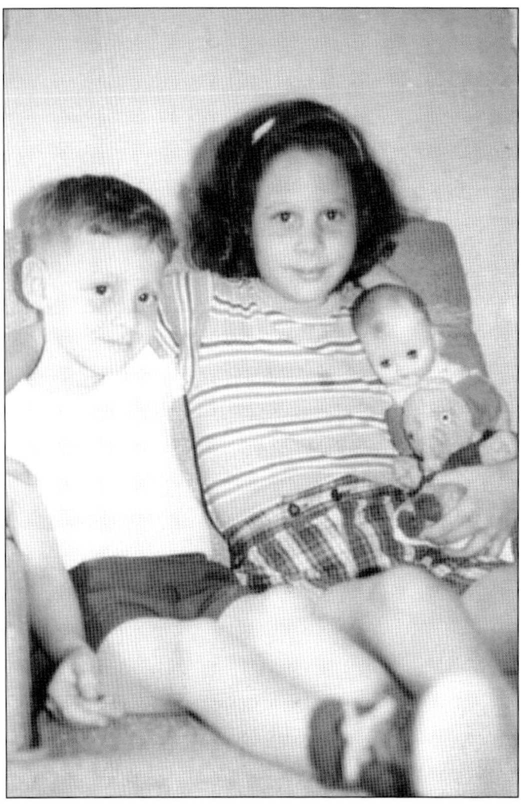

Seen here is a family outing at Luquillo Beach, about 40 minutes east of San Juan, on the Atlantic. Jose Pedrogo's sister Irma Pedrogo and her husband, Phillip, are at left. Carmen Julia Alvarez is at center, and Rosa Cordero Pedrogo is on the right with an assortment of nieces and nephews. This photograph was taken shortly before Jose and Carmen Pedrogo left Puerto Rico for Miami in the early 1950s. (Courtesy of Carmen Pedrogo.)

In 1956, Jose Pedrogo relocated his family to North Miami Beach. An accountant by trade, Pedrogo opened an office in North Miami where Puerto Ricans were also starting to move at that time. His children Carmen and Jose Carlos are pictured here in the family home at 1840 NE 173rd Street. This photograph was taken right after Christmas 1959. (Courtesy of Carmen Pedrogo.)

Jose Pedrogo's wife, Carmen, and their children Carmen and Jose Jr. are pictured here in front of their home in North Miami Beach on a Sunday morning in the late 1950s. The family was heading for Mass at St. Lawrence Catholic Church in North Miami. The family was active in the church and their children participated in Boys Scouts and Brownies there. (Courtesy of Carmen Pedrogo.)

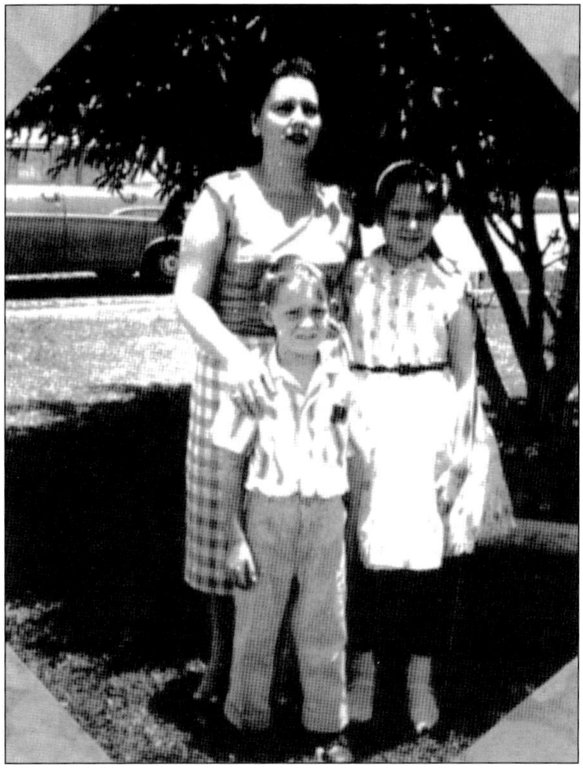

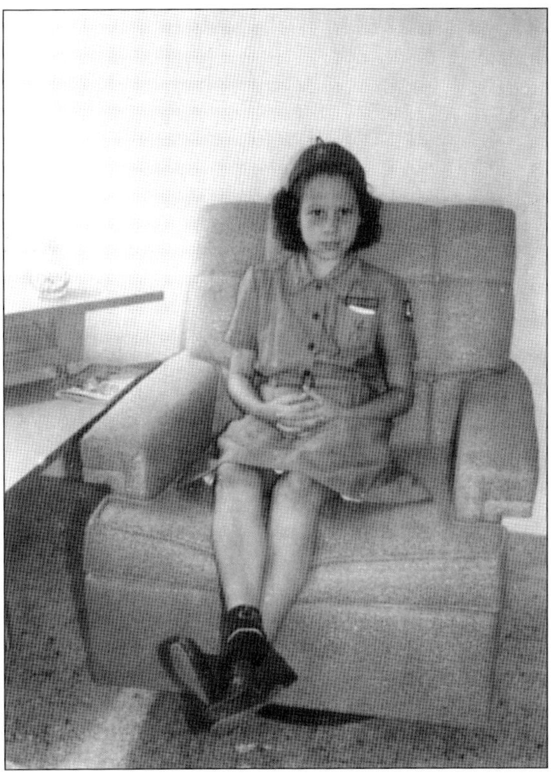

Pictured here is Carmen Pedrogo as a Brownie. She sits in her living room around 1960. Brownies are young Girl Scouts, generally between the ages of 7 to 11. The Brownies met at St. Lawrence Catholic Church in North Miami. (Courtesy of Carmen Pedrogo.)

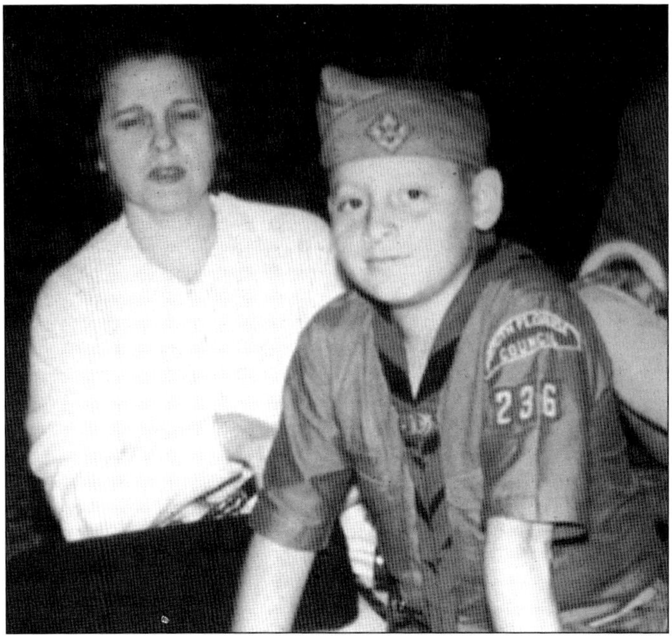

Pictured here is Carmen Pedrogo, with her son Jose Carlos, as a Boy Scout at a campsite around 1964. No doubt both Jose Sr. and Carmen saw the value of their son's participation in scouting and the values of civic participation and community service that it provides. Carmen and Jose Pedrogo Sr. also instilled these values in their children by participating in and supporting Puerto Rican organizations in Miami. (Courtesy of Carmen Pedrogo.)

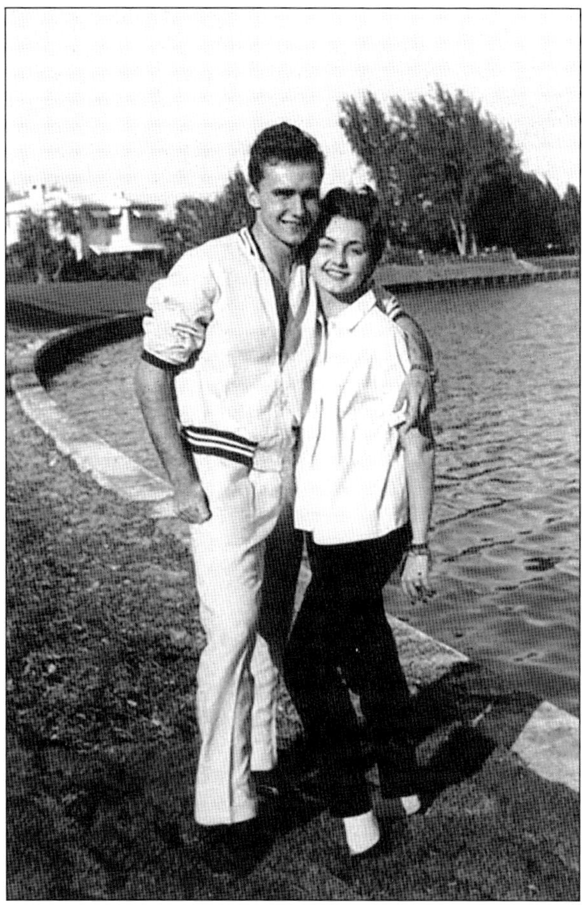

Maurice A. Ferre was born in Puerto Rico and came to Miami in 1942. He was elected to the Florida House of Representatives in 1967 and then to the Miami City Commission in 1968. In 1972, Ferre became the first Hispanic mayor of Miami. He and his wife, Mercedes, are pictured here in their 20s. (Courtesy of History Miami Museum.)

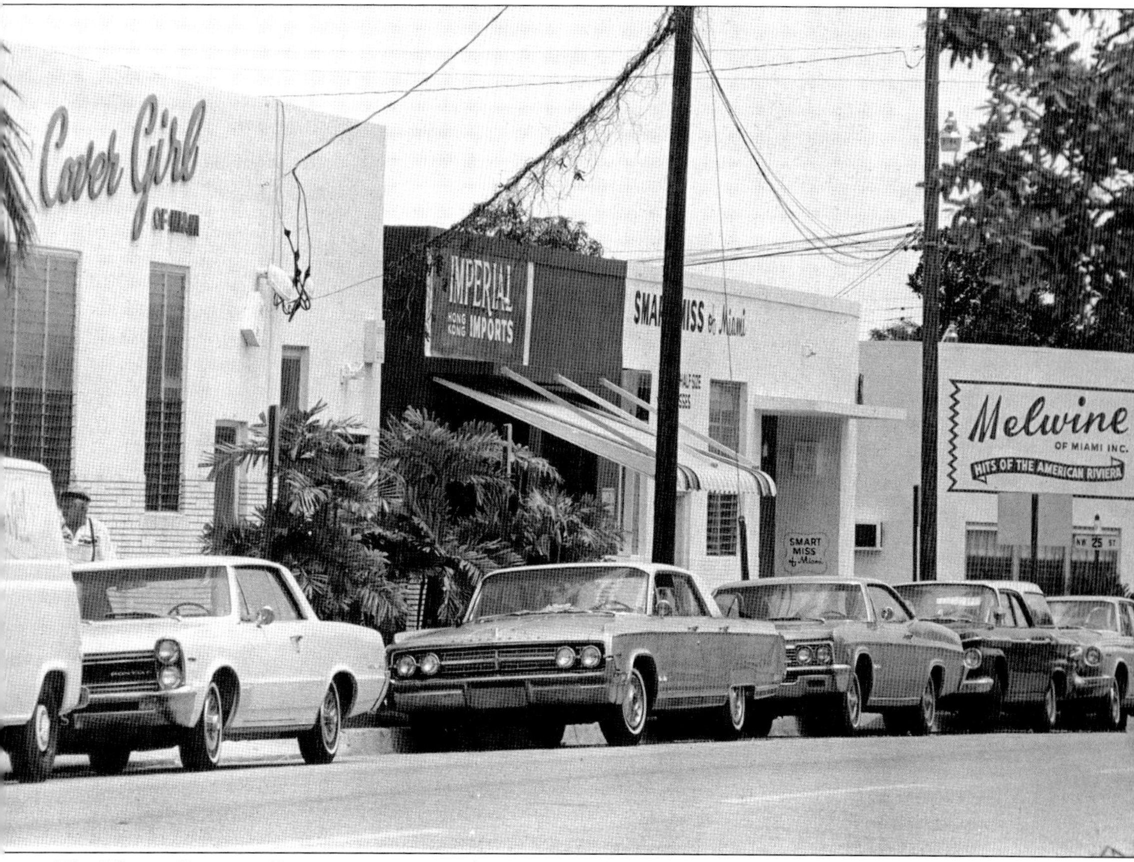

The Miami Garment District was centered in Wynwood during the 1950s–1970s. The factories were in and around NW Fifth Avenue and NW Twenty-Fourth and NW Twenty-Fifth Streets. During this period, more than 40 women who worked there were Puerto Rican, like Dorothy Quintana, and many others actually lived in the neighborhood. Some of the factories that had outlets like the one featured in this photograph from 1971 were in Wynwood. (Courtesy of Casey Piket.)

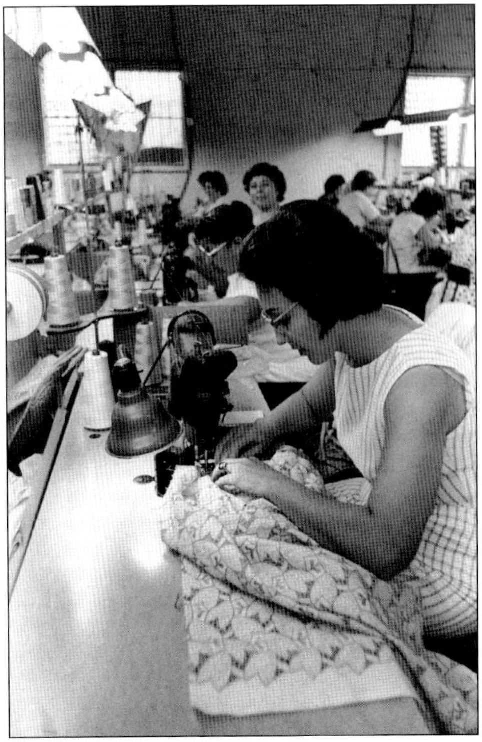

Pictured here are Puerto Rican and other Latina garment workers in a factory in Wynwood. The Garment Districts thrived with the influx of skilled seamstresses who moved from New York and other factory cities in the Northeast. Puerto Rican women made up approximately 40 percent of all garment workers in Miami in the 1950s and 1960s. This photograph is from 1965. (Courtesy of History Miami Museum.)

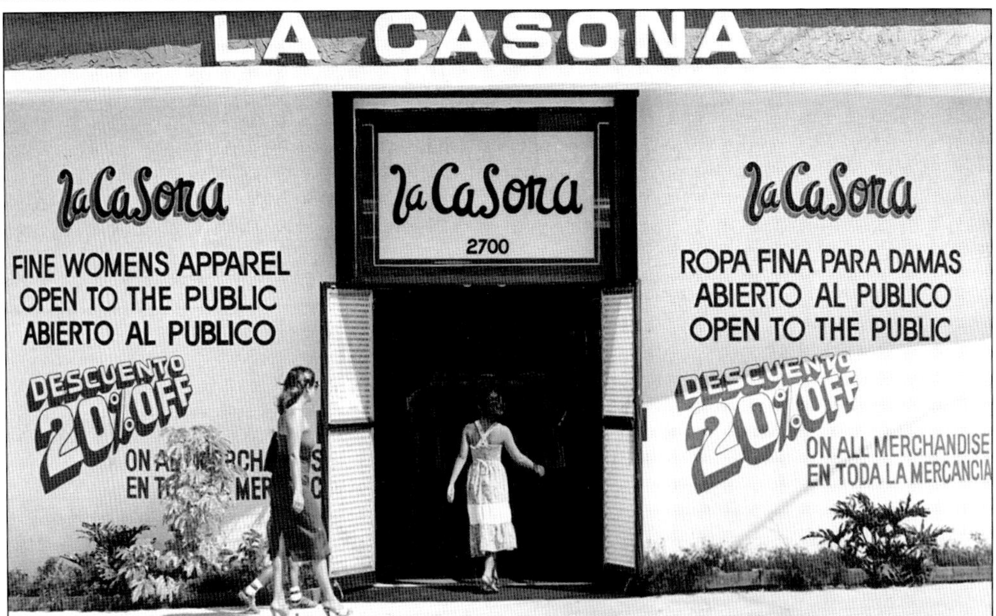

Many of the factories in Wynwood worked with outlets like La Casona, at 2700 NW Second Avenue in the heart of Puerto Rican Wynwood. It not only provided quality clothing at a lower cost, but also jobs for local residents. In this picture from the 1960s, women and children are going into the store. Local garment factories also offered union-made clothing. The International Ladies Garment Workers Union followed the garment workers to Miami and organized them. (Courtesy of Casey Piket.)

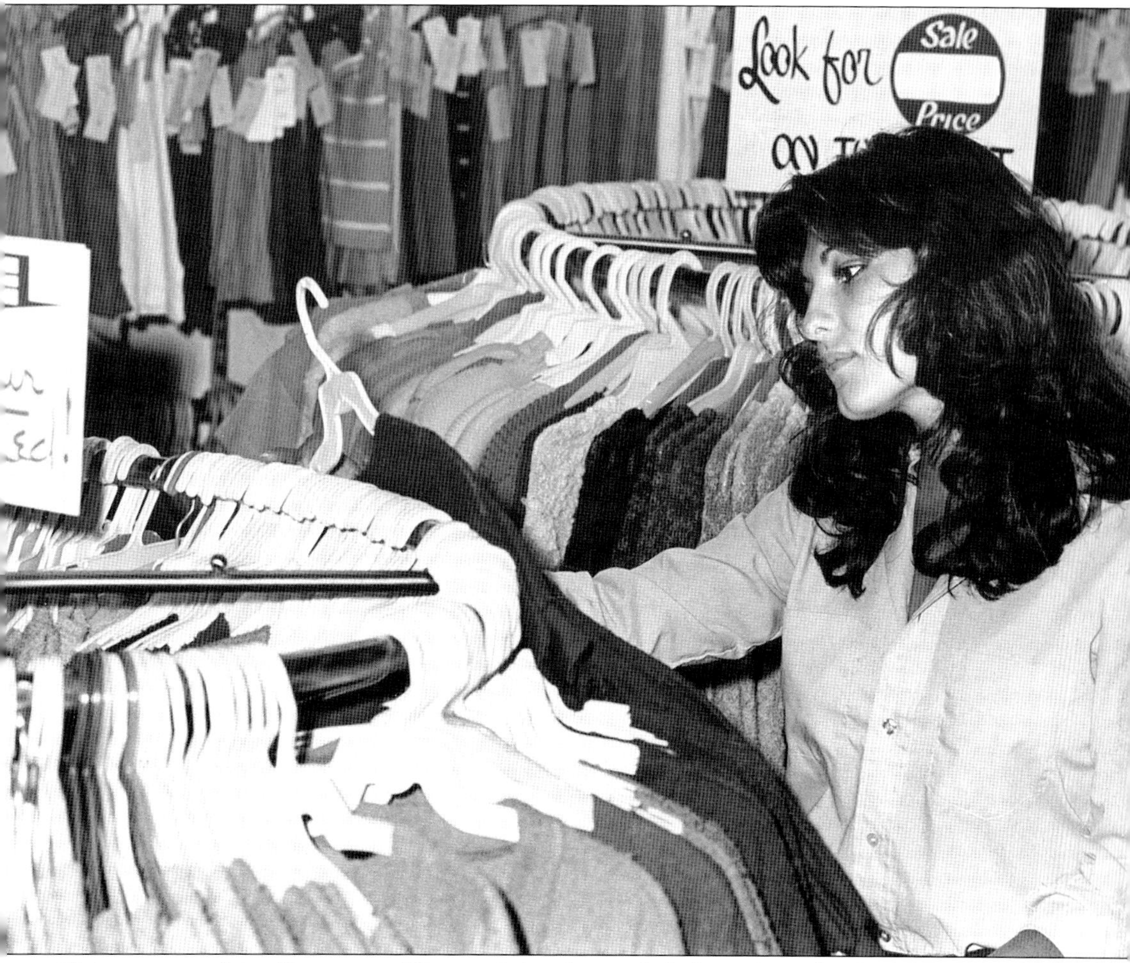

This was one of the 17 stores in Wynwood that featured clothing from the Garment District. Producers like Daisy's Originals and Pops for Kids were among the factories that sold their products. Sometimes, the factories featured small fashion shows where children would model some of the products. (Courtesy of Casey Piket.)

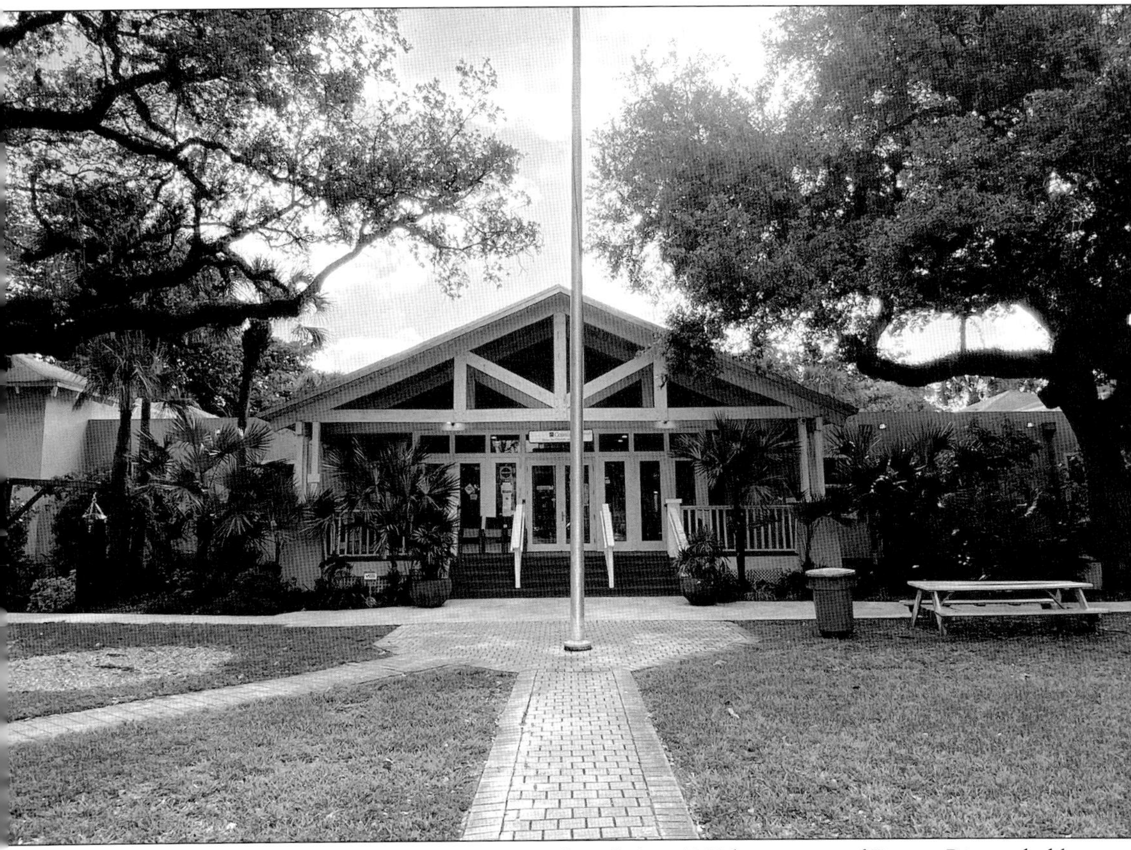

Casa Puerto, the House of Puerto Rico, was founded in 1971 by a group of Puerto Ricans led by Juan and Iris Corbella and Jaime and Esther Machado. It was located at 2810 NW South River Drive. The facility was spacious and contained several buildings, including a large dining/dancing area. It also had conference rooms for meetings and ample parking, as well as an outdoor picnic area. (Author photograph.)

Two

Wynwood, a Puerto Rican Barrio in Miami

In the 1940s, Miami and South Florida became ever more attractive for Puerto Ricans. Reasons for this included the return of servicemen from the island who had been stationed in the city and surrounding region in World War II and found the environment attractive, as did wealthy Puerto Rican investors, farm laborers, garment workers, and those attracted to employment in the burgeoning hotel industry. Between 1940 and 1960, the Puerto Rican population in Miami increased to more than 30,000.

Greater numbers of migrants moved to Miami, especially to Wynwood, a 1920s-era community with a strong blue-collar base, by the early post–World War II era. Wynwood lies three miles north of downtown Miami. Migrants were drawn there primarily by the prospect of employment in the growing garment industry. Others worked in the burgeoning hotel industry in Miami and Miami Beach. By the early 1950s, garment manufacturers from the North began relocating to the South, particularly to Wynwood, as well as to Hialeah in northwest Dade.

Also, a number of wealthy Puerto Rican families, including the Ferres, whose son Maurice would become the first Hispanic mayor of Miami, settled south of downtown in the late 1940s. Along with some Puerto Rican investors and bankers, they created a neighborhood called Little San Juan on leafy Brickell Avenue. Meanwhile, the working-class Puerto Rican population of the city settled in Wynwood. Another group of Puerto Rican migrants in Miami and other parts of Florida were farmworkers. By 1953, Puerto Ricans represented a steady portion of the state's agricultural labor force.

In the meantime, as the number of Puerto Rican residents of Wynwood grew, the neighborhood took on the trappings of a typical Puerto Rican community. The main street, NW Second Avenue, was the locale for several small "mom and pop" businesses, including a laundromat, an eatery, and a bodega, which carried a wide array of foods and other goods.

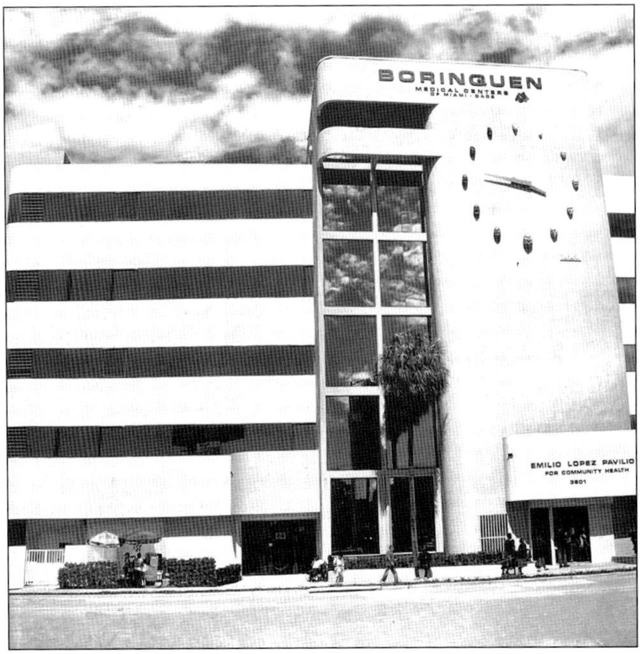

The late 1960s and 1970s turned out to be times of great energy and challenges for Puerto Ricans in Miami. In Wynwood, the need for better city services led to the formation of the United Puerto Ricans of Miami (UPRM). The group was led by Emilio Lopez, who as counselor at Robert E. Lee Junior High School found a lack of adequate healthcare services among his students and their families. As a result, he launched an organizing effort that led to the formation of the Borinquen Clinic, pictured here in 1972. Lopez became its first executive director. (Courtesy of Paul Velez.)

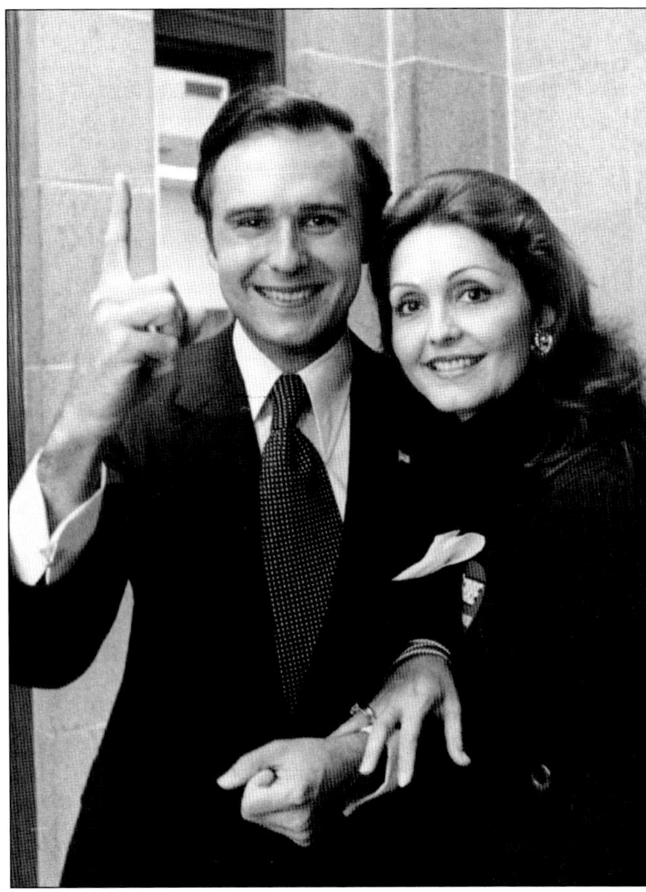

In 1972, Maurice A. Ferre became the first Hispanic mayor of Miami. He served 12 years as mayor and oversaw the transformation of Miami as a gateway city to and from Latin America. He and his wife, Mercedes, are pictured here. (Courtesy of History Miami Museum.)

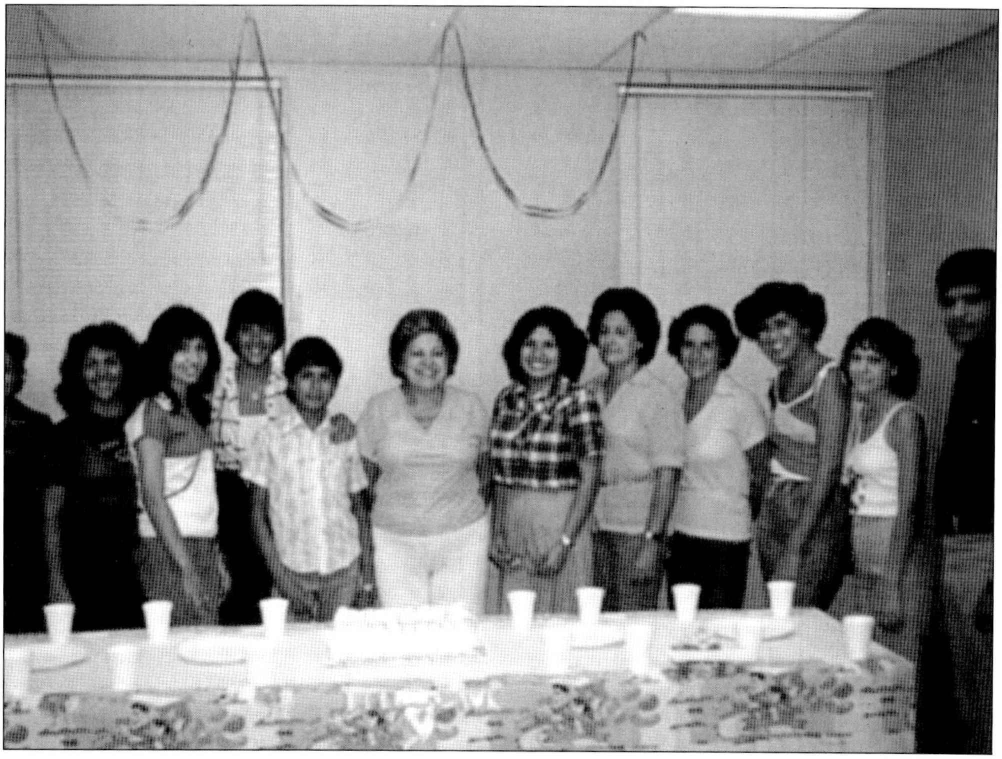

The Eugenio Maria De Hostos Wynwood Neighborhood Center was established in Wynwood in 1974 to provide a multitude of services to seniors and youth along with a small daycare. Located at 2901 NW Second Avenue in the hub of the Puerto Rican enclave, it is named after a Puerto Rican educator and patriot of the 19th century. On this day, the staff was celebrating the birthday of the executive director, Haydee Miranda. (Courtesy of Gil Garcia.)

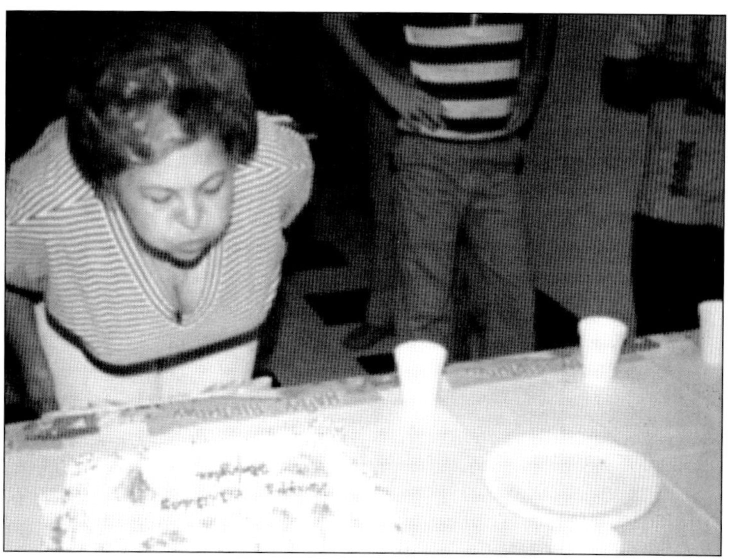

Haydee Miranda blows out the candles on her birthday cake in the 1970s. The de Hostos Center served as a clearinghouse for newly arriving Puerto Ricans. The space was often used by other community groups for meetings and activities. (Courtesy of Gil Garcia.)

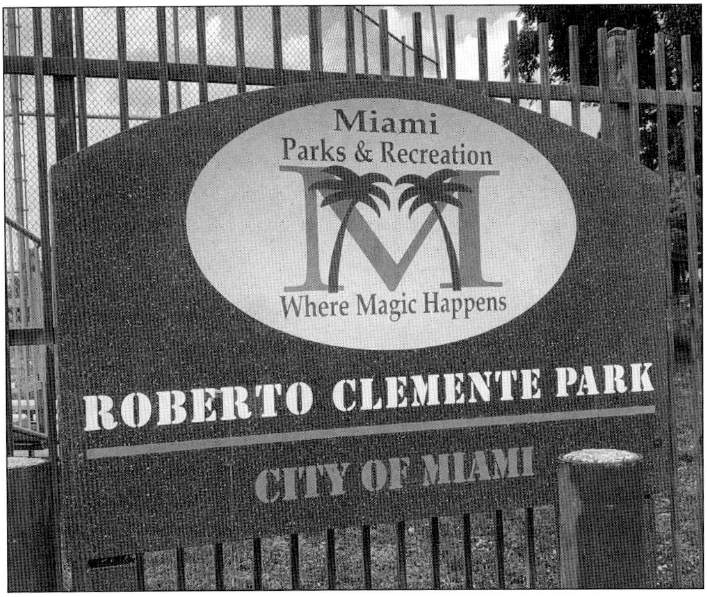

On December 31, 1972, Roberto Clemente, "the Great One," Afro Puerto Rican star outfielder for the Pittsburgh Pirates, perished. He was on a humanitarian mission to Nicaragua when his plane crashed after taking off from the San Juan airport. The City of Miami and the Puerto Rican community renamed the park at NW Thirty-Fourth Street in Wynwood after Clemente. (Courtesy of Luz Sofia Vazquez-Hernandez.)

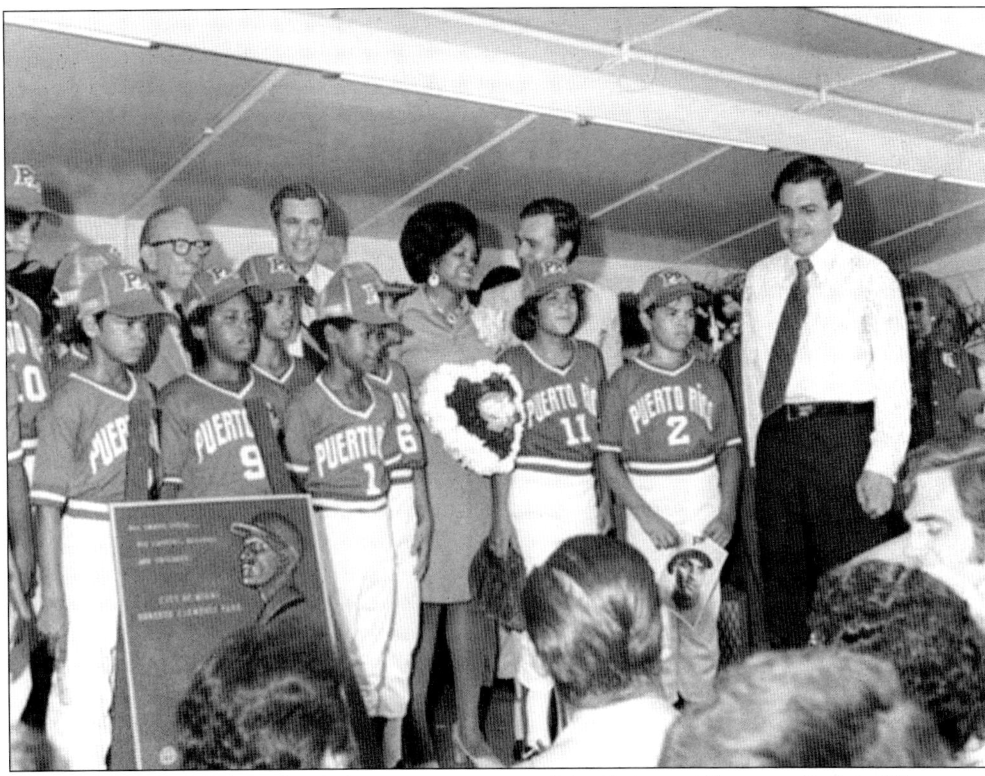

This picture was taken at the dedication ceremony of the Roberto Clemente Park in Wynwood, hosted by newly installed mayor Maurice A. Ferre in 1974. The mayor welcomed Vera Clemente, the wife of Roberto Clemente (center), US congressman Claude Pepper (left, with glasses), Florida governor Ruben Askew (right of Pepper), and the governor of Puerto Rico, Rafael Hernandez Colon (right). A Little League baseball team poses with the group. (Courtesy of Florida State University Archives.)

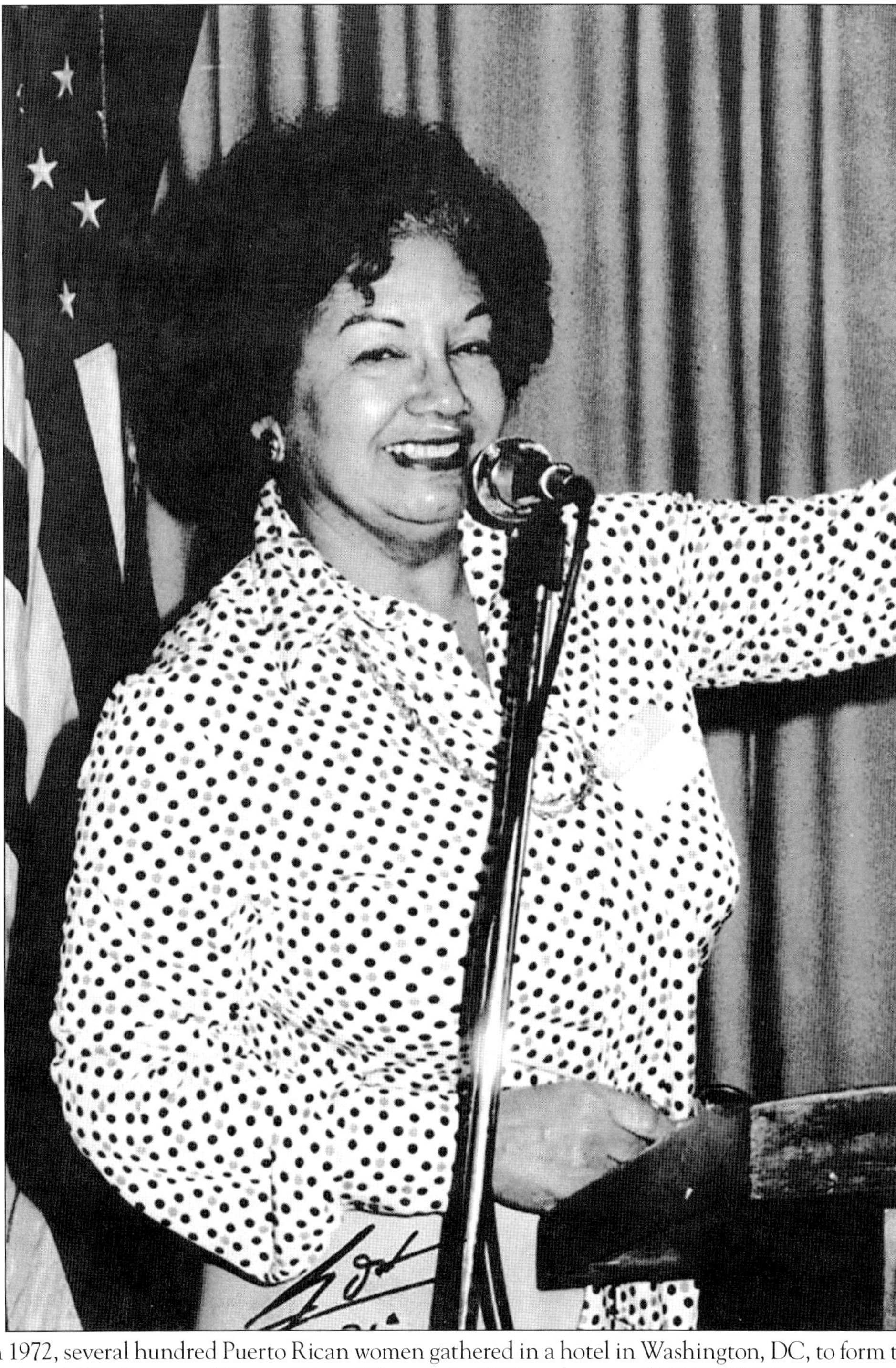

In 1972, several hundred Puerto Rican women gathered in a hotel in Washington, DC, to form the National Conference of Puerto Rican Women. In 1977, a chapter of NACOPRW was organized in Miami. Community leader Dr. Alicia Baro became a co-founder and president of the Miami chapter. In this photograph, she addresses the group for the first time as president. (Courtesy of NACOPRW.)

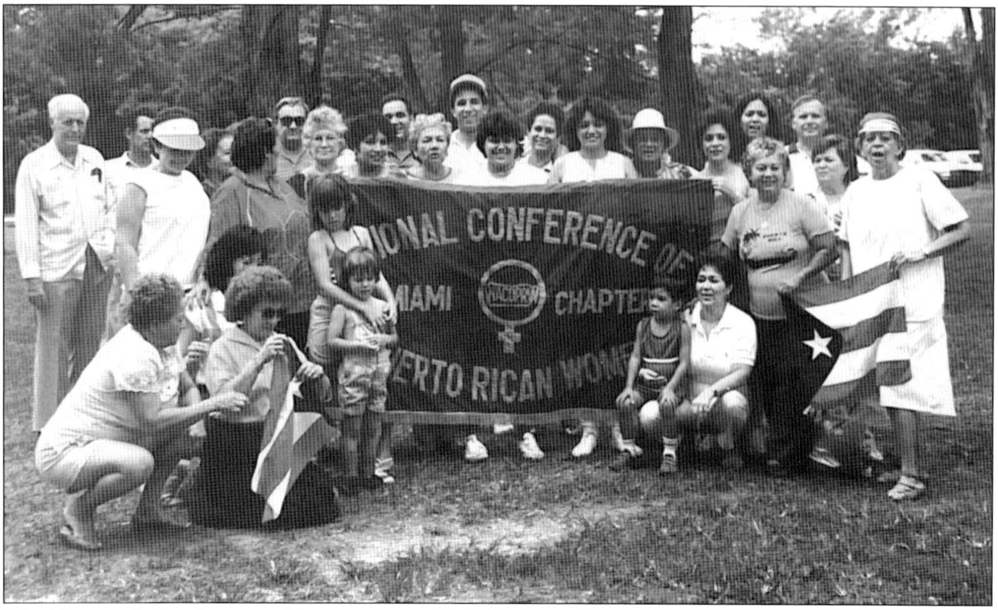

The National Conference of Puerto Rican Women–Miami Chapter began to implement a number of signature events on an annual basis. Here is a photograph from the first annual picnic, held at Tropical Park in Miami in June 1978. The outings were not only family gatherings but often included meetings or speakers on important subjects. The Miami chapter became an important organization for Puerto Rican and Hispanic women. (Courtesy of NACOPRW.)

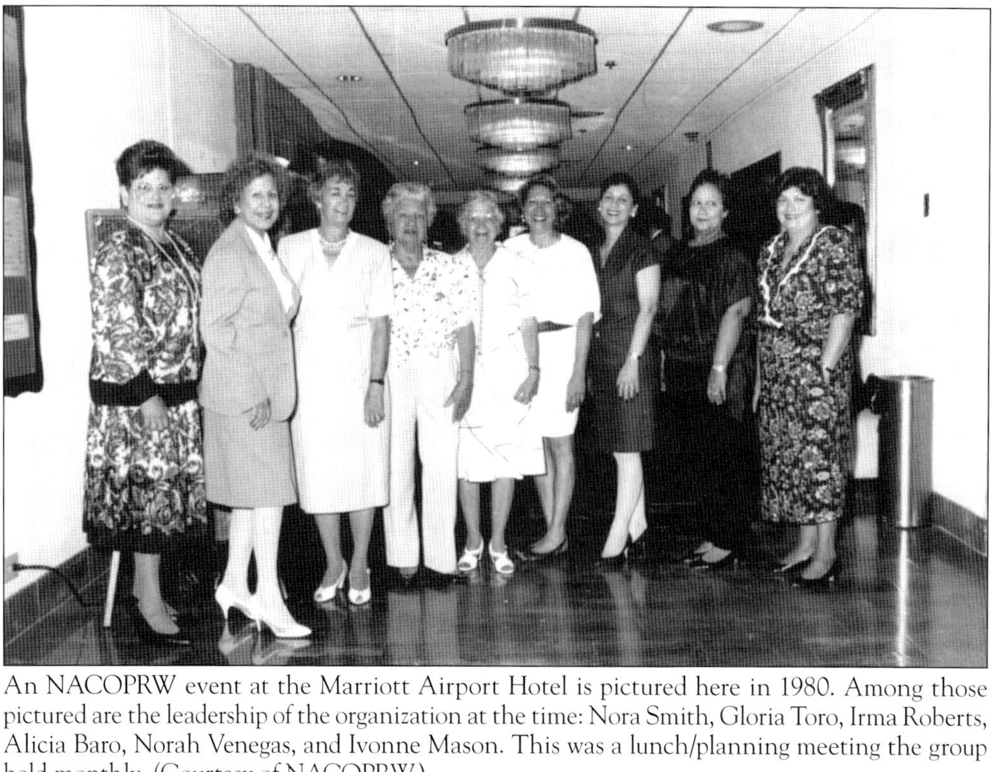

An NACOPRW event at the Marriott Airport Hotel is pictured here in 1980. Among those pictured are the leadership of the organization at the time: Nora Smith, Gloria Toro, Irma Roberts, Alicia Baro, Norah Venegas, and Ivonne Mason. This was a lunch/planning meeting the group held monthly. (Courtesy of NACOPRW.)

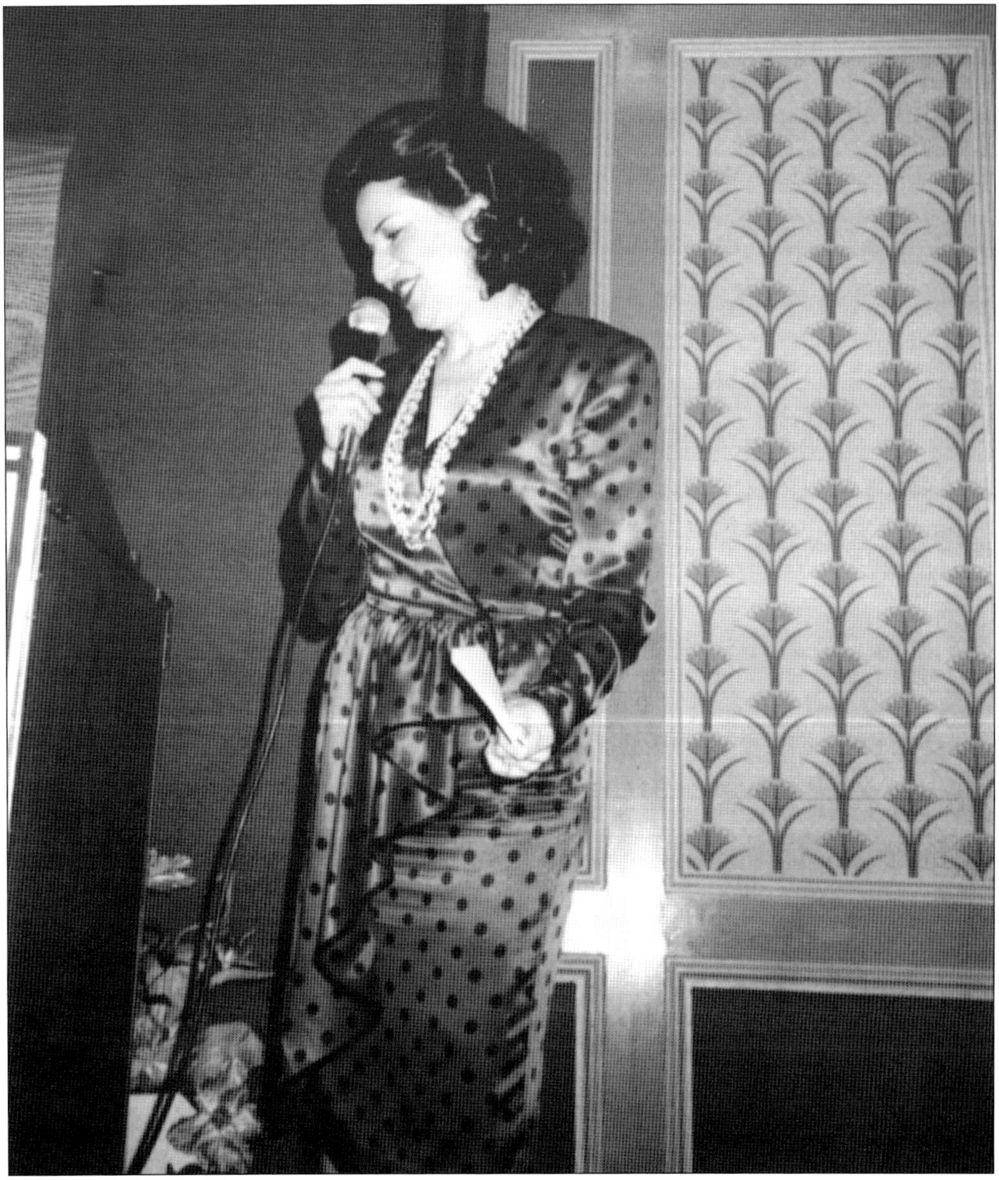

This photograph was taken during an NACOPRW event honoring Marta Casals Istomin, wife of the Spanish cellist Pablo Casals. Marta was born Marta Montanez Martinez in Humacao, Puerto Rico; from a young age, she trained on the cello with her uncle Rafael Montanez. At the age of 15, she met Pablo Casals and became his student. They married in 1957, and later founded the Casals Festival. (Courtesy of NACOPRW.)

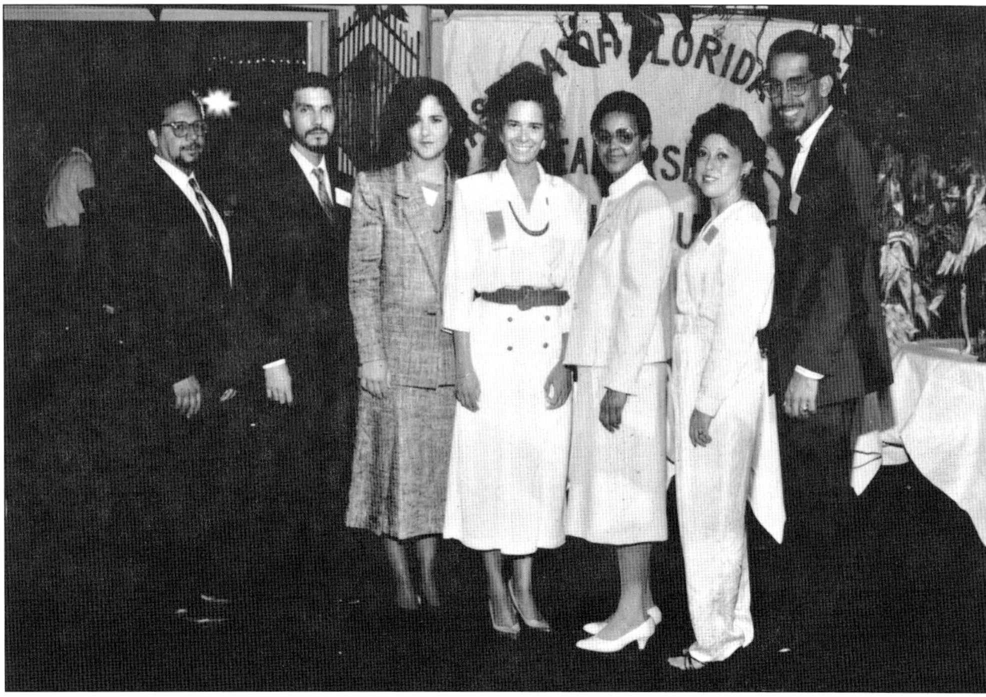

Puerto Rican educators started ASPIRA of Florida in 1981. ASPIRA, a national Latino leadership organization for youth, was founded by Dr. Antonia Pantoja in New York in 1961 to assist Puerto Rican youth to graduate from high school, go to college, and give back to the community. This 1985 photograph shows a fundraising gala with ASPIRA staff (from left to right) Felix Diaz, Raul Martinez, unidentified, executive director Victoria Hernandez, Iris Corchado, unidentified, and Willie Ramos. (Courtesy of ASPIRA of Florida.)

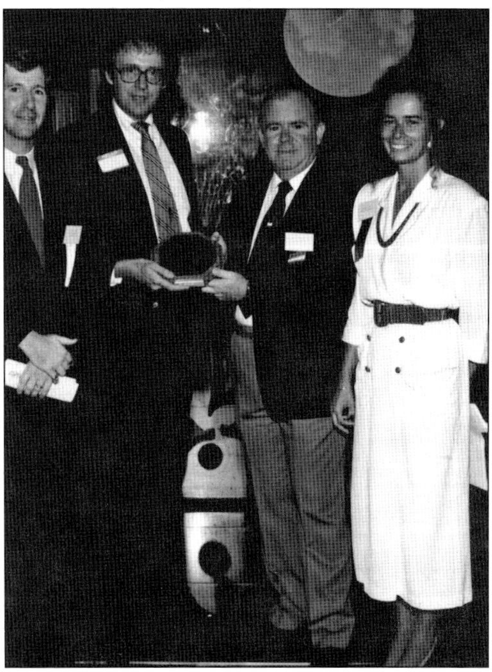

Seen here is a fundraising event at the Miami Metro Zoo in 1986. From left to right are ASPIRA board member Chas Scurr, supporter Seth Gordon, board chair Dr. Luis Martinez-Perez, and executive director Victoria Hernandez. Raising funds for discretionary operations was very important for ASPIRA, as most grants did not cover this cost. (Courtesy of ASPIRA of Florida.)

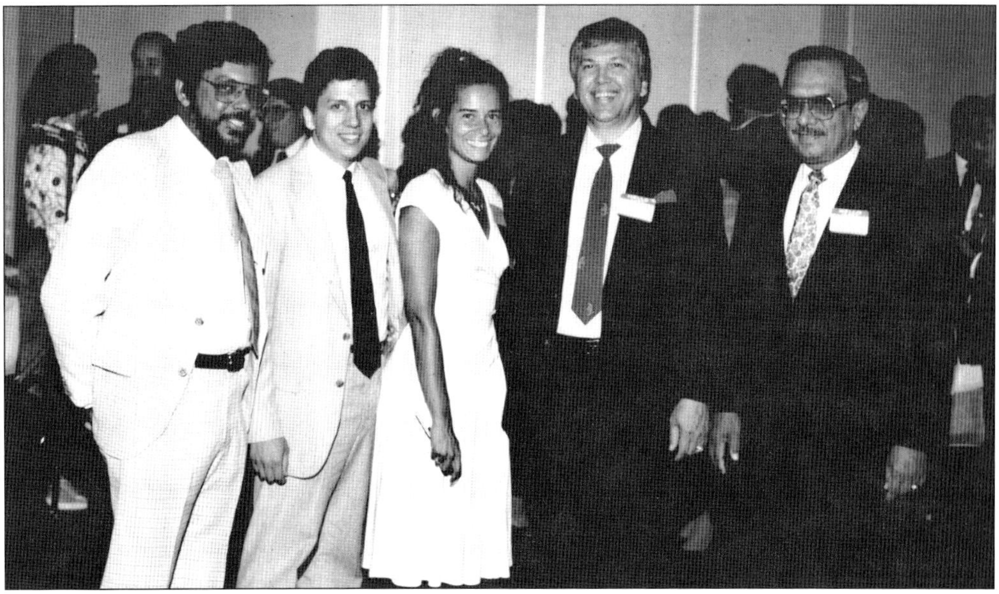

In 1986, ASPIRA of Florida's status changed from being an affiliate to a full associate. This granted it certain privileges, such as full representation on the national board. The executive director of ASPIRA of Florida is flanked by several national board members who flew to Miami for this event. (Courtesy of ASPIRA of Florida.)

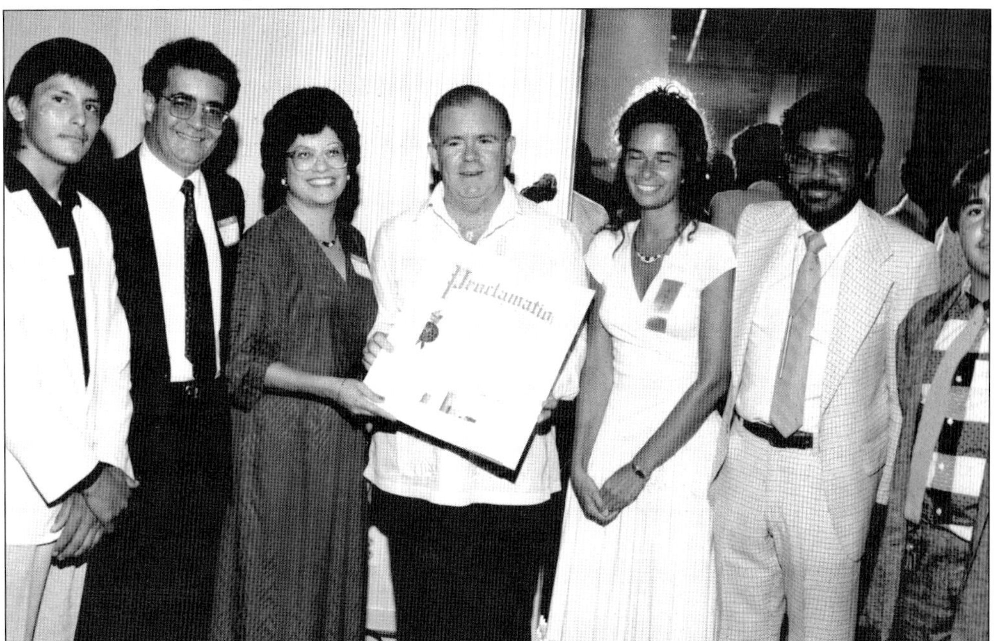

In the same event in which ASPIRA received its associate status in 1986, the City of Miami presented the organization with a proclamation commemorating the occasion. From left to right are an unidentified Aspirante (a student who participated in ASPIRA programs), Dr. Juan Rosario, national executive director of ASPIRA; an unidentified representative from the City of Miami; Dr. Luis Martinez-Perez, chair of the board; Victoria Hernandez, executive director; and an unidentified member of the national board. (Courtesy of ASPIRA of Florida.)

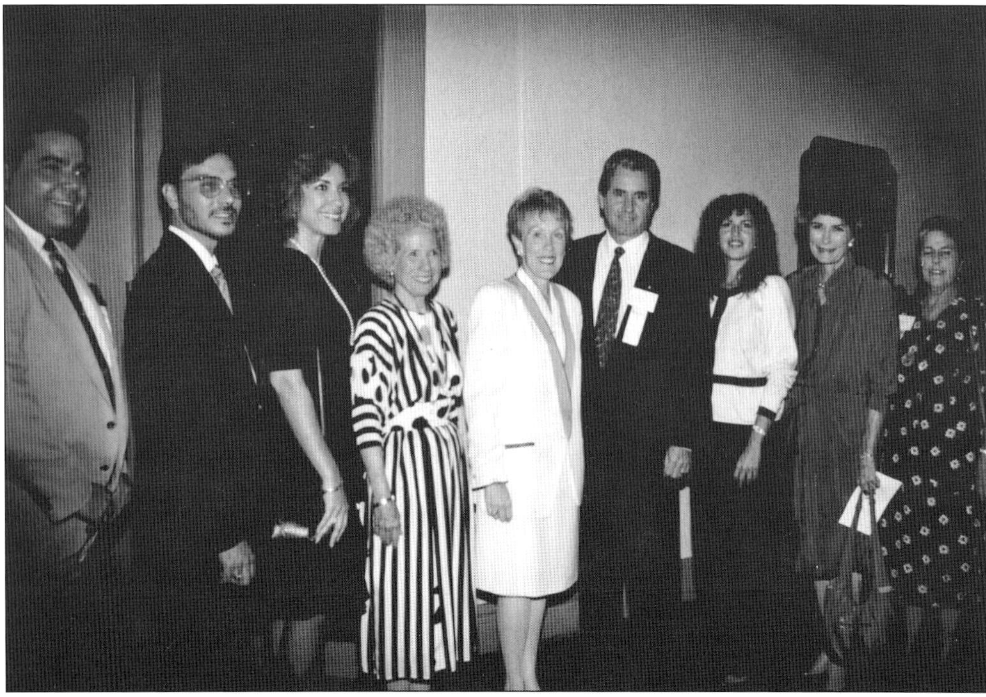

In 1986, the Florida commissioner of education, Betty Castor, visited ASPIRA, and a reception was held in her honor. From left to right are Jimmy Morales (Miami Beach law enforcement officer working the Youth Gang Prevention Project detail), Raul Martinez (hired to lead ASPIRA's Youth Gang Prevention Project), unidentified, Betsy Kaplan (Miami–Dade County Public School Board), Betty Castor (Florida education commissioner), Lee Ramos (ASPIRA of Florida board member and architect), unidentified, Janet McAliley (Miami–Dade County Public School board), and Yvette Arteaga-Morgan (ASPIRA board). (Courtesy of ASPIRA of Florida.)

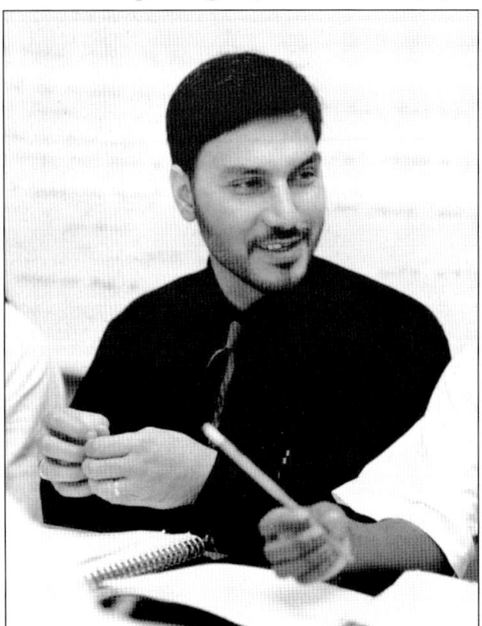

Raul Arnaldo Martinez was born and raised in Puerto Rico. He moved to Miami in the late 1970s. In 1986, he was hired by ASPIRA as a senior youth counselor to run a gang prevention program. Martinez was assigned to work in South Beach, an area that had active youth gangs. He succeeded in getting several gangs to sign truces and to improve opportunities for youth in the neighborhood. This photograph was taken around 1988. (Courtesy of ASPIRA of Florida.)

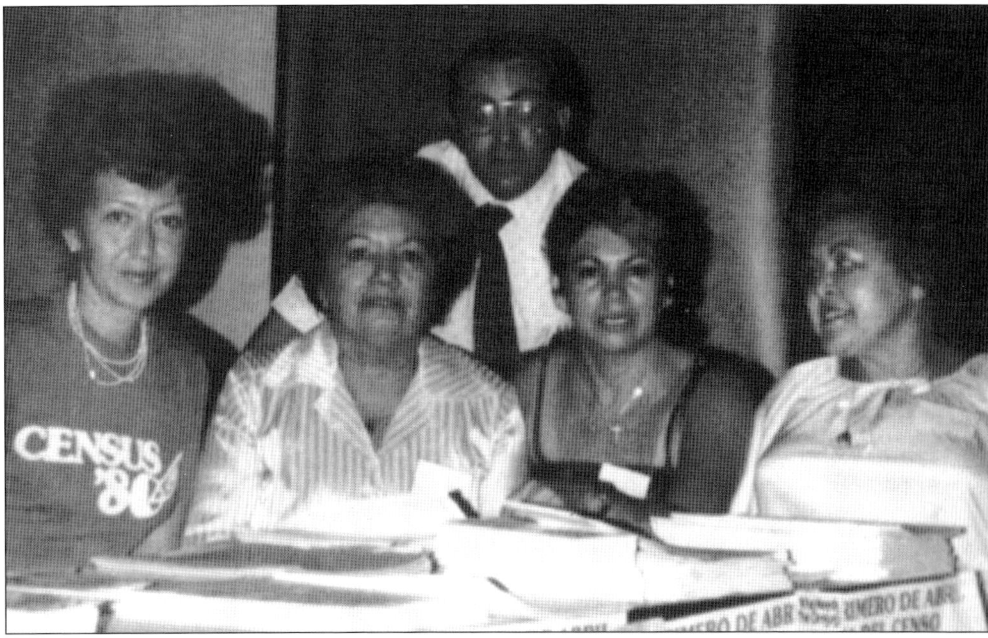

NACOPRW was very active in assisting the US Census Bureau's efforts in gathering data for the 1980 Census. In this photograph, Dr. Alicia Baro and several members of her group are working to help get the word out about the importance of the Census in the Latino community. (Courtesy of NACOPRW.)

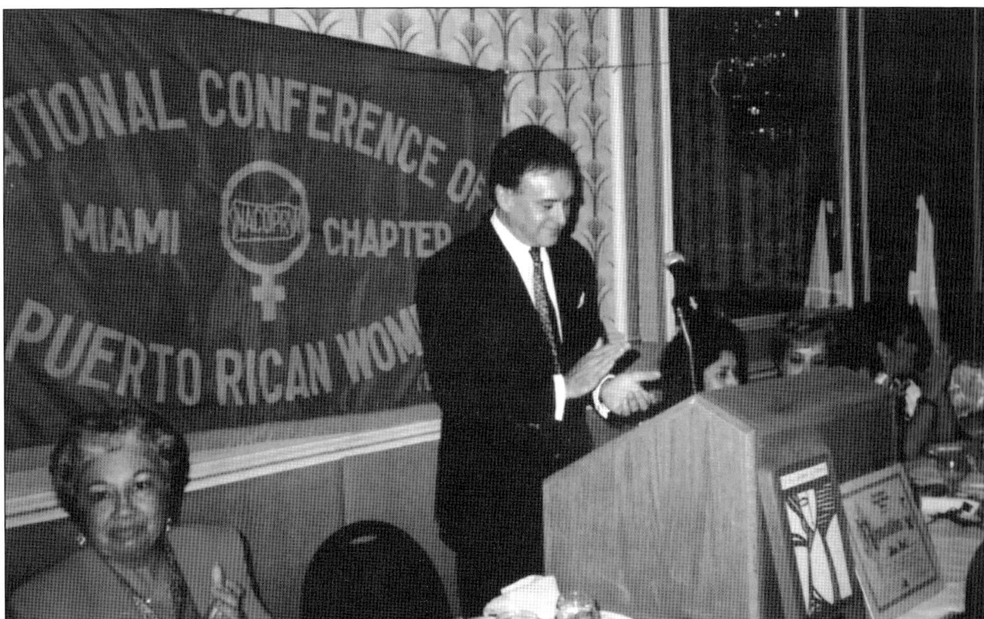

Mayor Maurice Ferre was a huge supporter of NACOPRW during and after his six terms in office (1973–1985). In fact, according to Dr. Alicia Baro, it was Ferre who encouraged her to organize a chapter of NACOPRW in Miami. At this 1980s fundraising event, Ferre presented the organization with a proclamation from the City of Miami for its work in the community. (Courtesy of NACOPRW.)

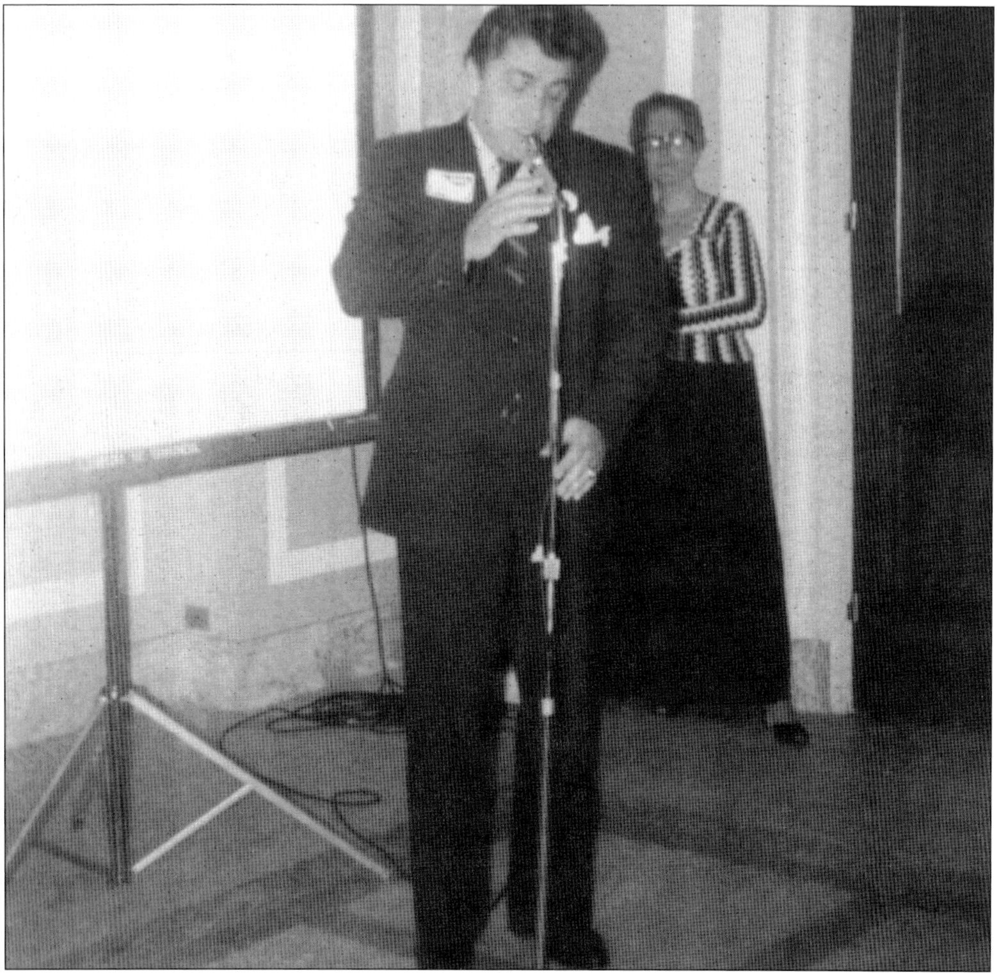

US Congressman Robert "Bobby" Garcia was a Puerto Rican politician born and raised in the South Bronx. He was a Korean War veteran who served as a radio operator. He was first elected to the New York State Assembly (1966–1967) and then became state senator (1967–1978). When Herman Badillo, the first Puerto Rican elected to Congress from New York, stepped down to run for mayor of New York, Garcia replaced him. He served in Congress for 22 years (1978–1990). In this c. 1980 photograph, Congressman Garcia addresses a meeting of NACOPRW. (Courtesy of NACOPRW.)

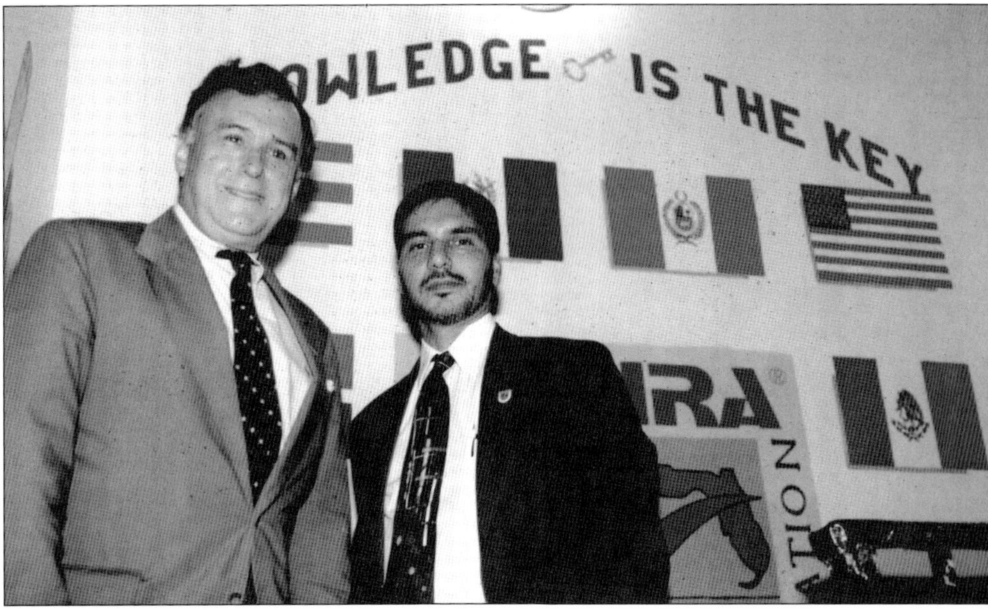

Mayor Maurice Ferre was a big supporter of ASPIRA, and worked very closely with Raul Martinez, who was in charge of youth leadership. Martinez also recognized the importance of leaders like Mayor Ferre, Dr. Baro, and Emilio Lopez, and continued to engage them and invite them to meetings of Aspirantes. It was good for these high school students to hear from leaders and learn about the struggles and successes of the Puerto Rican community in Miami. In addition, Ferre and Martinez represented two generations of Puerto Rican leaders as well as the transitions occurring in the community during the 1980s. (Courtesy of ASPIRA of Florida.)

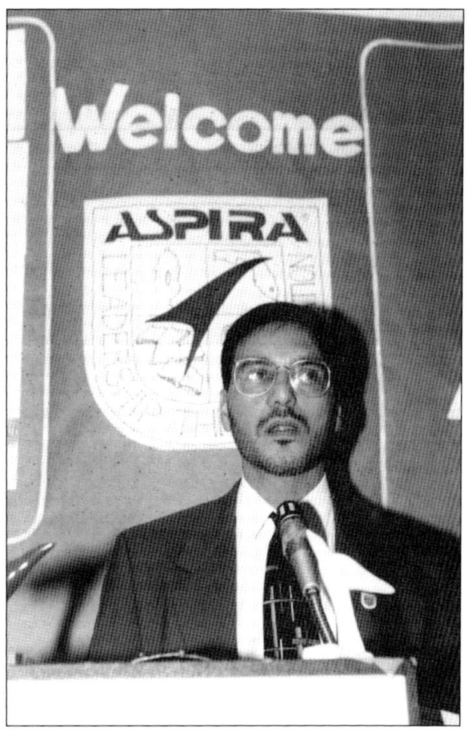

When this photograph was taken in the late 1980s, Raul A. Martinez had taken the helm of ASPIRA of Florida. When Victoria Hernandez left ASPIRA in 1988, she recommended Martinez to the board. Over the next 25 years, Martinez expanded the organization's programming across three South Florida counties. (Courtesy of ASPIRA of Florida.)

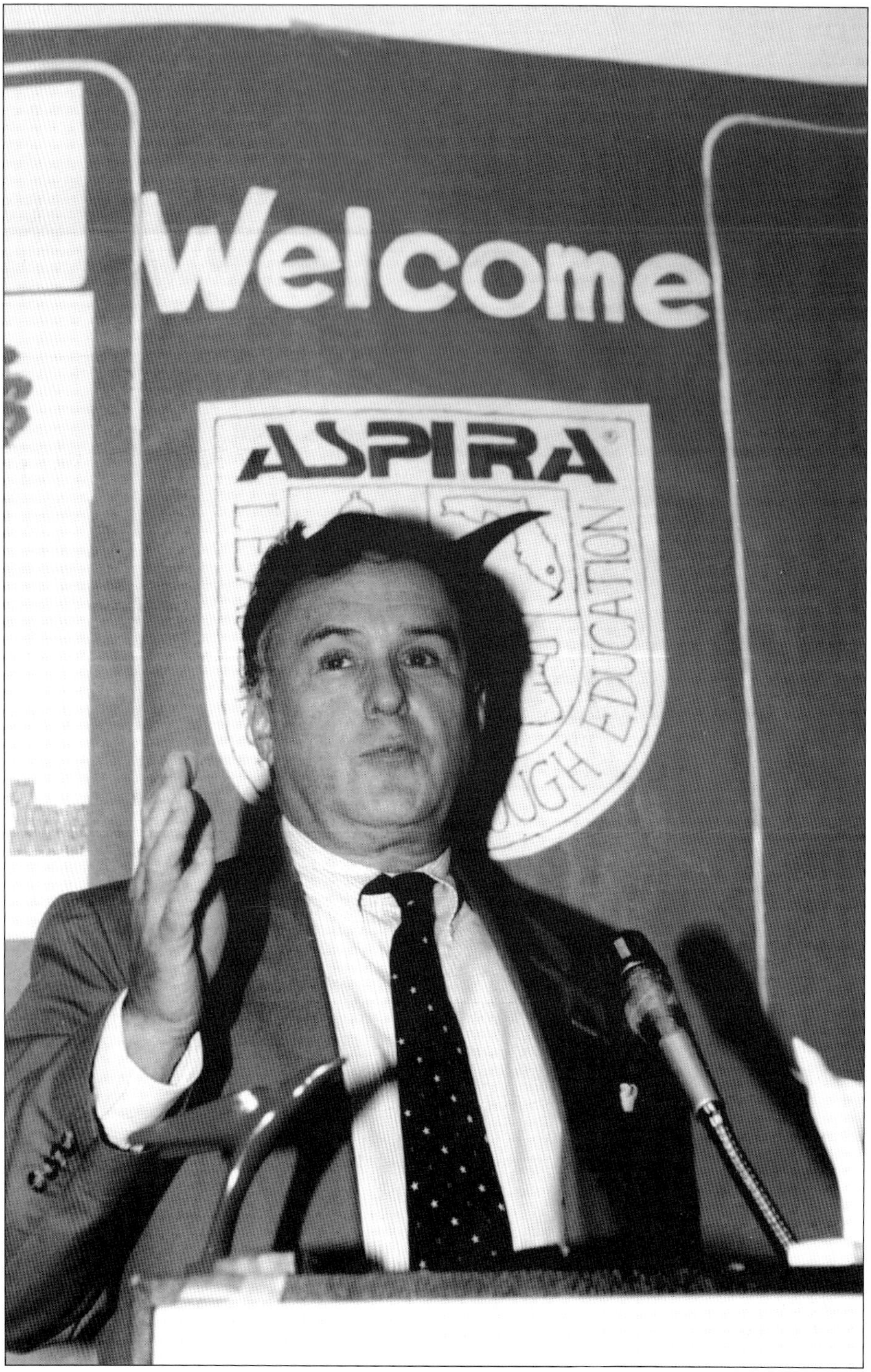

Maurice Ferre, seen here around 1989, was a very sought-after speaker. He was engaging and intelligent and could quote philosophers while discussing international trade or transportation (one of his specialties). He could talk to students about their goals and aspirations and of the importance of giving back to the community. (Courtesy of ASPIRA of Florida.)

Three

POLITICS AND CIVIC LIFE

Beginning in the 1950s and for the next 70 years, Puerto Ricans in Miami–Dade County formed a myriad of political and civic organizations. Both Dorothy Quintana and Dr. Alicia S. Baro were involved in the struggles and evolution of Puerto Ricans in Miami for more than 50 years. Many of the Puerto Rican organizations in the city, like ASPIRA of Florida and NACOPRW, were incubated in Wynwood. The oldest of these groups, the Organización de Demócratas Puertorriqueños/Organization of Puerto Rican Democrats (ODP), was founded in 1955, also in Wynwood, to address the civil rights of Puerto Rican farmworkers in Homestead and discrimination against Puerto Ricans in Wynwood. The ODP's challenges were great, since working and living conditions for these laborers were often horrific.

During the 1960s, vocal demands by residents of Wynwood for a social services center, particularly one catering to the elderly, resulted in the construction of the Eugenio Maria De Hostos Senior Citizens Center on a large corner lot at NW Second Avenue and Twenty-Ninth Street. The center's namesake was a prominent 19th-century advocate of Puerto Rican independence. Standing across the street from the complex was the Borinquen Health Clinic (its name was derived from the indigenous name for the island of Puerto Rico), led by Emilio Lopez and founded in 1972.

Another effect of the growth of the Puerto Rican diaspora in Miami was felt politically. In the 1950s and 1960s, Puerto Ricans were considered an important voting bloc. In 1967, Maurice A, Ferre, the son of one of the investment families in Miami, was elected a Florida state representative. In a special election in 1972, he was elected the first Hispanic mayor of Miami. Ferre's election opened the door for other Latino politicians, especially for Cubans, who followed him as mayor. Since then, several Puerto Ricans have been elected to the statehouse and as mayors and judges. In addition, in the 1980s and 1990s, other prominent Puerto Rican businesses and educational institutions have opened franchises in Miami. Among them are the Banco Popular, an important banking institution on the island, Carlos Albizu University, and Ana G. Mendez University, which have been serving Miami for decades.

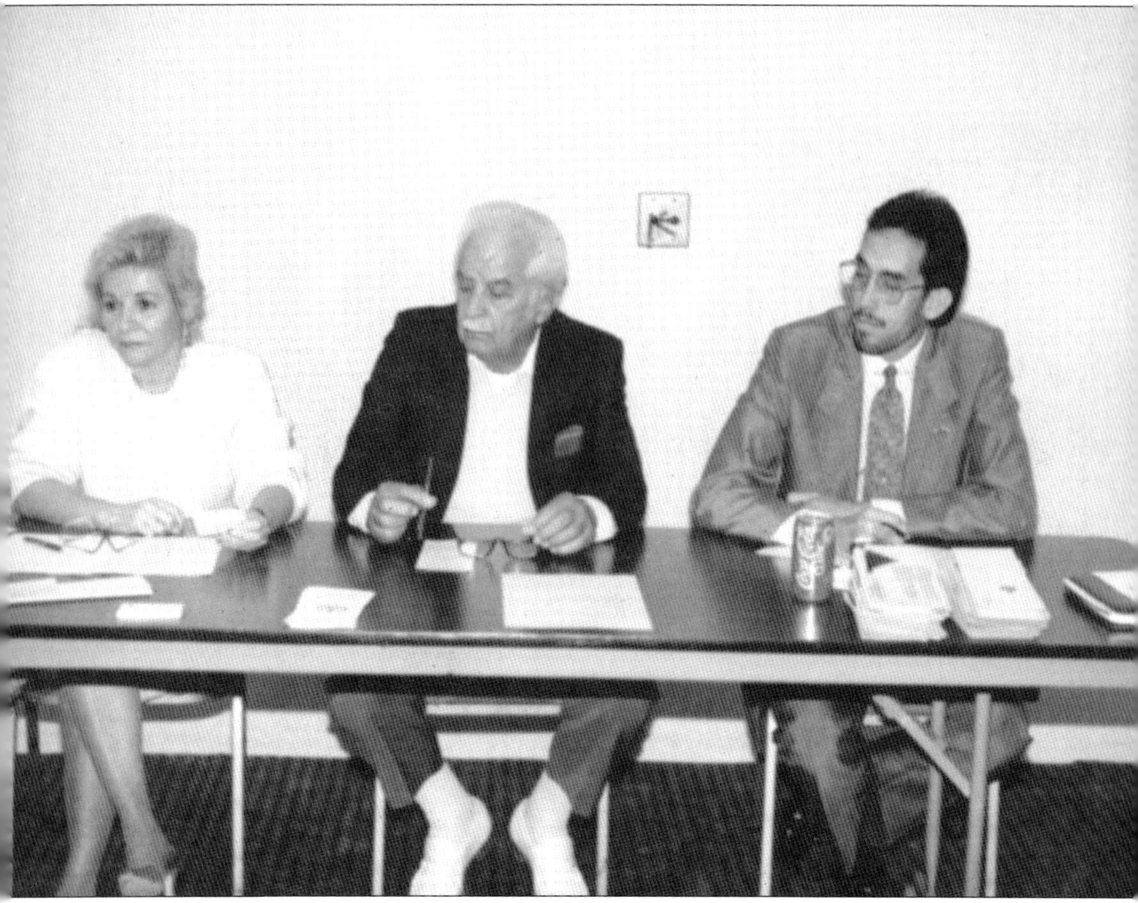

The Puerto Rican Democrat Organization was formed in 1955 by brothers Felix Aguirre and Jose Ramon. Felix was president, Jose was vice president, and Alicia Baro was secretary. They formed to fight the mistreatment of Puerto Rican farmworkers in Homestead. Aguirre owned the Pan American Pharmacy at North Miami Avenue and NW Fifth Street. Pictured here around 1988 from left to right are an unidentified ODP member, Jose Baro, and Willie Ramos. (Courtesy of Luis De Rosa.)

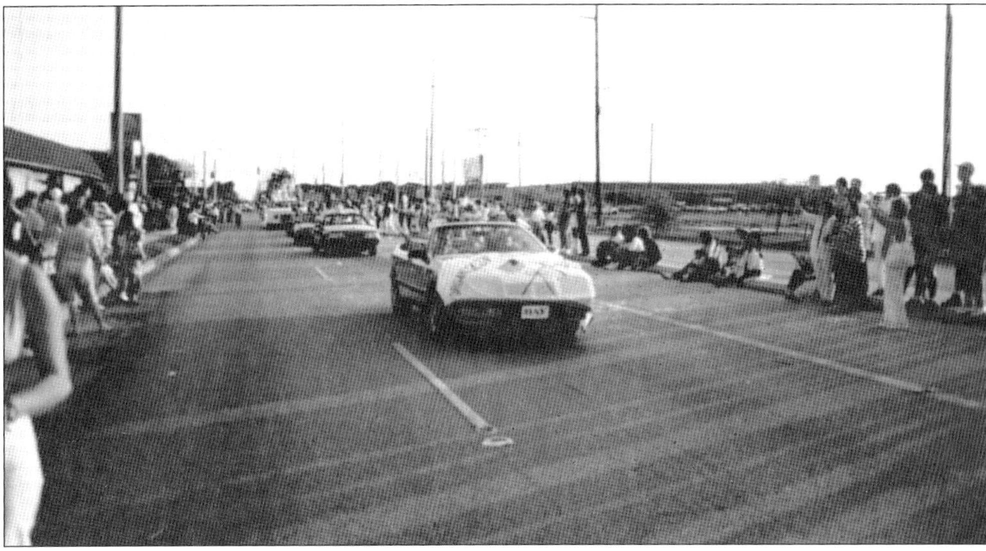

This image was captured during the Festival of Saint John the Baptist in Miami. It has been a tradition in Puerto Rico for many centuries to celebrate the patron Saint of Puerto Rico's birthday. Legend has it that it was June 24 when he was born. The holiday begins on the eve of his birth, with Puerto Ricans flocking to the beaches and, right before midnight, dunking themselves backward into the water three times to cleanse their sins and hope for good fortune. Many Puerto Rican communities have followed this tradition. Led by Gil Garcia, a group of Puerto Ricans began this celebration in 1980. The festival always included artists like Ismael Miranda. (Courtesy of Gil Garcia.)

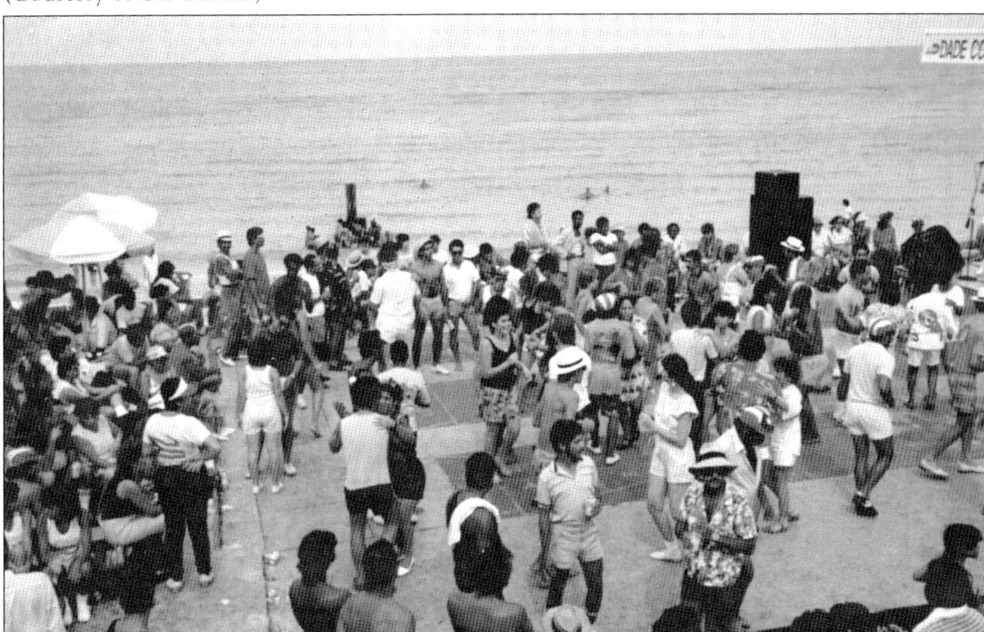

Revelers enjoy the Fiesta San Juan Bautista while performers from the island play in this annual event in 1980. These events were usually held either at the Waikiki Hotel or the Marco Polo Hotel in North Miami Beach. Attendees would dance into the night, and then many would walk down to the beach to jump into the water backward near midnight. (Courtesy of Gil Garcia.)

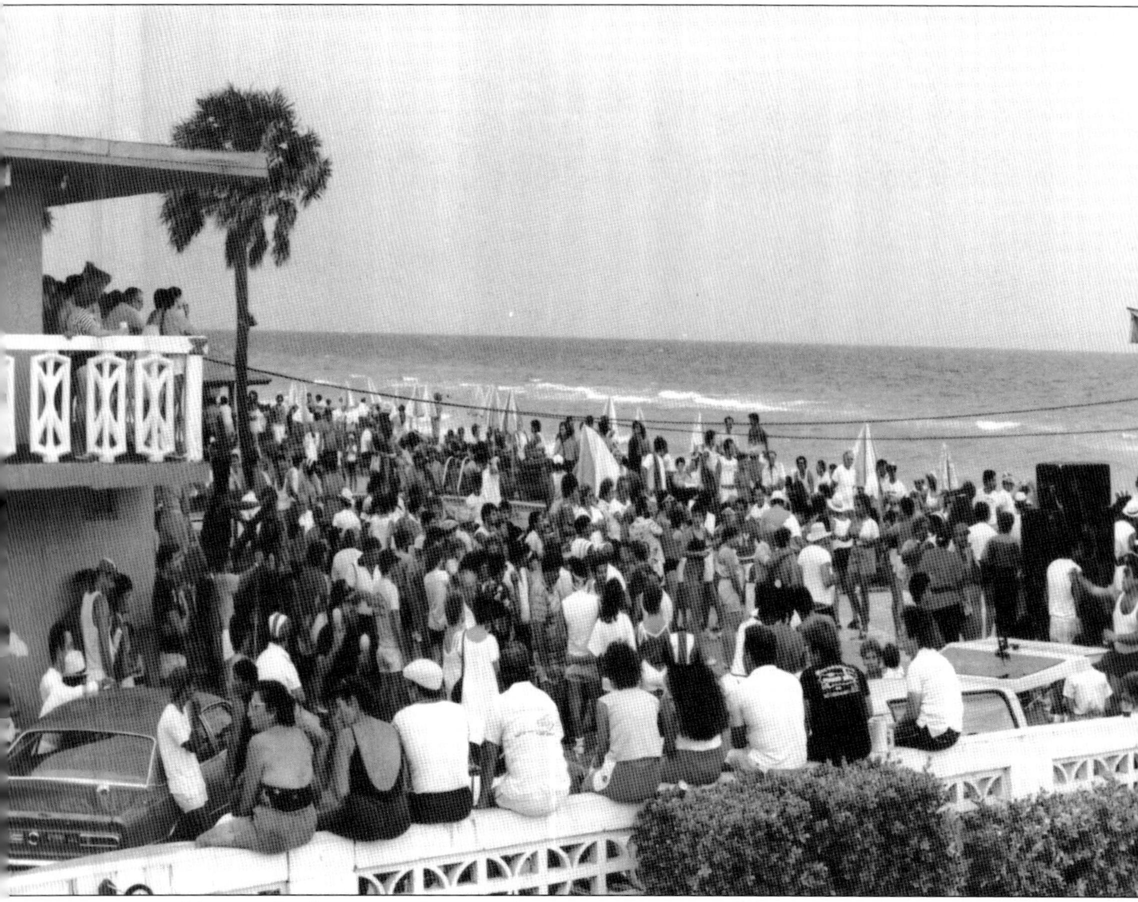

Pictured here is the first annual Fiesta of San Juan Bautista celebrated in North Miami Beach in 1981. These events became very popular and were well attended. Over the years, more vendors would attend, and premier orchestras would perform, including some of the top names in the business, like El Gran Combo. (Courtesy of Gil Garcia.)

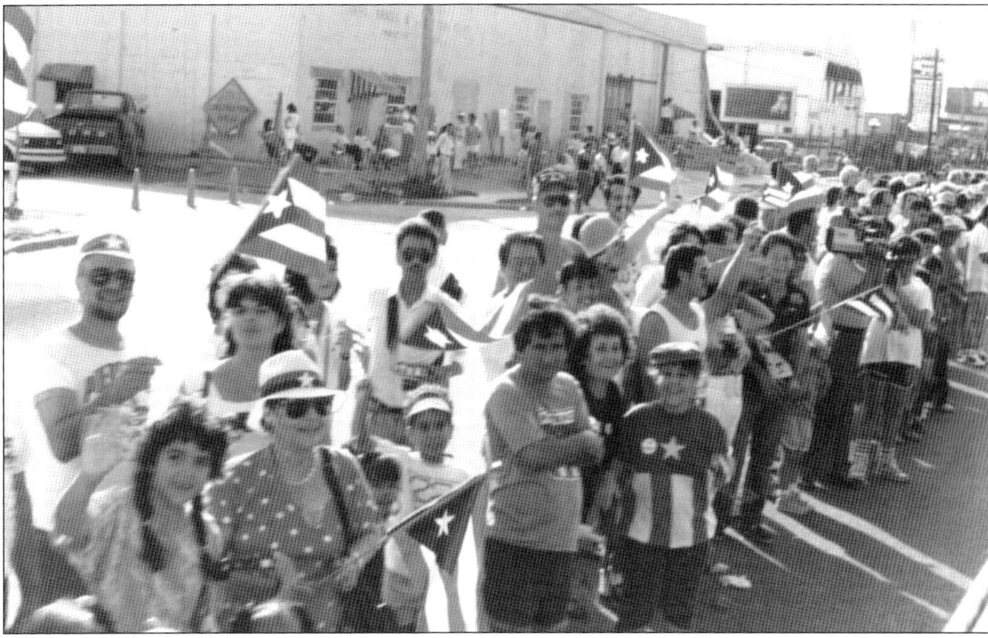

In the 1980s, the San Juan Club, another organization formed in Miami, began organizing Puerto Rican Day parades. The parades included many different floats as well as dignitaries from the island. Pictured here are folks waiting for the floats to come by. The parade would end near the site of the San Juan Festival, where the participants would blend in with the attendees. (Courtesy of Gil Garcia.)

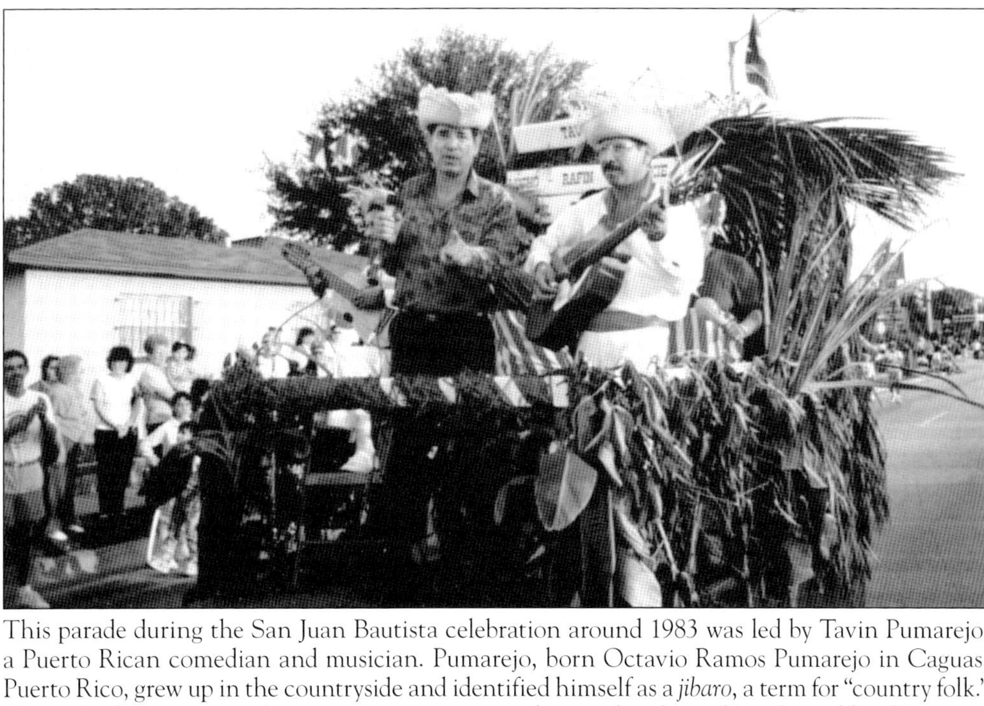

This parade during the San Juan Bautista celebration around 1983 was led by Tavin Pumarejo, a Puerto Rican comedian and musician. Pumarejo, born Octavio Ramos Pumarejo in Caguas, Puerto Rico, grew up in the countryside and identified himself as a *jibaro*, a term for "country folk." He used a folksy vernacular, sometimes exaggerated, to endear himself to the public. (Courtesy of Gil Garcia.)

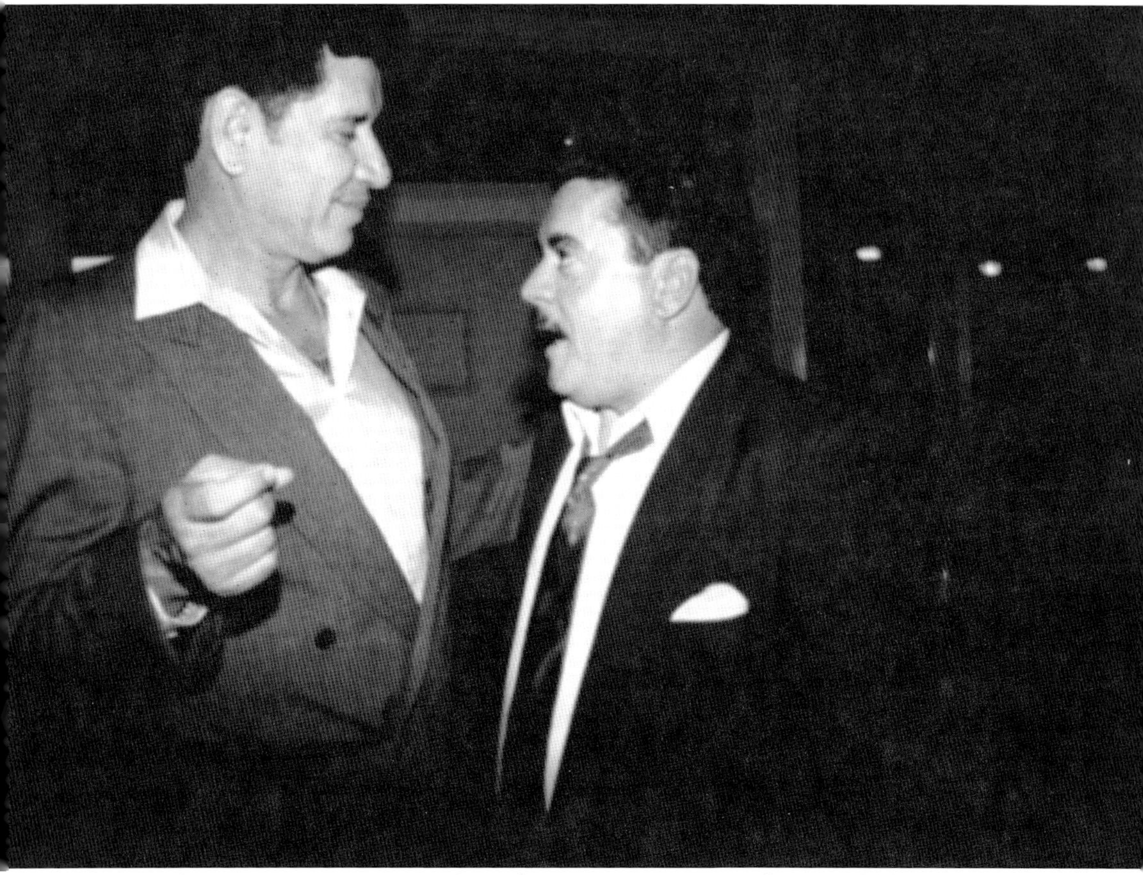

After the Puerto Rican Day parade at the San Juan Bautista, there would be a reception with the honored guest from Puerto Rico. Pictured here is Tavin Pumarejo joining in the festivities and speaking with one of the organizers. Pumarejo not only sang but did comedy as well. He was well-received as a native son. He was a popular figure in television on the island. (Courtesy of Gil Garcia.)

Dr. Carlos Albizu-Miranda was the first Puerto Rican to earn a doctorate degree in the United States, in the 1950s. A prominent leader in his discipline, he founded the first graduate program on the island, the Caribbean Center. In 1985, he came to Miami to establish a campus of the Miami Institute of Psychology. After his passing, the center was renamed Carlos Albizu University, now located in Doral. (Courtesy of Dr. Teresa Albizu.)

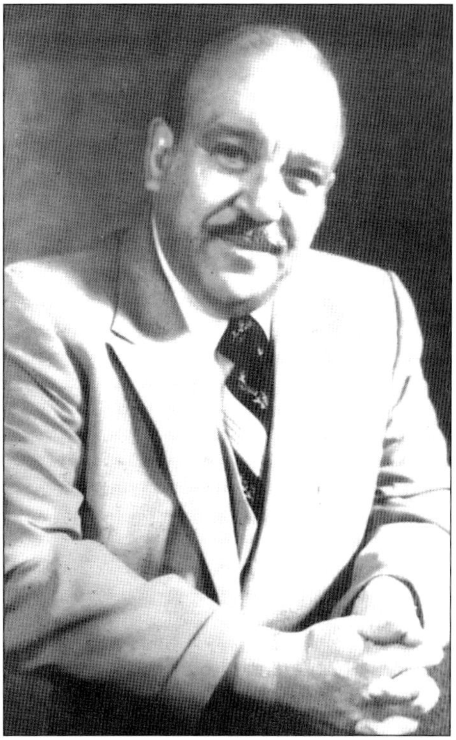

Pictured here is Dr. Alicia S. Baro with NACOPRW on a boat ride around Biscayne Bay in Miami around the 1980s. These events were very popular forms of bringing together members to eat and discuss matters of importance; they could invite family members, including their children and grandchildren. (Courtesy of NACOPRW.)

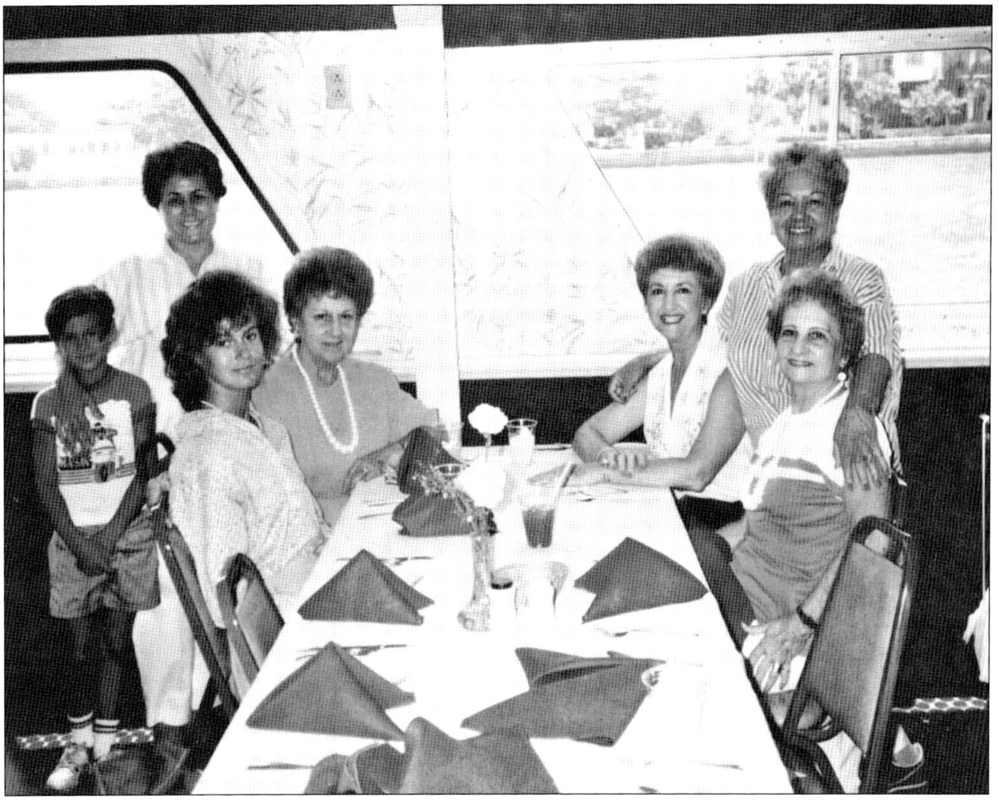

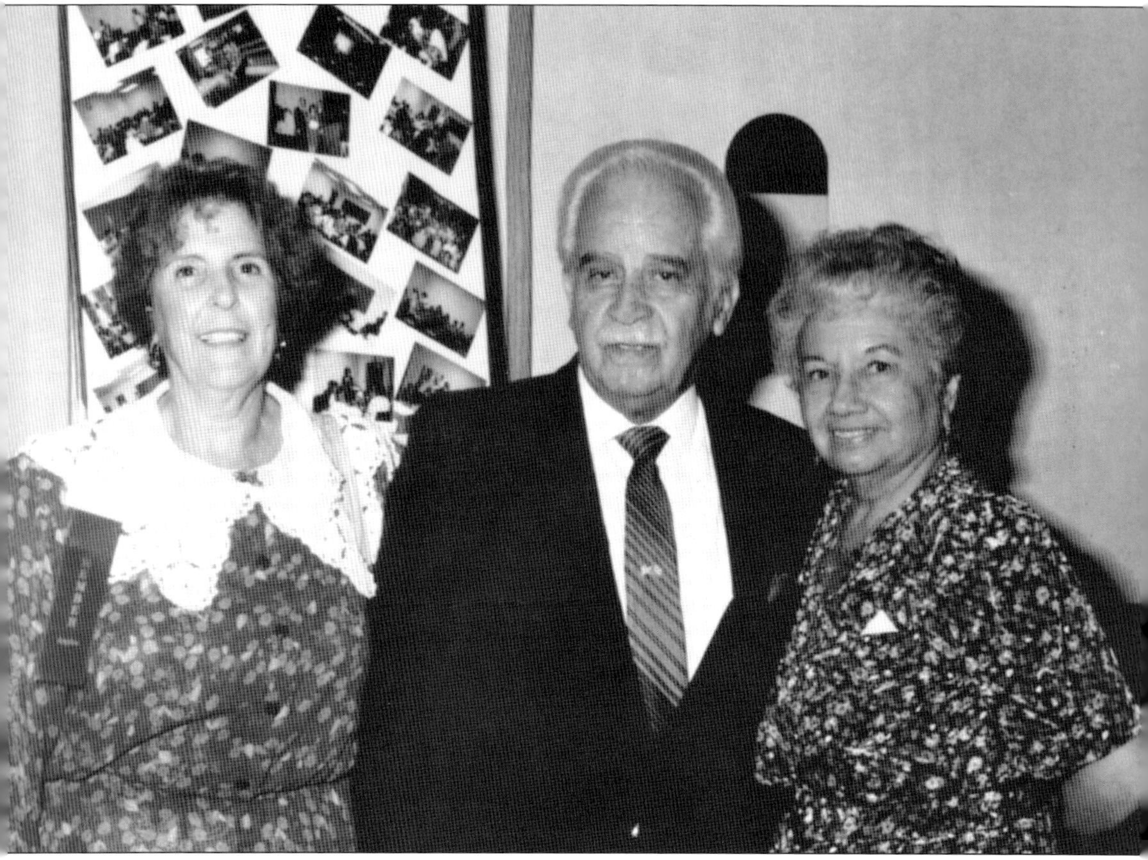

Pictured from left to right are Dr. Ivette Morgan, Jose Baro, and Dr. Alicia S. Baro at a function of the Puerto Rican Democratic Organization. The group was active from 1955 until the early 2000s. The ODP usually had candidates' forums or brought in speakers to talk about policy issues that affected the local Puerto Rican community. (Courtesy of Luis De Rosa.)

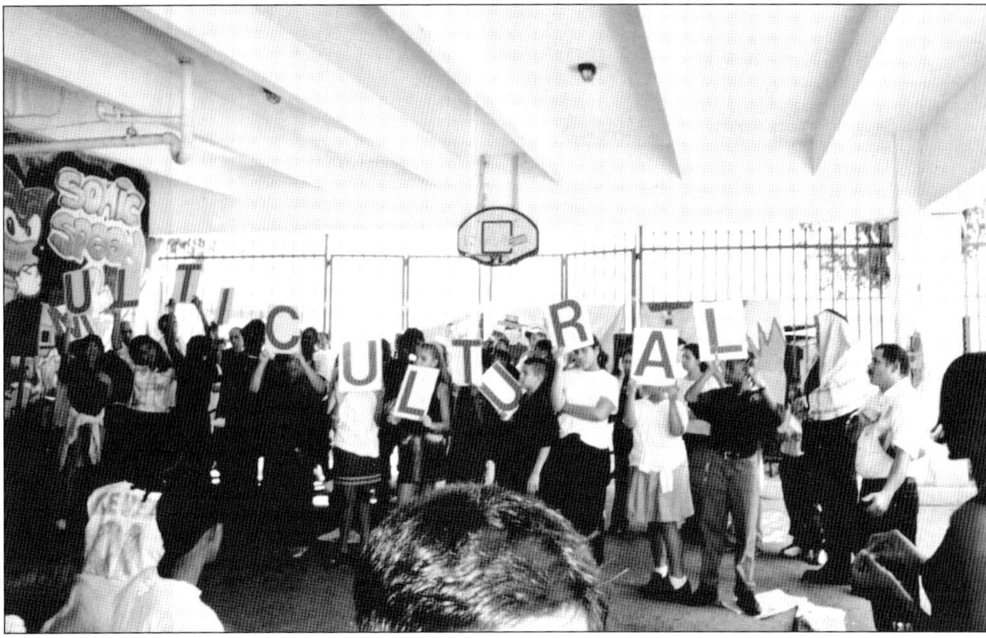

Pictured here are Aspirantes celebrating Multicultural Day. While ASPIRA was founded as a Puerto Rican organization to address the high dropout rates of students in New York in 1961, by the 1980s, it had expanded its outreach to many Latino students and, as in Miami, to Haitian American students as well. (Courtesy of ASPIRA of Florida.)

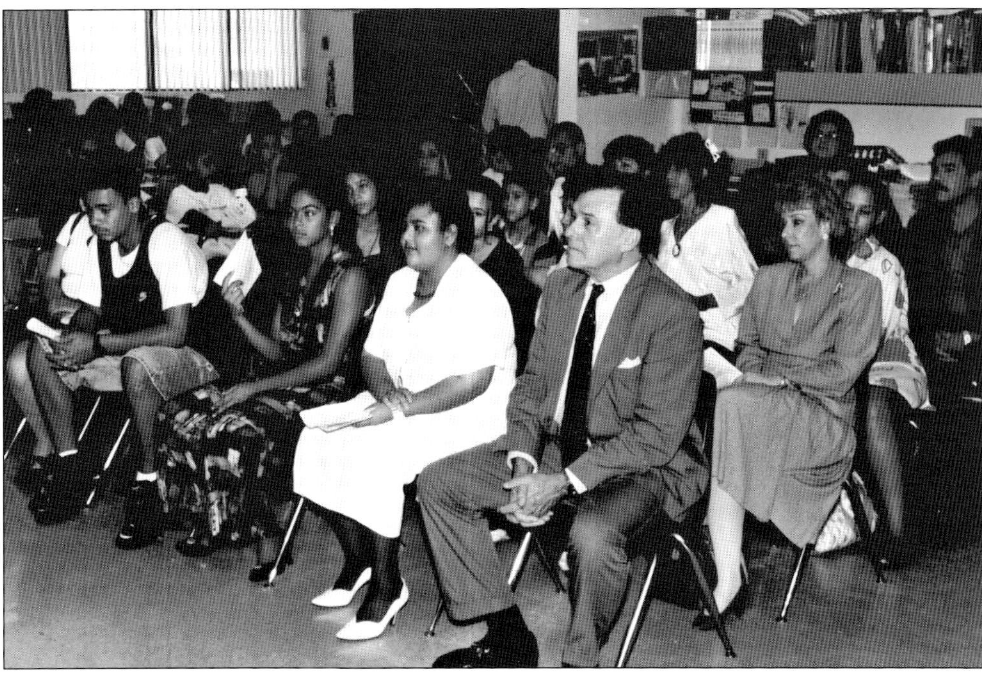

Seen here is a school assembly at the Eugenio Maria de Hostos ASPIRA Middle School in Wynwood. Former mayor Maurice Ferre is sitting in the audience, waiting to speak to students, teachers, and staff. Ferre was always a welcome speaker at special events at ASPIRA, especially on Puerto Rican Days in the 1980s. (Courtesy of ASPIRA of Florida.)

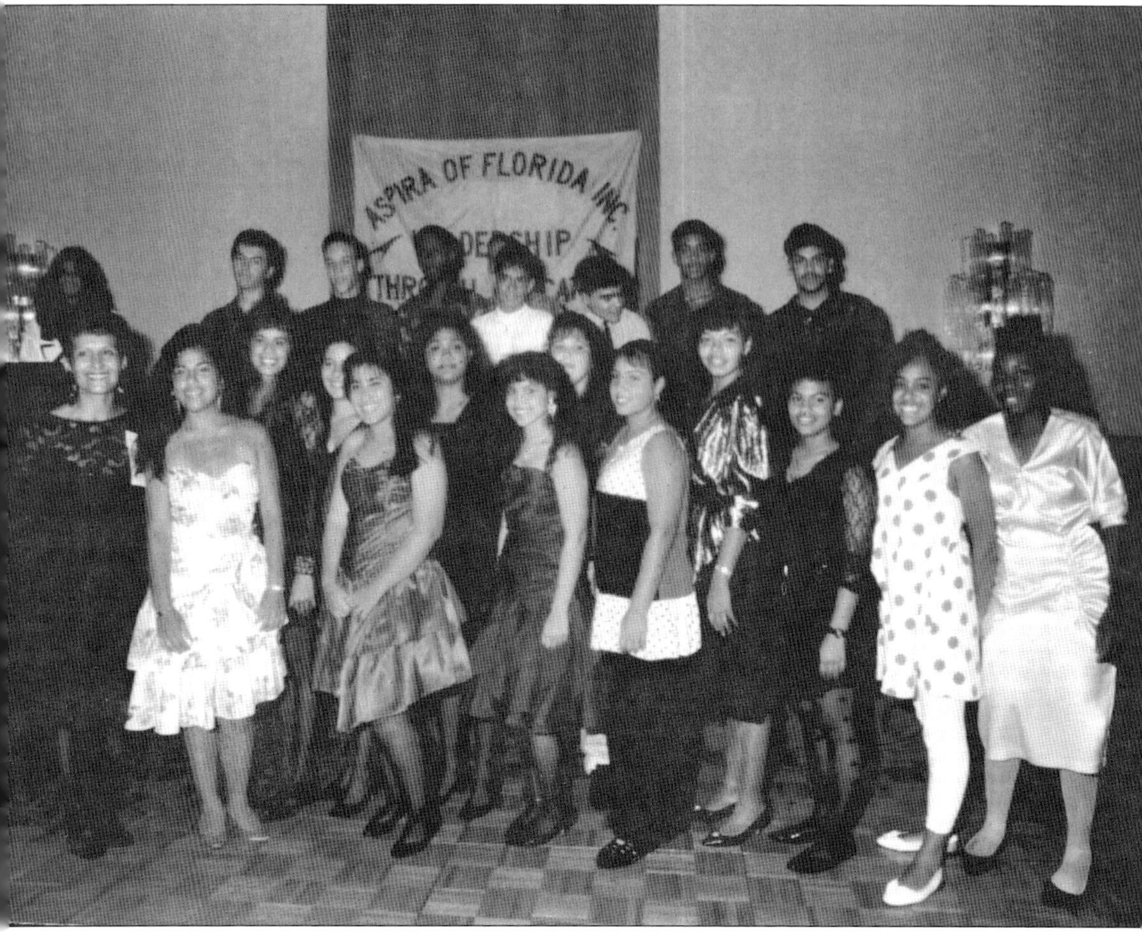

Pictured here is a ceremony of a Miami Beach school ASPIRA club. The school-based clubs were at the heart of the ASPIRA model of teaching students about history, culture, academic achievement, and leadership. Each club always had a school-based counselor or teacher advisor, like US Army veteran Nancy Snell, seen here at far left. (Courtesy of ASPIRA of Florida.)

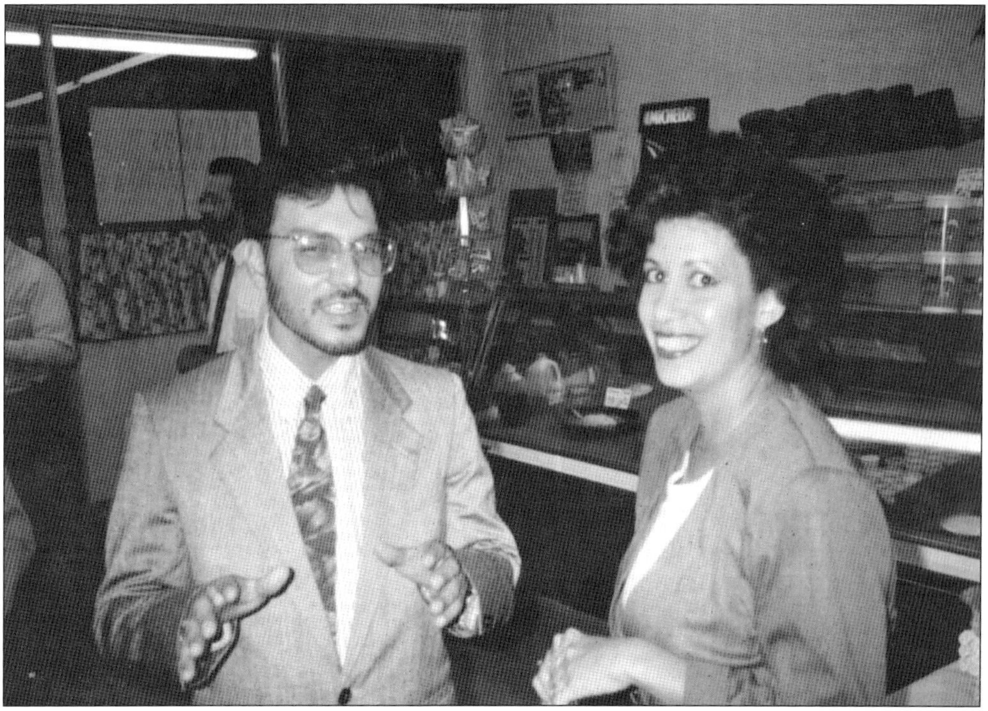

Pictured here is Raul Martinez, ASPIRA CEO, chatting with ASPIRA deputy director William Ramos's girlfriend, Raquel, during a break in a staff celebration around 1990. The event was held at a Puerto Rican restaurant on Eighth Street, the famous Calle Ocho, in Miami. (Courtesy of ASPIRA of Florida.)

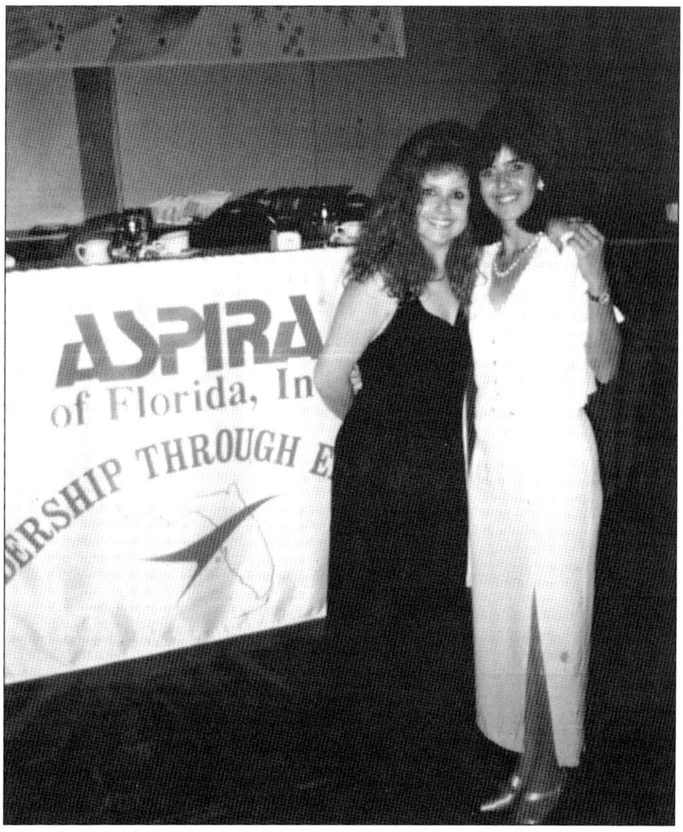

Pictured here is Syndia A. Nazario with an Aspirante at an awards ceremony in the 1990s. Nazario was a counselor and director with the ASPIRA North division. She began her career as a preschool teacher and worked to develop leaders through education. (Courtesy of ASPIRA of Florida.)

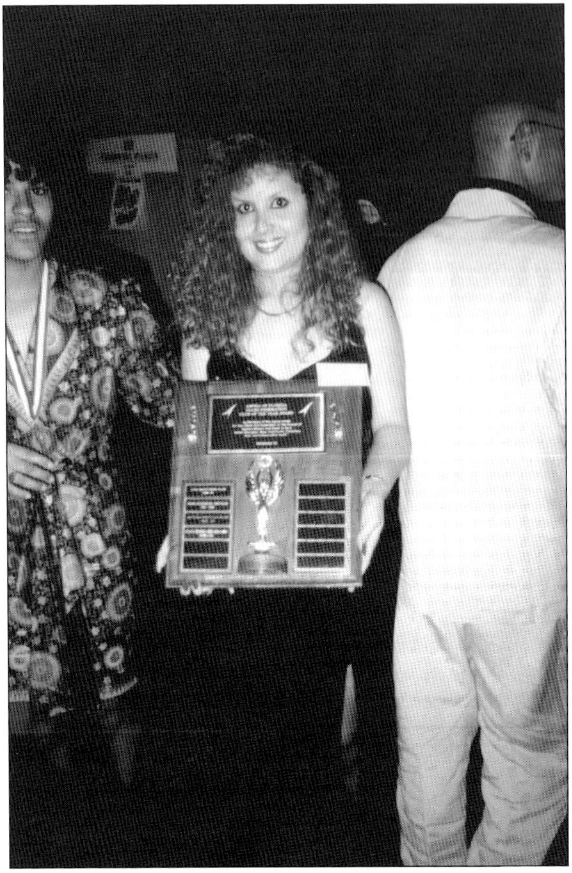

Pictured here is Syndia A. Nazario as a director of the ASPIRA North Division, receiving recognition for her work. When ASPIRA expanded its operations into the cities of Miramar and Pembroke Pines in Broward County, Nazario was tapped to lead. Her success led Ana G. Mendez University of Puerto Rico to recruit her when they decided to expand to South Florida. (Courtesy of ASPIRA of Florida.)

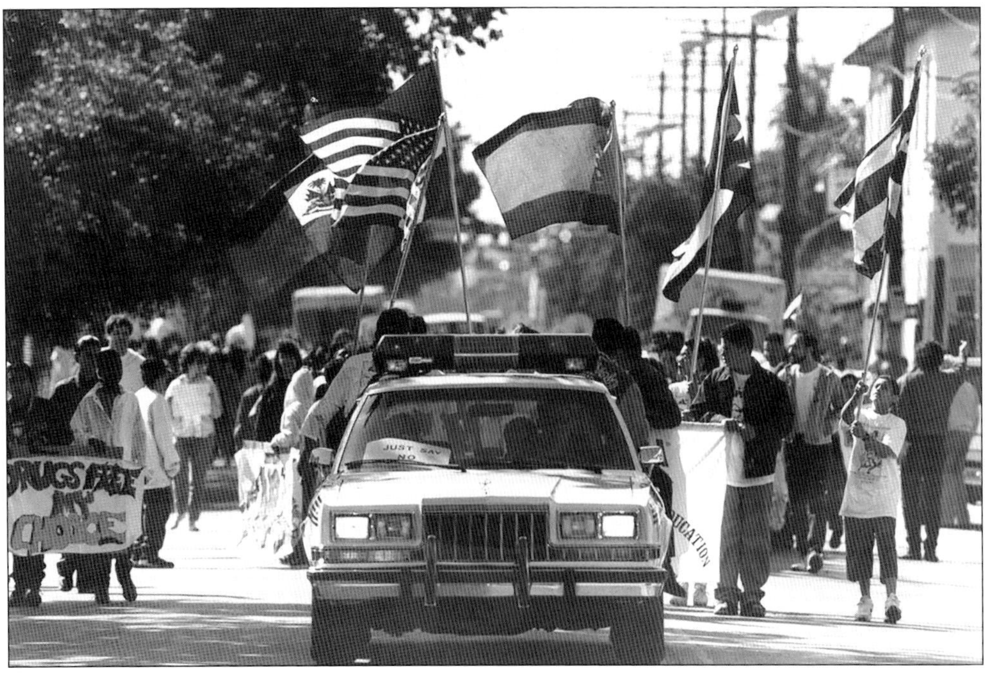

Pictured here is a march through the streets of Wynwood in 1990 to advocate for a drug-free community. Residents were reacting to the infestation of illegal drugs on Miami streets, especially in minority communities. It was the time of the crack cocaine epidemic, and Wynwood felt its wrath. (Courtesy of Casey Piket.)

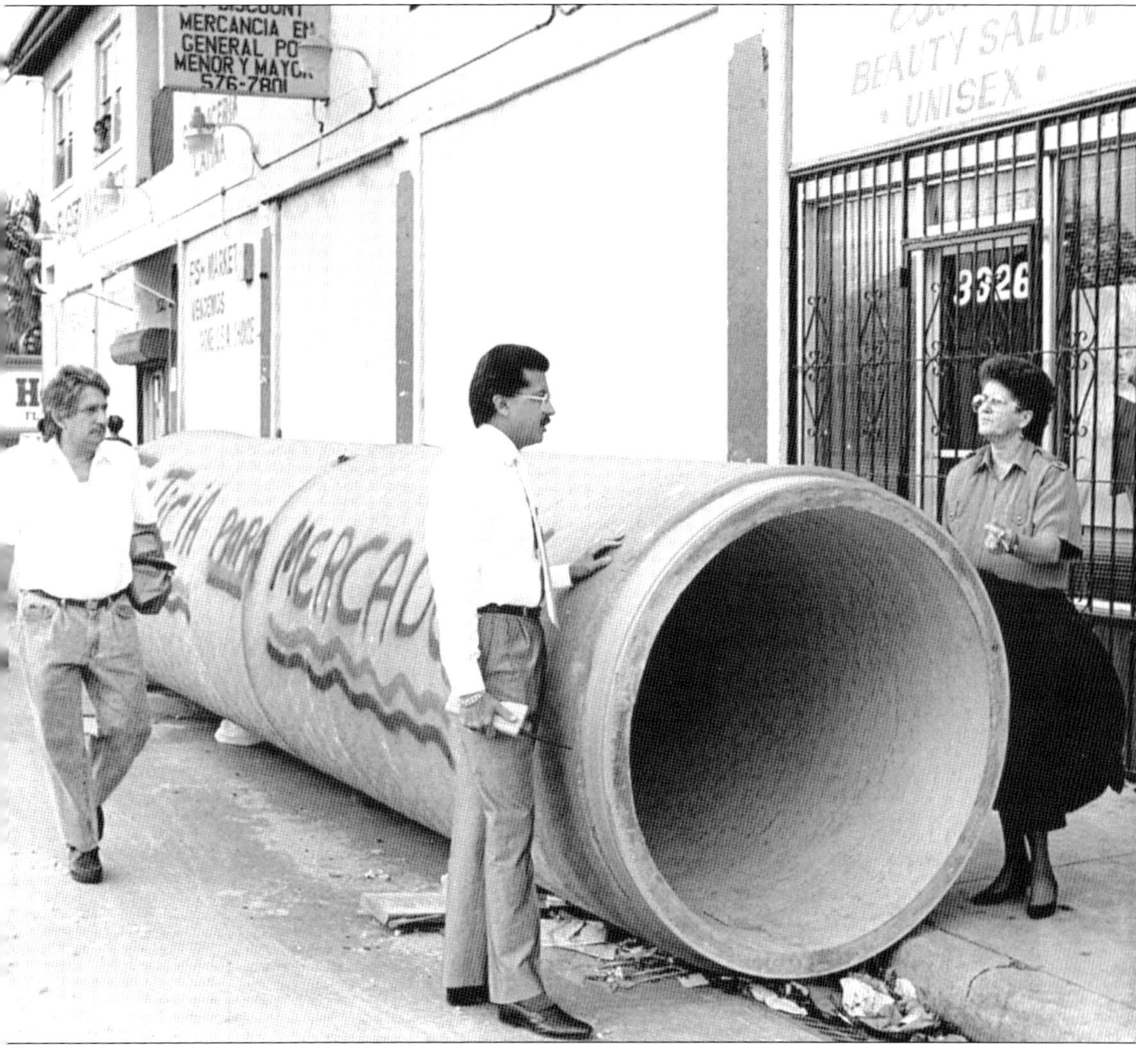

At left is Eleno Alvarez, owner of Robert Supermarket on NW Second Avenue between NW Thirty-Third and Thirty-Fourth Streets. He is walking toward Freddie Santiago, owner of a travel agency, and Elena Alvarez as they discuss construction issues in the community. Along the side of the water main, someone wrote, "Justice for Mercado," the Puerto Rican beaten to death by police in 1988. (Courtesy of Casey Piket.)

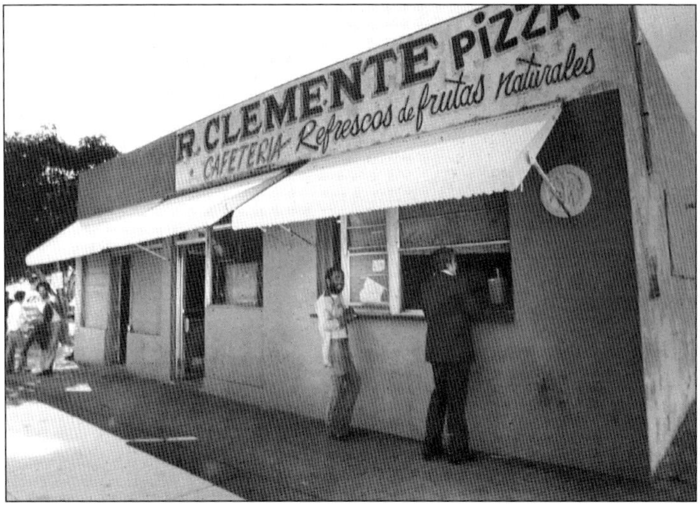

Pictured here is one of the many Puerto Rican–owned businesses in the 1980s. The cafeteria/pizzeria carries the name of Puerto Rican baseball great Roberto Clemente, whose name is also on the baseball field just a few blocks away. Note some deterioration of the buildings. When the garment factories left Wynwood, the community was hit hard. (Courtesy of Casey Piket.)

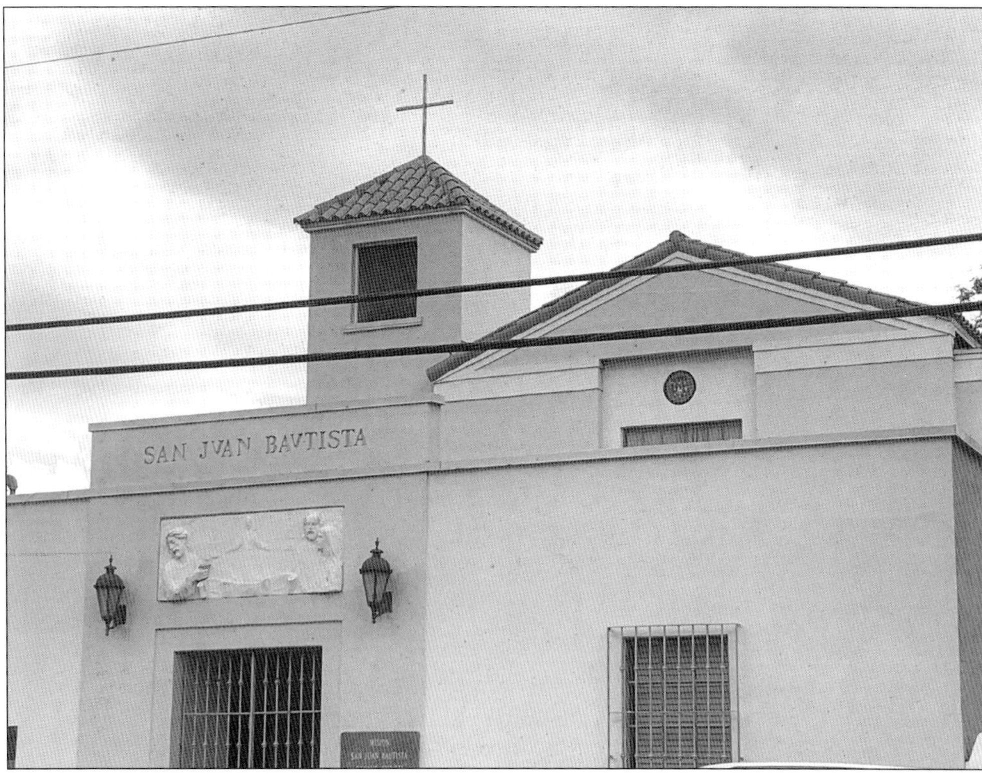

The Mission of Saint John the Baptist/Mision de San Juan Bautista is in the heart of the Puerto Rican settlement in Wynwood at 3116 NW Second Avenue. The mission was the first launched by the Corpus Christi Catholic Church in nearby Allapattah. It was under the guidance of Father Menendez to open a mission in Wynwood in the late 1980s. (Courtesy of Luz Sofia Vazquez-Hernandez.)

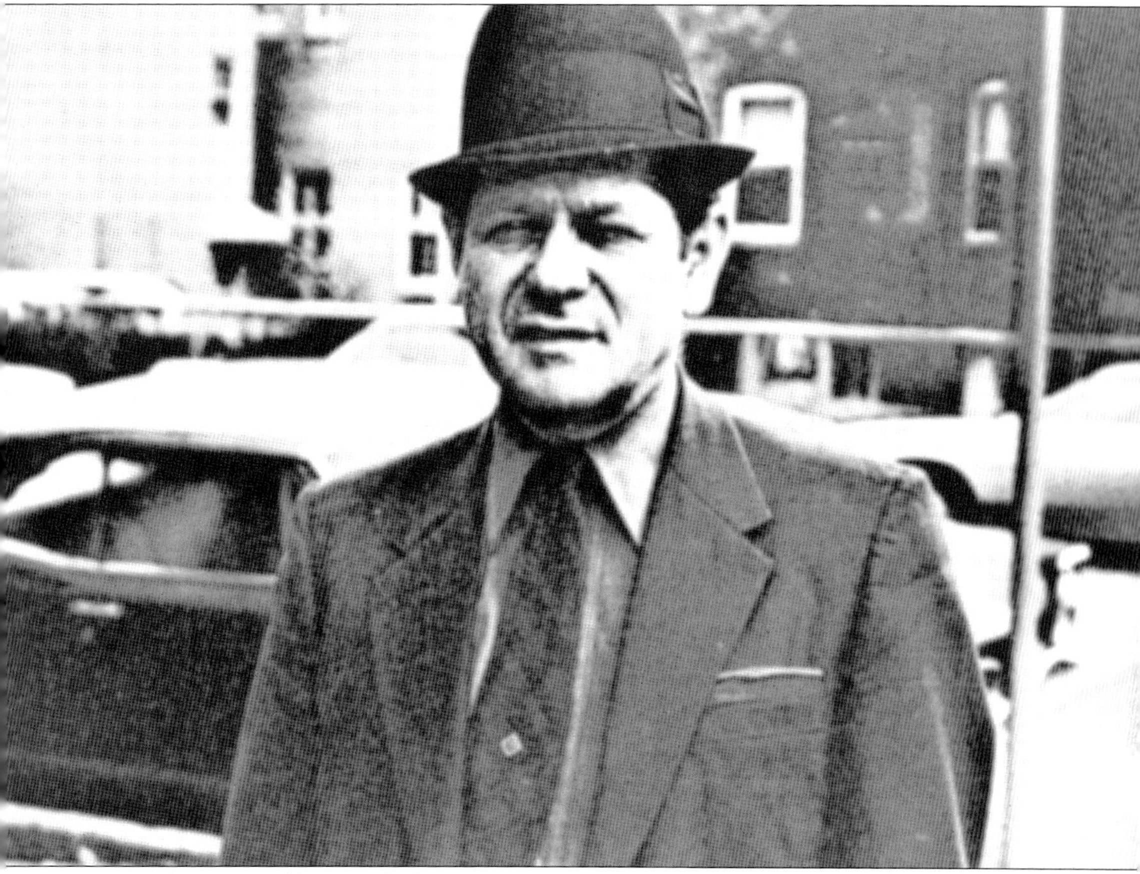

Gregorio Velez, pictured here in the late 1960s in Chicago, was born in Puerto Rico. He moved to the Windy City in 1952 and worked for Western Bell Telephone Company. He raised his family in Chicago and became a lay deacon for the Catholic archdiocese. In the late 1970s, he moved to Miami and continued his work at Corpus Christi in Allapattah and was involved with the San Juan Mission in Wynwood. (Courtesy of the Velez sisters.)

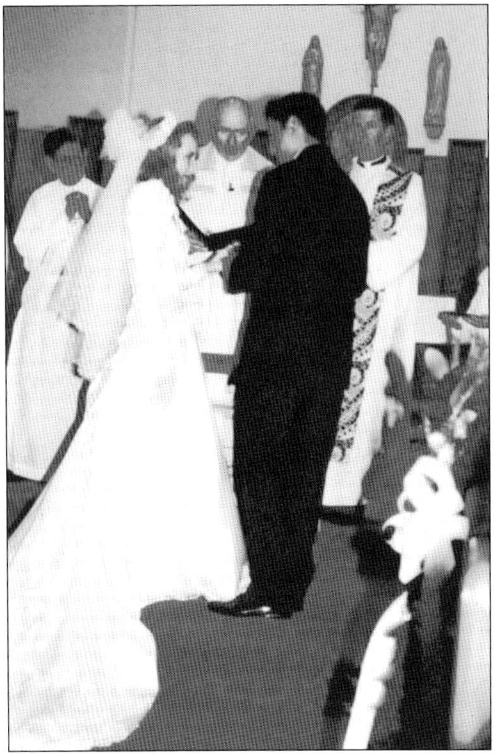

Deacon Velez is pictured helping to officiate a wedding at Corpus Christi Catholic Church in Allapattah in the 1980s. Velez also contributed to the Mission San Juan Bautista and was involved in community projects in Wynwood. (Courtesy of the Velez sisters.)

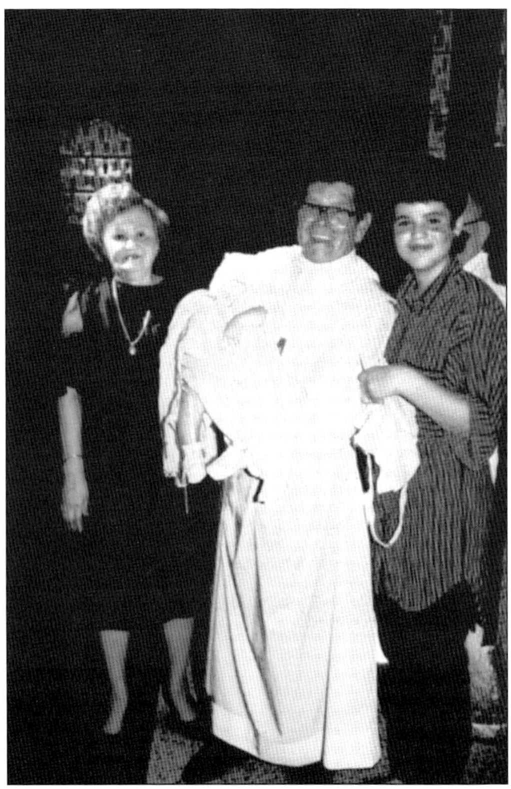

In 1985, Deacon Velez was able to officiate his grandson Ricky's baptism, pictured here. This brought joy to his daughter Nilda and her husband, Raul Ruiz. The baptism took place at the Corpus Christi Church in Allapattah. (Courtesy of the Velez sisters.)

In the late 1980s, Deacon Gregorio Velez became involved in a project in Wynwood to address abandoned houses and other problems dealing with the physical deterioration of the neighborhood. Economic decline and lack of investments in the community brought drug infestations and gang-related problems. Velez was cited in the Catholic newspaper for the archdiocese of Miami for his exemplary work in the community. (Courtesy of the Velez sisters.)

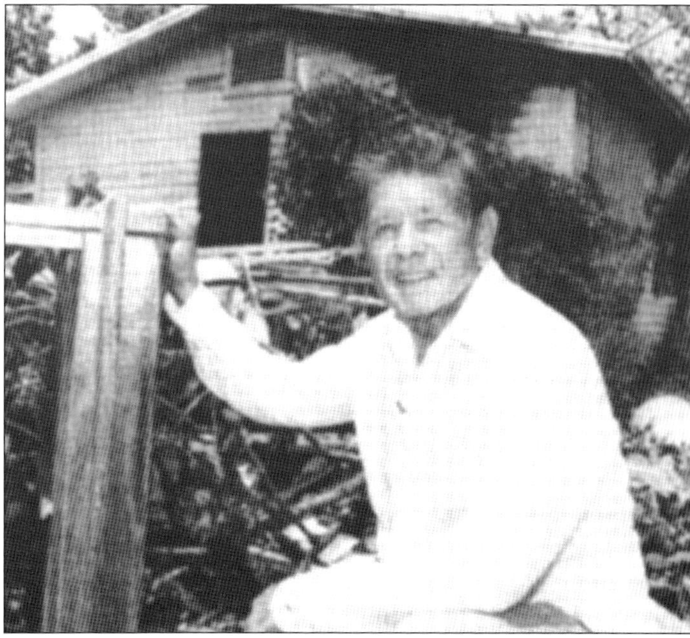

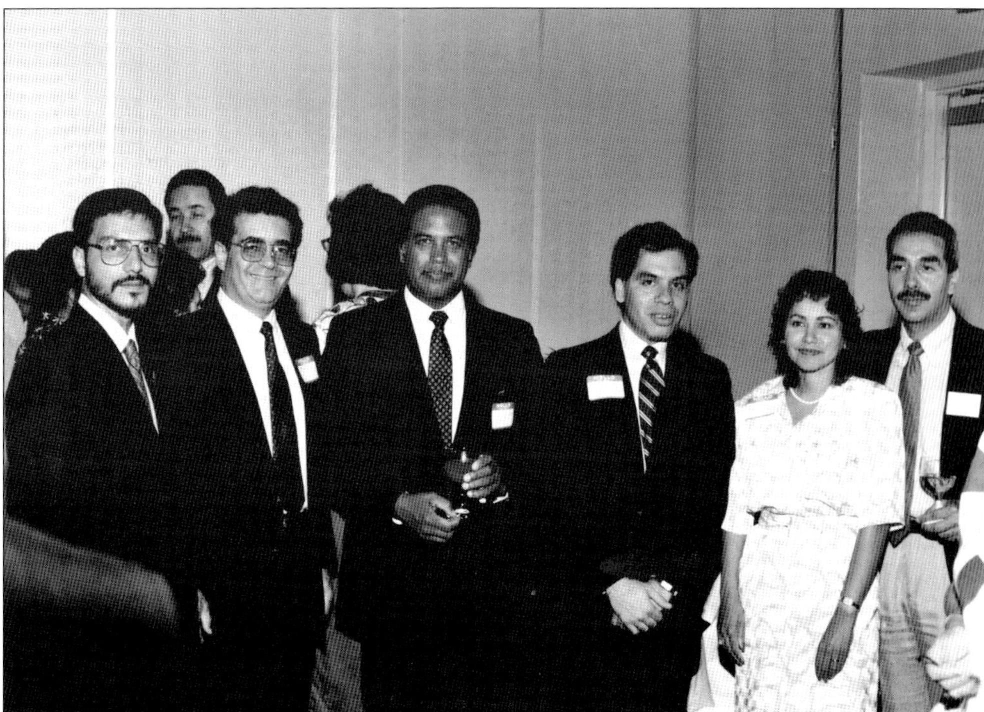

Twice a year, the ASPIRA national board meets to plan and discuss progress and challenges nationally and at the local levels. In this picture from 1990 are ASPIRA CEO Raul Martinez (far left) and directors of associates in Puerto Rican communities in the United States. Attending these meetings were also the chairs of the local boards of directors as well as the presidents of the ASPIRA Clubs Federation. (Courtesy of ASPIRA of Florida.)

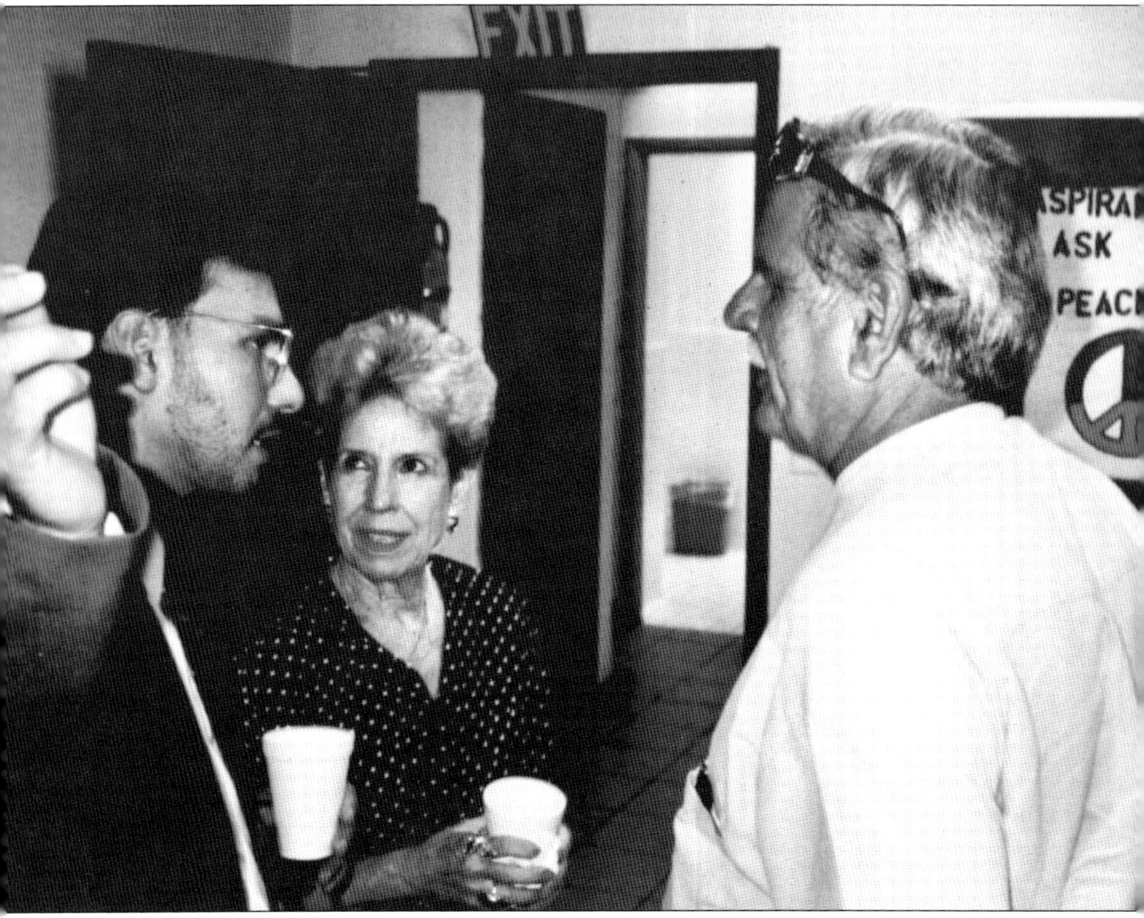

Pictured here are Emilio Lopez, longtime leader of the Puerto Rican community of Wynwood and founder of the Borinquen Health Clinic, visiting ASPIRA offices to meet with executive director Raul Martinez and school board member Betty Kaplan in 1990. Martinez often sought out Lopez for advice or to speak to Aspirantes about the campaigns of Puerto Ricans in Wynwood, especially in regard to the establishment of the clinic. (Courtesy of ASPIRA of Florida.)

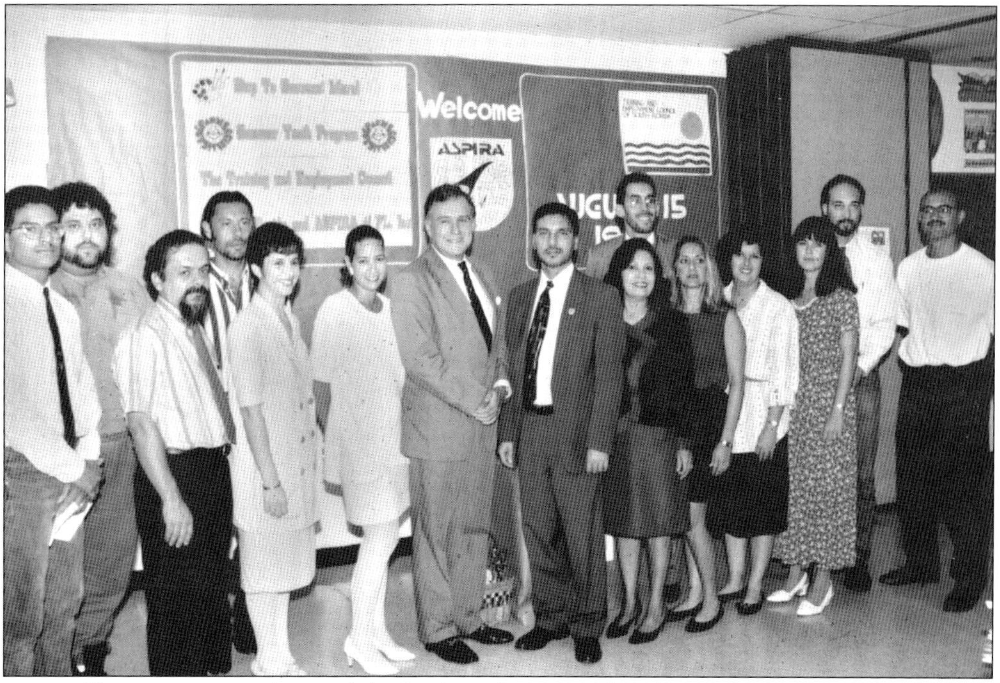

Pictured here in 1993 are the youth leadership advisors and teachers from the ASPIRA Accolade Alternative Middle School, ASPIRA's first school in Wynwood, during a visit from Maurice Ferre. The advisors had a chance to hear him speak and have a warm exchange of ideas. From left to right are (first row) Eduardo Lacayo, advisor; Carlos Salgado, art teacher; Aymet Chaples, ASPIRA COO, Mara Teresa Jimenez, South Division director; Maurice Ferre; Raul Martinez; Aida Diaz, principal; Sara Bajar, advisor; Loyda Lorenzo, reading teacher; Vivian Rowe, social studies teacher; unidentified; and Richard Lozada, advisor; (second row) Antonio Diaz, advisor; Alejandro Flores, language arts teacher; and William Ramos, ASPIRA deputy director. (Courtesy of ASPIRA of Florida.)

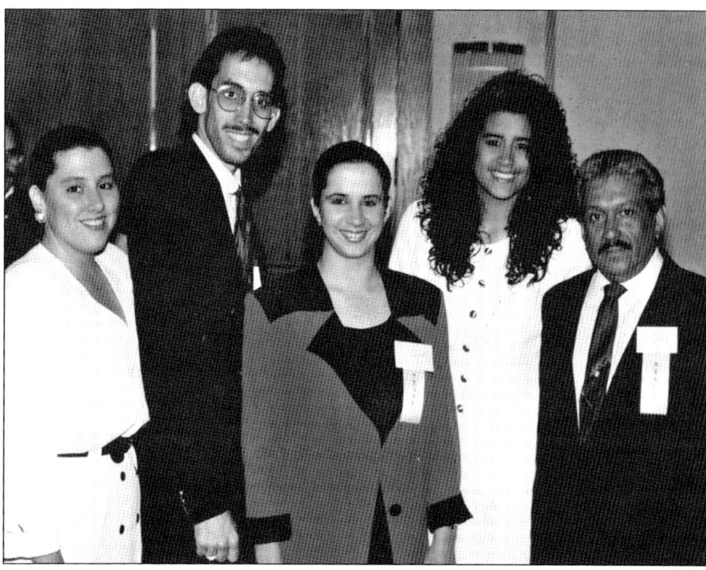

Pictured is the ASPIRA senior staff at the 1991 youth conference. From left to right are Cathy Anaya, Palm Beach County division director; William Ramos, deputy director; Aymet Chaples, COO; Marisol Ramos, advisor; and Jose "Joe" Ardiera, advisor. This was a South Florida conference with hundreds of Aspirantes. (Courtesy of ASPIRA of Florida.)

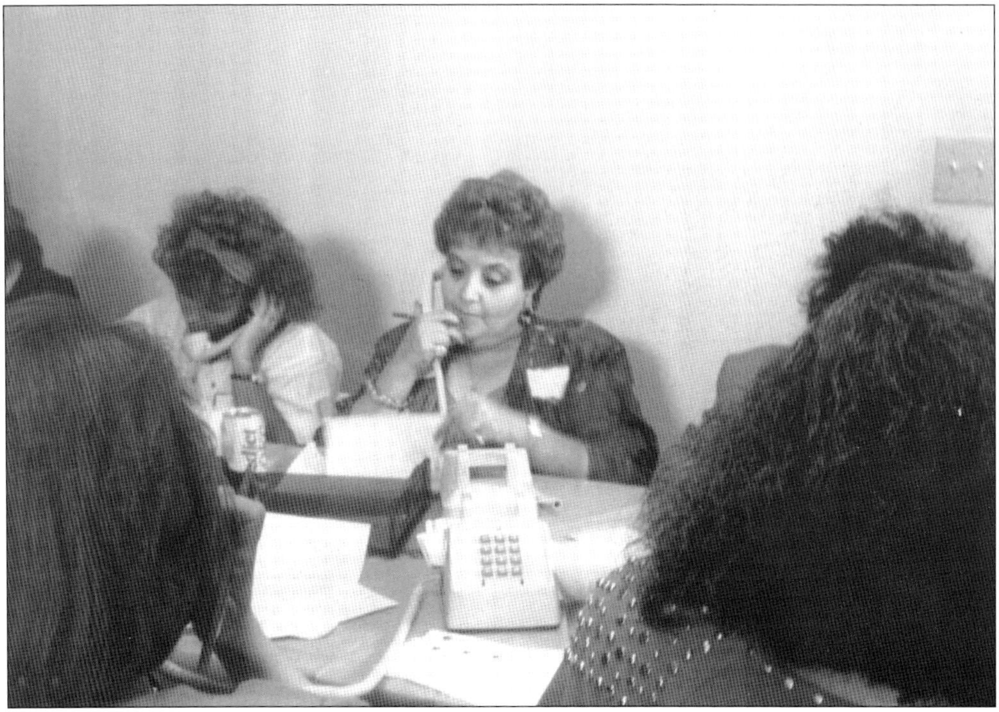

In August 1992, one of the most devastating hurricanes hit South Miami. Hurricane Andrew, a category 5 storm, struck near Homestead, the center of agricultural production in the region, and almost totally destroyed the Air Force base there. In a demonstration of solidarity with victims of the storm, members of NACOPRW's Miami chapters participated in a "phone-a-thon" in the studio of a local television station to help raise funds for those affected. (Courtesy of NACOPRW.)

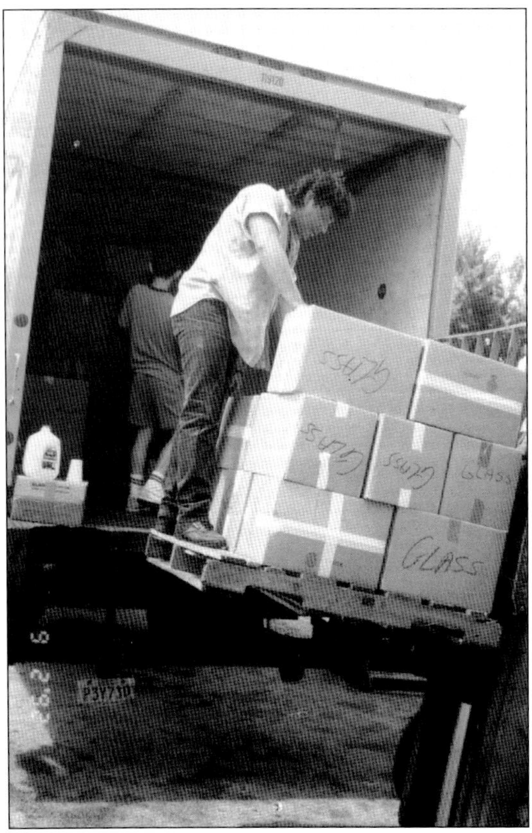

Many ASPIRA staff and parents helped to collect and load much-needed water and food in northern collection points. In South Miami, many ASPIRA staff helped to unload and distribute materials. Many also volunteered to work with the American Red Cross and other entities. (Courtesy of ASPIRA of Florida.)

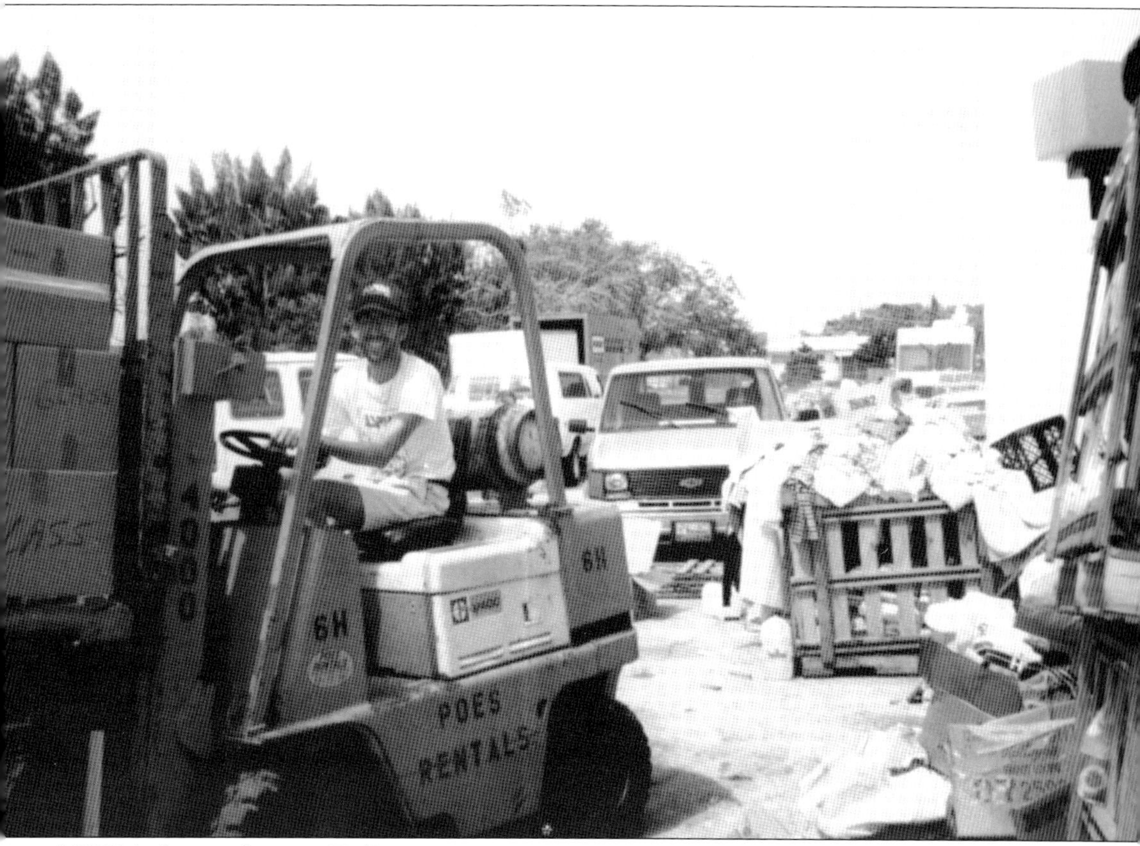

ASPIRA deputy director Willie Ramos, a Puerto Rican from Wynwood, drives a forklift to unload water for the victims of the hurricane. Some years later, Ramos left ASPIRA and began to work for city politicians in Miami. Later, he worked in Washington, DC, and in 2009, Pres. Barack Obama named Ramos deputy secretary of the Department of Commerce. (Courtesy of ASPIRA of Florida.)

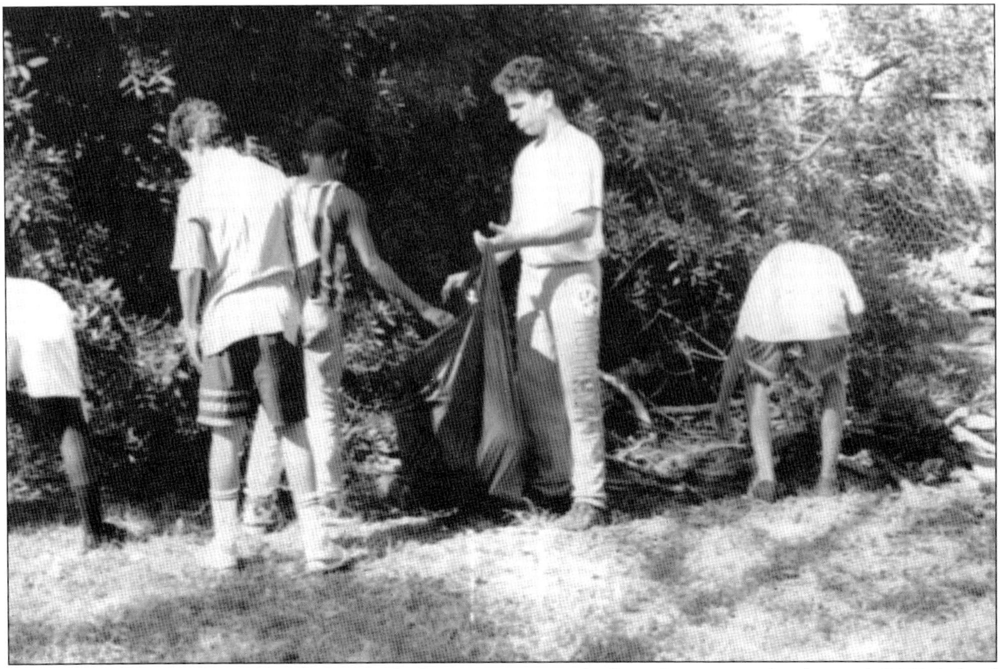

ASPIRA of Florida also mobilized to help in Homestead after Hurricane Andrew. ASPIRA had an operational center in Homestead and ran programs there. Many of ASPIRA's students and families were affected by the storm. Some Aspirantes were left homeless. These ASPIRA students helped by clearing debris. (Courtesy of ASPIRA of Florida.)

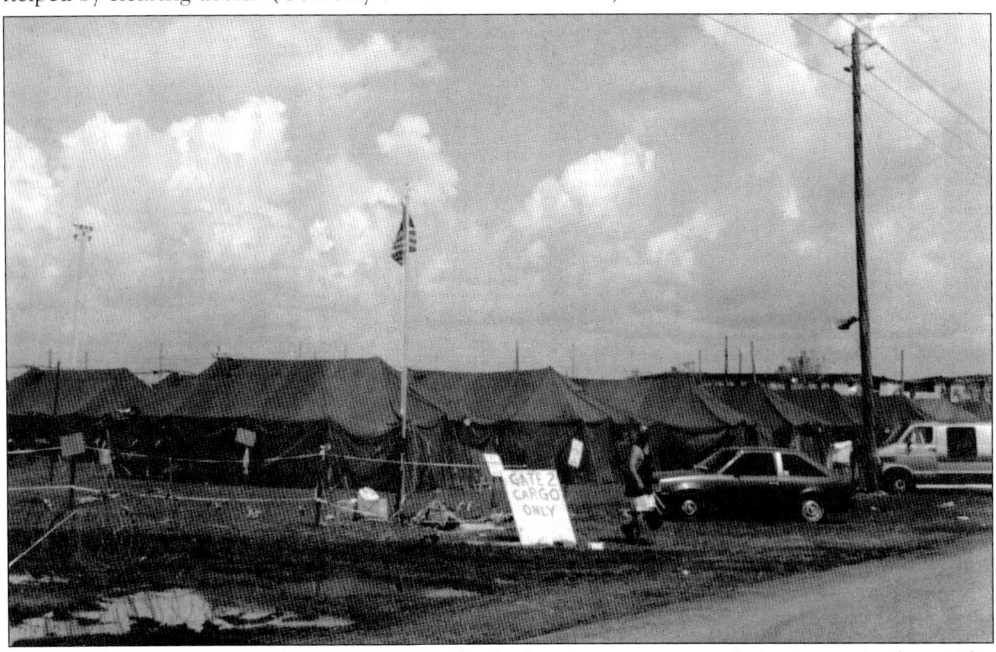

Pictured here are some of the tent cities established to house victims of Hurricane Andrew. The US Marines set up 108 tents in Harris Field in Homestead to house over 1,500 people left homeless by the storm. Working with the Salvation Army and the Red Cross, ASPIRA volunteers worked in this camp. (Courtesy of ASPIRA of Florida.)

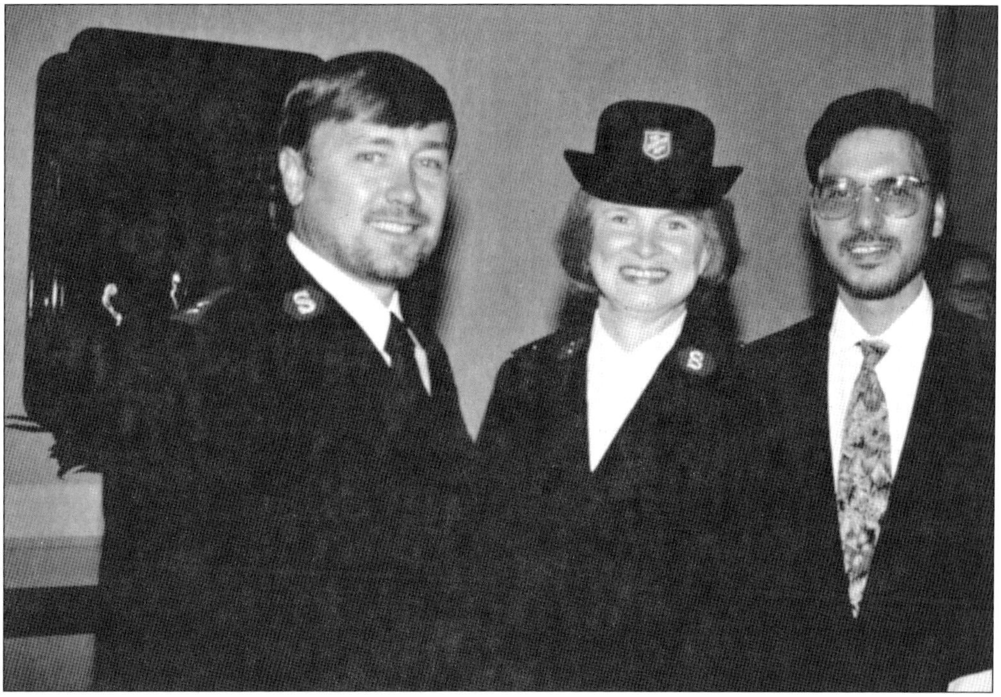

In response to the work done by ASPIRA in disaster relief after Hurricane Andrew in 1992, Maj. Wayne McHargue, director of Salvation Army Disaster Services in Florida, and his team recognized the efforts of ASPIRA. ASPIRA deployed its entire staff to work at the Salvation Army warehouse in the aftermath of the storm. (Courtesy of ASPIRA of Florida.)

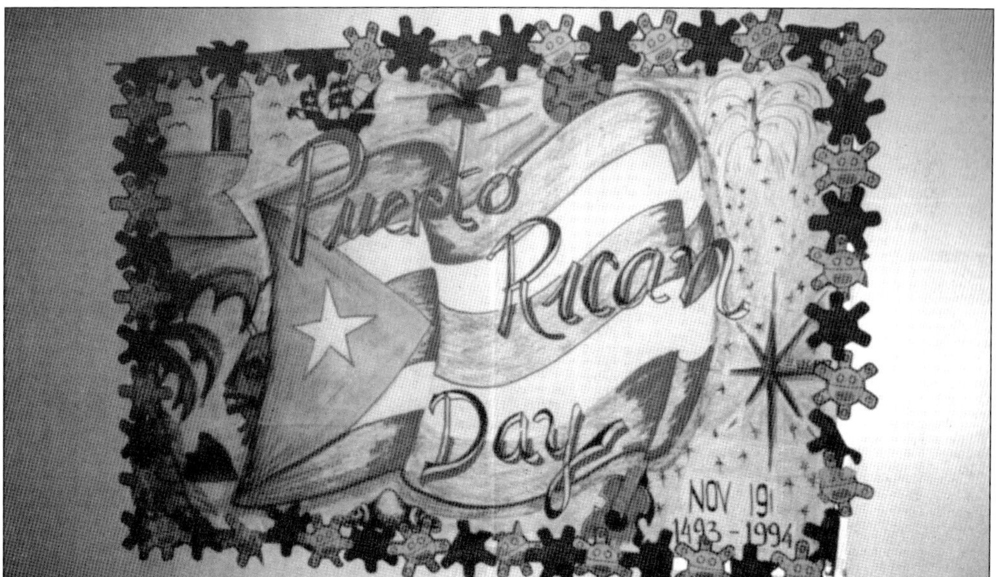

ASPIRA's mission includes empowering Puerto Ricans through advocacy, education, and leadership development of its youth. This includes immersing youth in their culture and history. This poster is from a Puerto Rican Heritage Month Celebration in the 1990s. The main day of the celebration is November 19. (Courtesy of ASPIRA of Florida.)

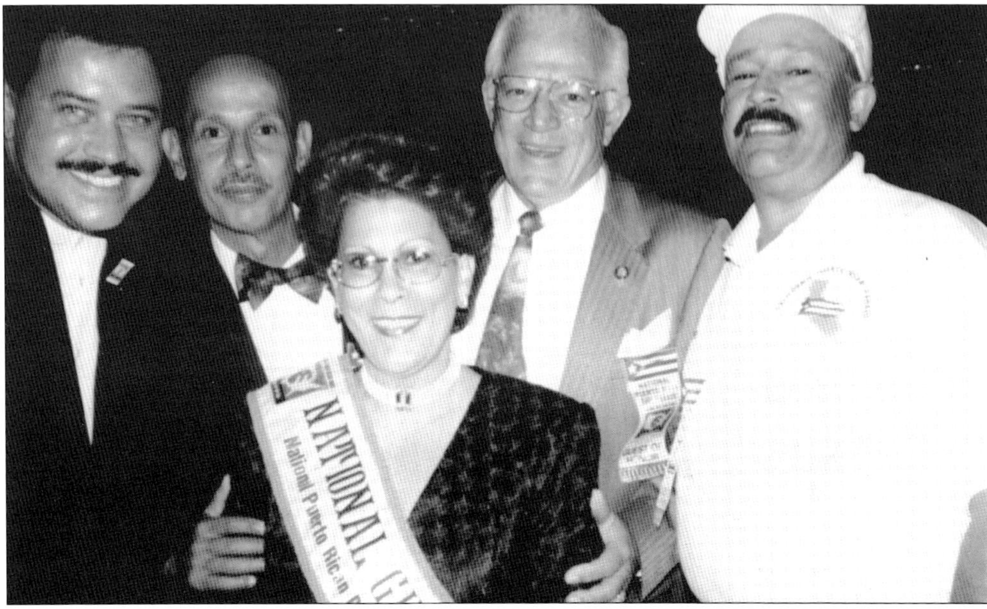

In 1992, Dr. Antonio Coello Novello, the US surgeon general, was selected as the grand marshal of the National Puerto Rican Day Parade in New York City. She is pictured with a delegation from Miami, including Luis De Rosa, president of the Puerto Rican Chamber of Commerce of South Florida. Dr. Novello was appointed by Pres. George H.W. Bush and served from 1990 to 1993. (Courtesy of Luis De Rosa.)

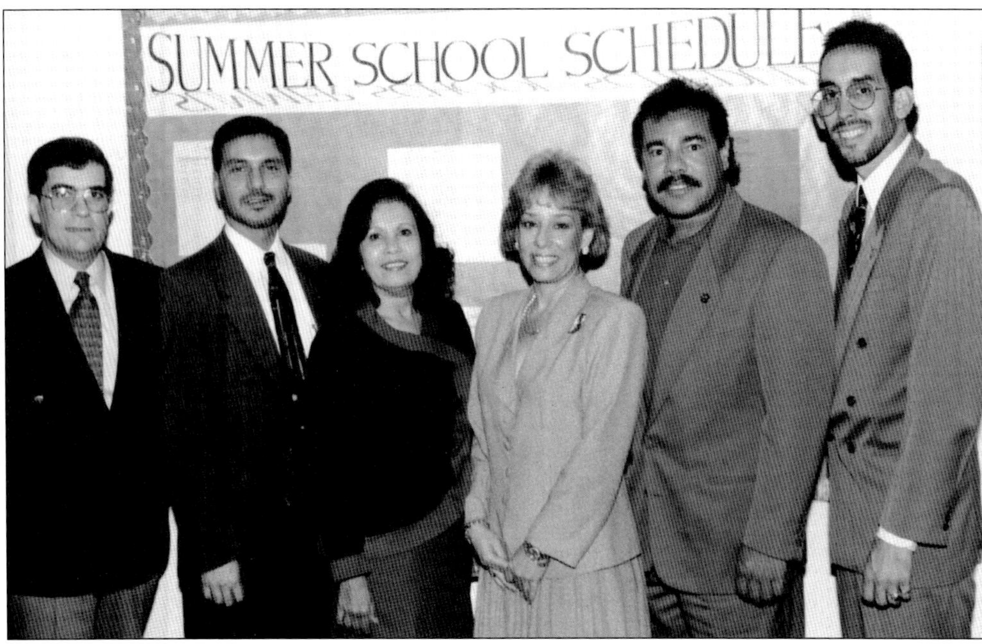

Pictured here on the first day of summer school in 1993 are ASPIRA CEO Raul Martinez (second from left); Dr. Aida Diaz, principal of the ASPIRA Accolade Alternative Middle School (to the left of Martinez); and William Ramos, deputy director of ASPIRA (far right), with community leaders. The alternative schools were the first schools ASPIRA managed, before the charter schools were developed. (Courtesy of ASPIRA of Florida.)

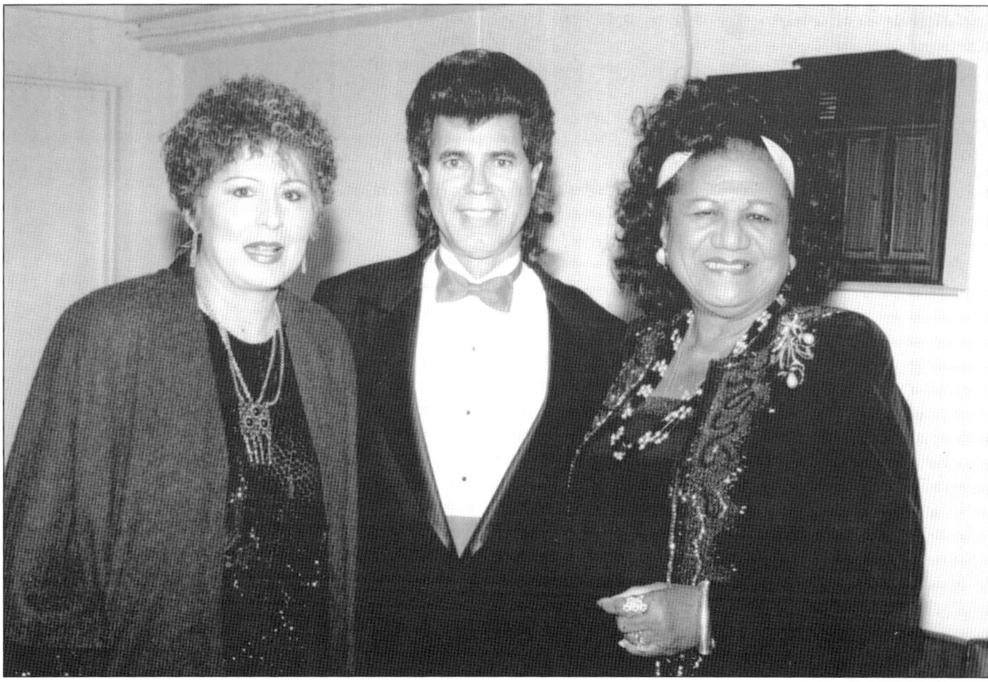

Ruth Fernandez (right), a famous Puerto Rican contralto singer, performed at the 1993 Puerto Rican Festival held at Hotel Biscayne in Miami. Fernandez was the first Afro Puerto Rican to perform at the Metropolitan Opera House in New York City and broke many racial barriers. She also spent time as a politician in the Puerto Rican Senate (1973–1981). (Courtesy of Luis De Rosa.)

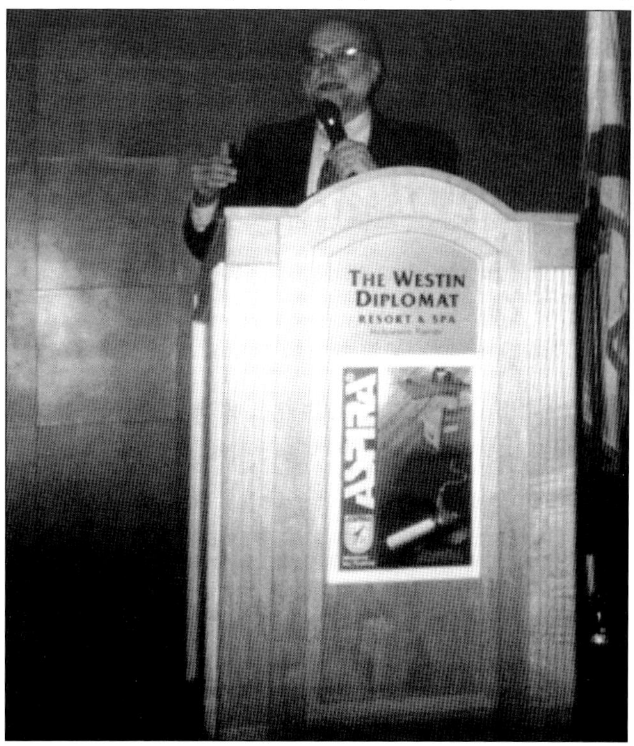

Ronald Blackburn Moreno speaks at an ASPIRA of Florida gala in Miami shortly after his appointment as the president and CEO of the ASPIRA Association in 1994. The association's national headquarters is in Washington, DC, and has affiliates in several states and Puerto Rico. Before coming to ASPIRA, Blackburn Moreno, born in Puerto Rico, served in several capacities at the Ana G. Mendez University and the Inter American University on the island. (Courtesy of ASPIRA of Florida.)

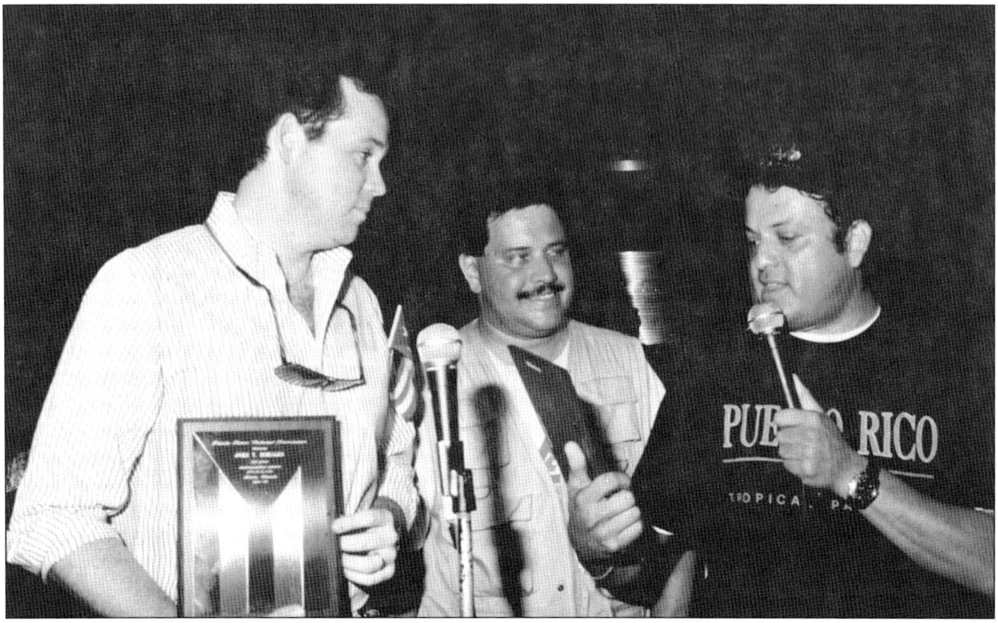

John T. Morales is a long-tenured broadcast meteorologist in South Florida. Born in New York to an Irish American father and Puerto Rican mother, he grew up in Puerto Rico. Morales has distinguished himself for three decades in weather broadcasts, including during Hurricanes Irma and Maria in 2017. In this 1994 picture, Morales is honored by the Puerto Rican Festival in Miami by Luis De Rosa; also pictured is Paul Rodriguez (right), the well-known Mexican American comedian and actor, in 1994. (Courtesy of Luis De Rosa.)

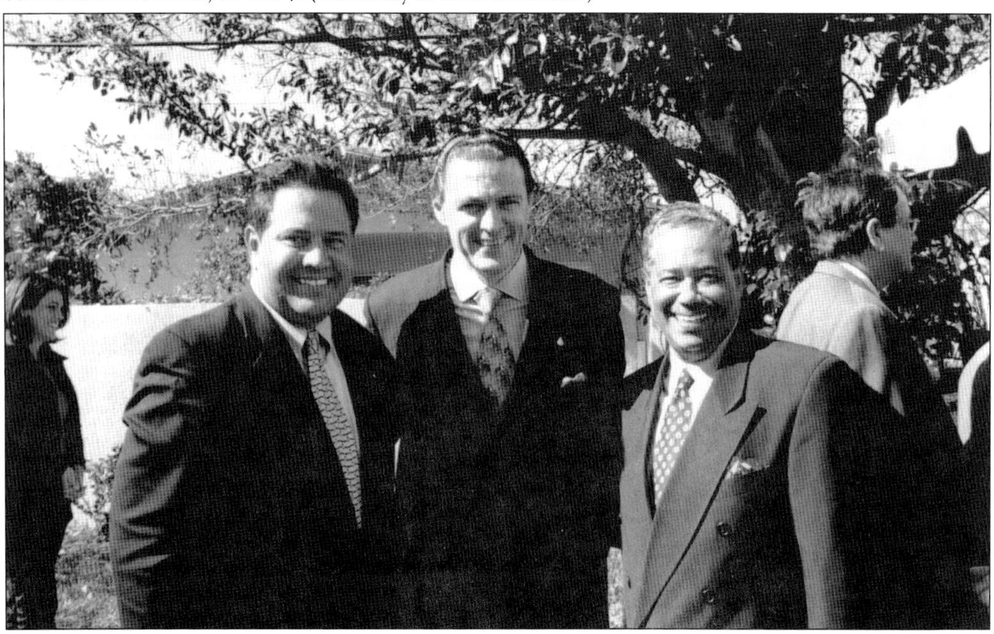

This image was captured during the opening of a new Miami branch of Banco Popular, the oldest banking institution in Puerto Rico. In this 1994 photograph is Richard Carrion IV, grandson of the founder and executive CEO. A grand opening was held outside the West Miami branch. (Courtesy of Luis De Rosa.)

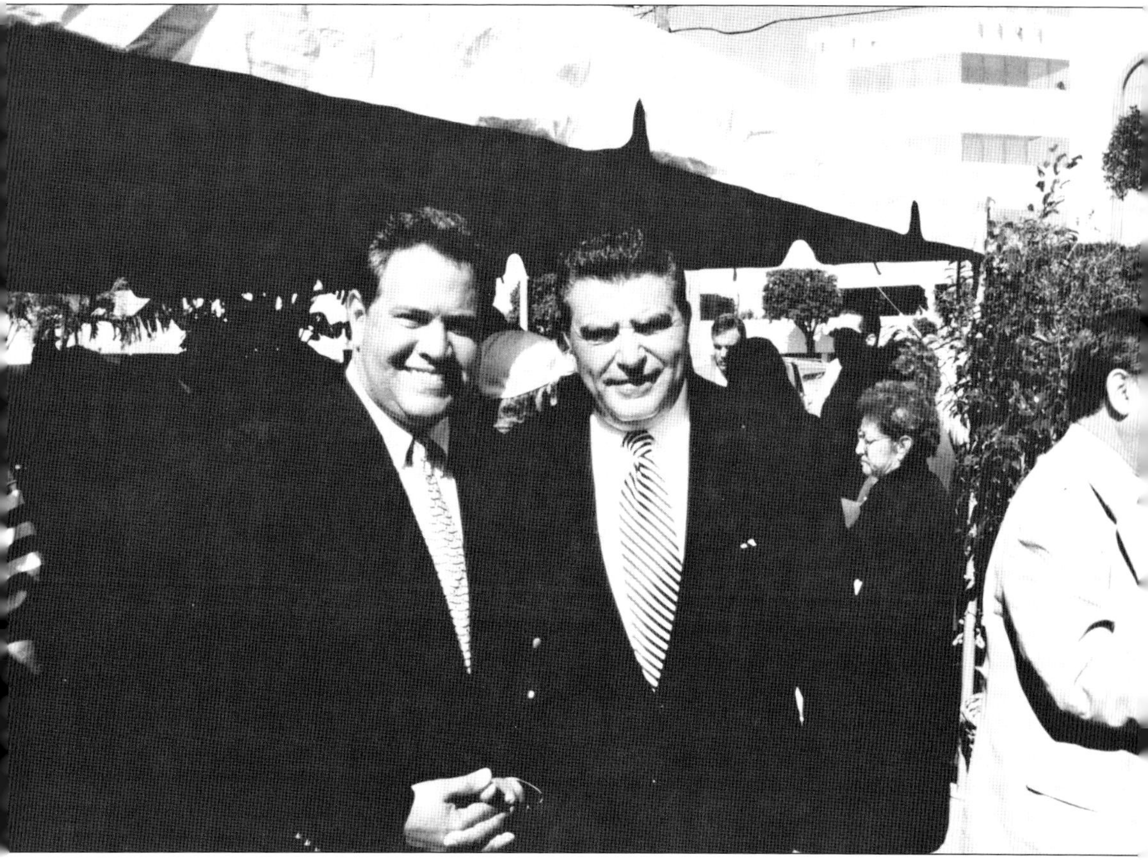

Don Francisco, the famous host of the television program *Sabado Gigante*, known throughout the Spanish-speaking world, and also a sponsor of Banco Popular, was present at the inauguration of the new branch. He is pictured at the ceremony along with Luis De Rosa in 1994. Born Mario Luis Kreutzberger Blumfield in Talca, Chile, in 1940 to German Jewish refugee parents, he spent more than 50 years hosting television programs produced in Miami. (Courtesy of Luis De Rosa.)

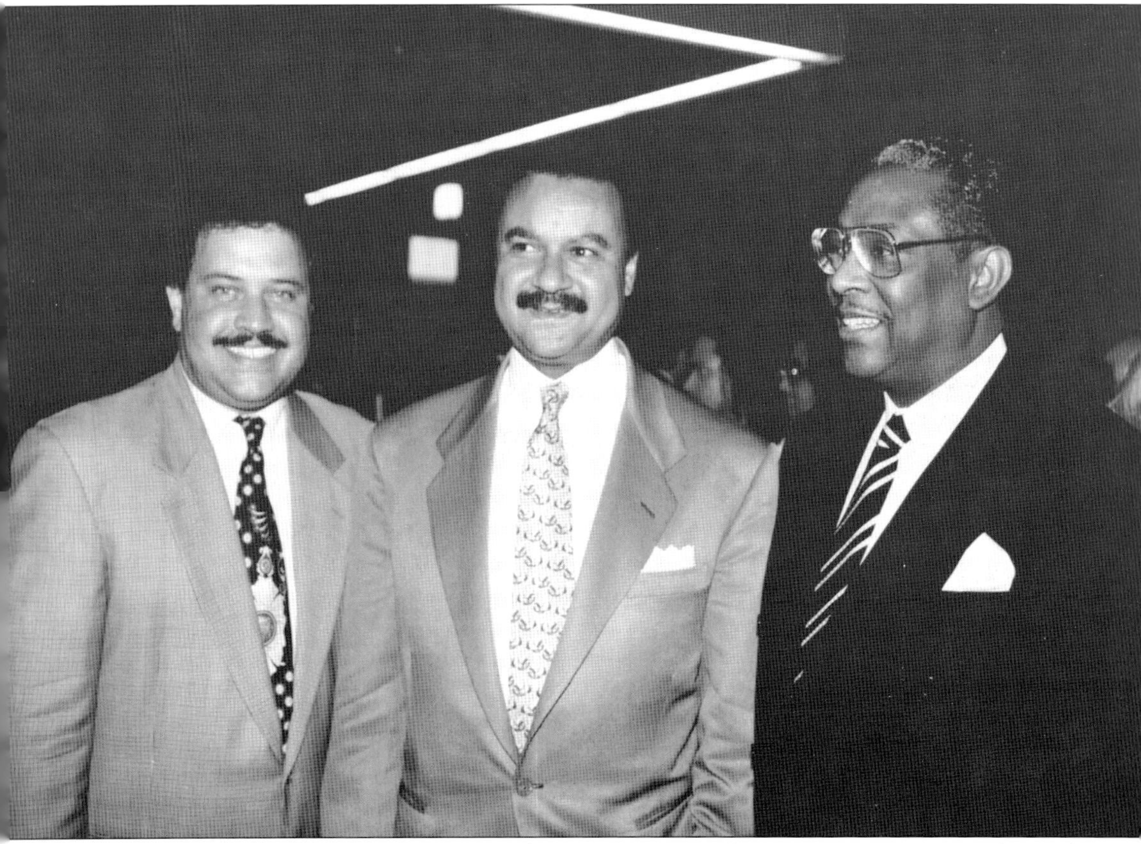

At this event in Miami in 1996 is special guest Secretary of Commerce Ron Brown (center), who served in Pres. Bill Clinton's first administration. Brown is flanked on the left by Luis De Rosa, president of the Puerto Rican Chamber of Commerce for South Florida, and on the right by Miami–Dade County commissioner Arthur E. Teele Jr. Some time after this event, Secretary Brown and 34 others perished in a plane crash in Croatia, where he was leading a trade delegation en route to Yugoslavia. (Courtesy of Luis De Rosa.)

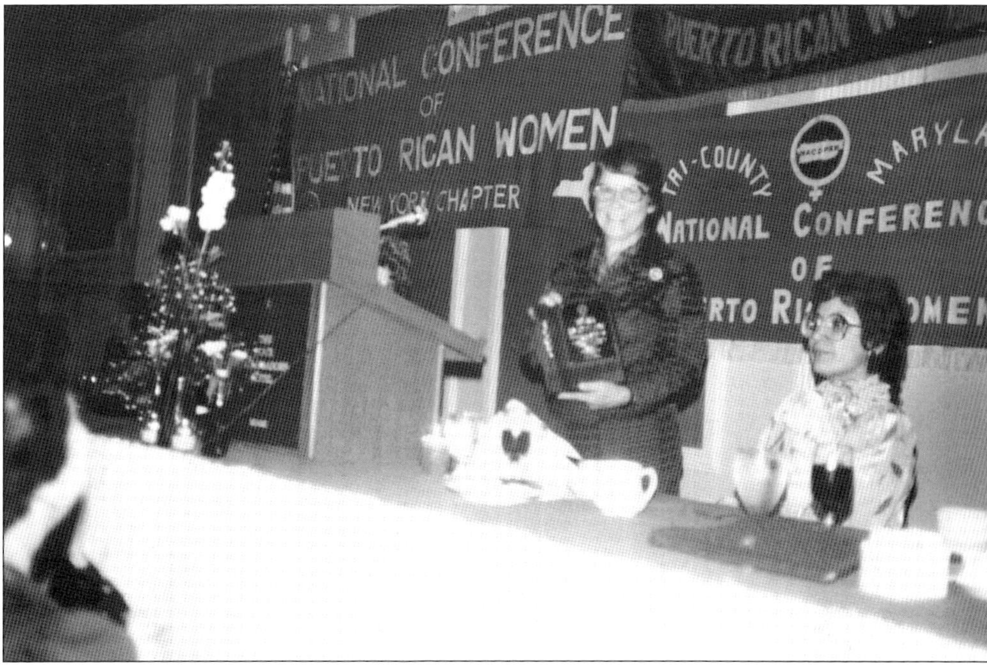

This NACOPRW conference honored Sister Isolina Ferre-Aguayo during Women's History Month. Sister Isolina was a Puerto Rican Catholic nun, recognized for humanitarian work among the poor in her home city of Ponce, Puerto Rico. She worked with young Puerto Rican gang members in New York and Philadelphia. Among her work in the poor community of La Playa in Ponce, she founded a small hospital, a school, and a resource center that created jobs. She was the aunt of Maurice Ferre and the sister of the governor of Puerto Rico, Luis A. Ferre. (Courtesy of NACOPRW.)

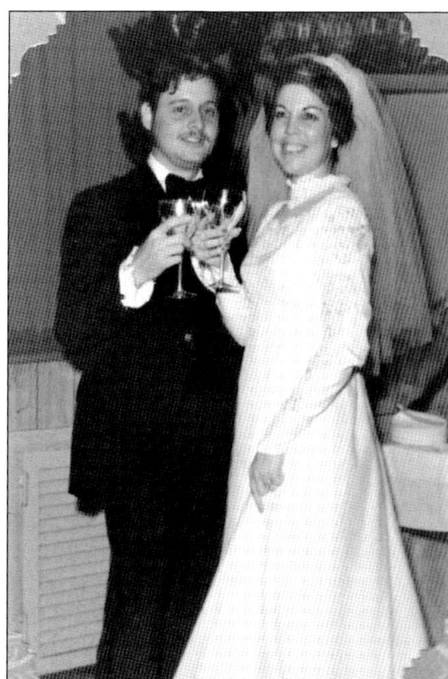

Pictured here is the wedding of Jose Carlos Pedrogo and Jane Elizabeth Padua in 1975. They were married at the Holy Family Parish in North Miami. Jose was still an architectural student at the University of Miami and did work for a local architectural firm. After graduation, he supervised construction. Jane worked in banking and earned a degree in finance from Florida International University. They presently live in Davie. (Courtesy of Carmen Pedrogo.)

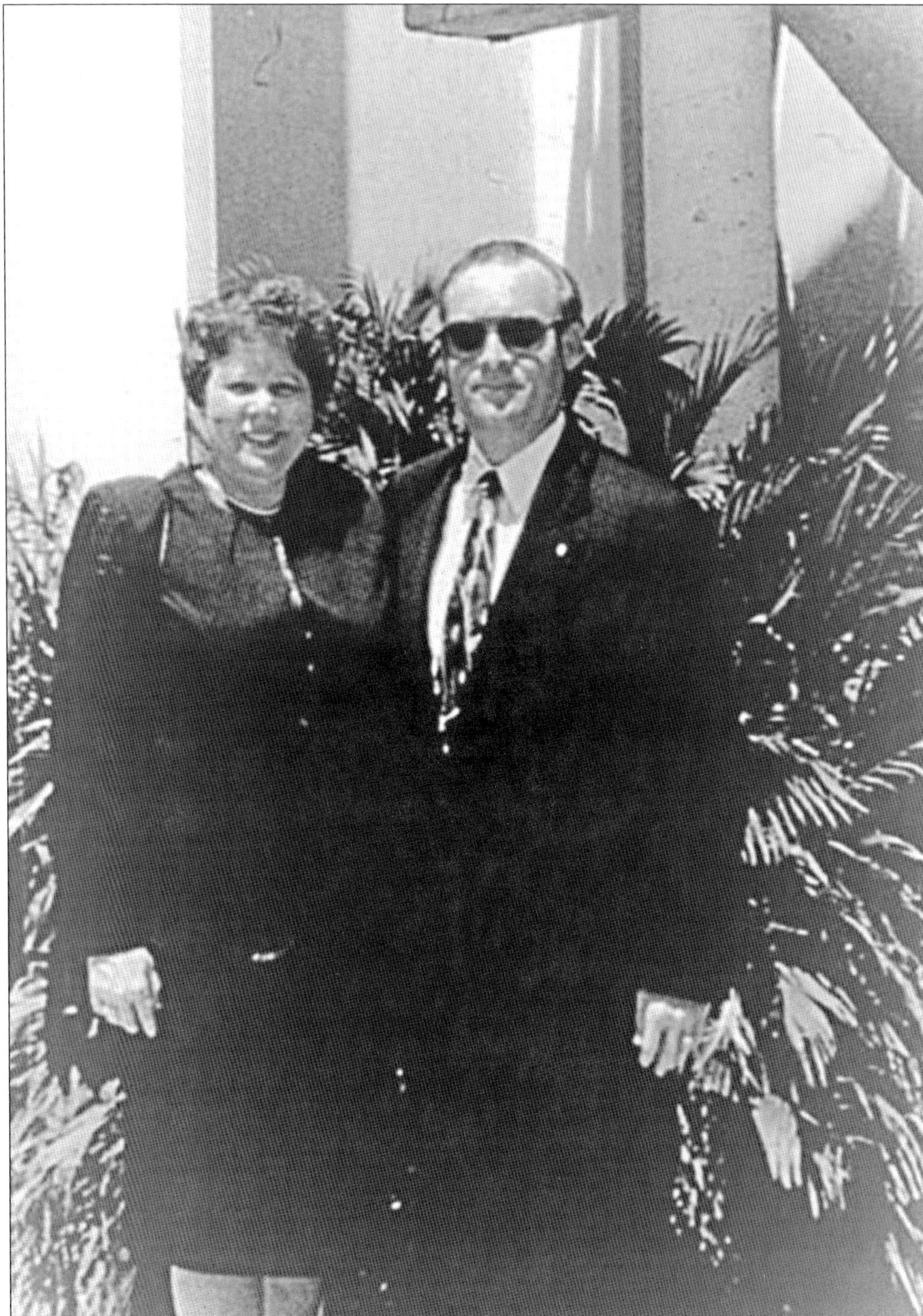

Carmen Pedrogo and her brother Jose Carlos are seen in 1995 at the wedding of John and Beth Carlsworth. The bride was Jose Pedrogo Sr.'s niece, the daughter of his sister Luisa. Luisa had been instrumental in her brother Pedrogo Sr. moving his family from Puerto Rico to Miami in the 1950s. (Courtesy of Carmen Pedrogo.)

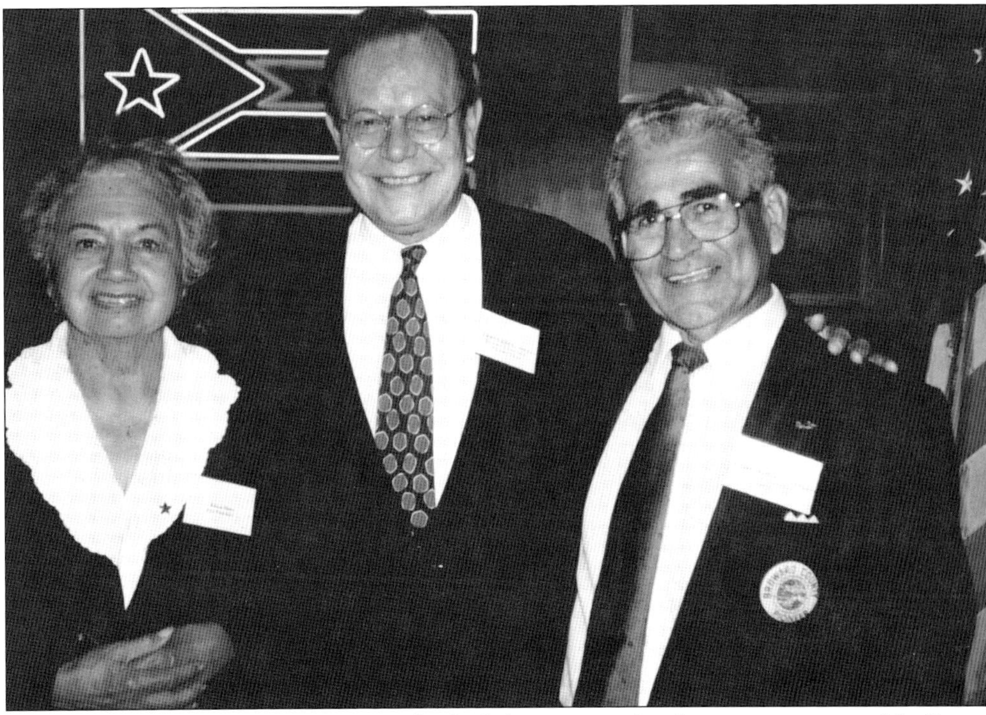

Dr. Alicia Baro (left) and Robert Camacho (right) are pictured with a representative of the Puerto Rico Statehood Commission in 1996. The purpose of this gathering was to discuss Puerto Rican voter registration in Miami with a focus on the upcoming elections. Camacho had lived in Miami since the 1940s. (Courtesy of Luis De Rosa.)

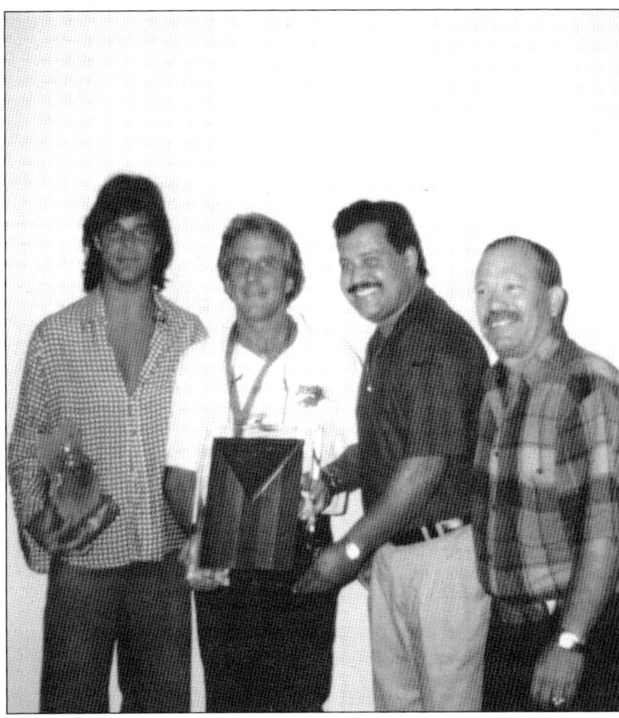

Miami radio station Power 96 and the Puerto Rican Chamber of Commerce honor Puerto Rican entertainer Ricky Martin (left) in 1996. Born in Puerto Rico, Martin was a sensation with the group Menudo from the ages of 12 to 17. (Courtesy of Luis De Rosa.)

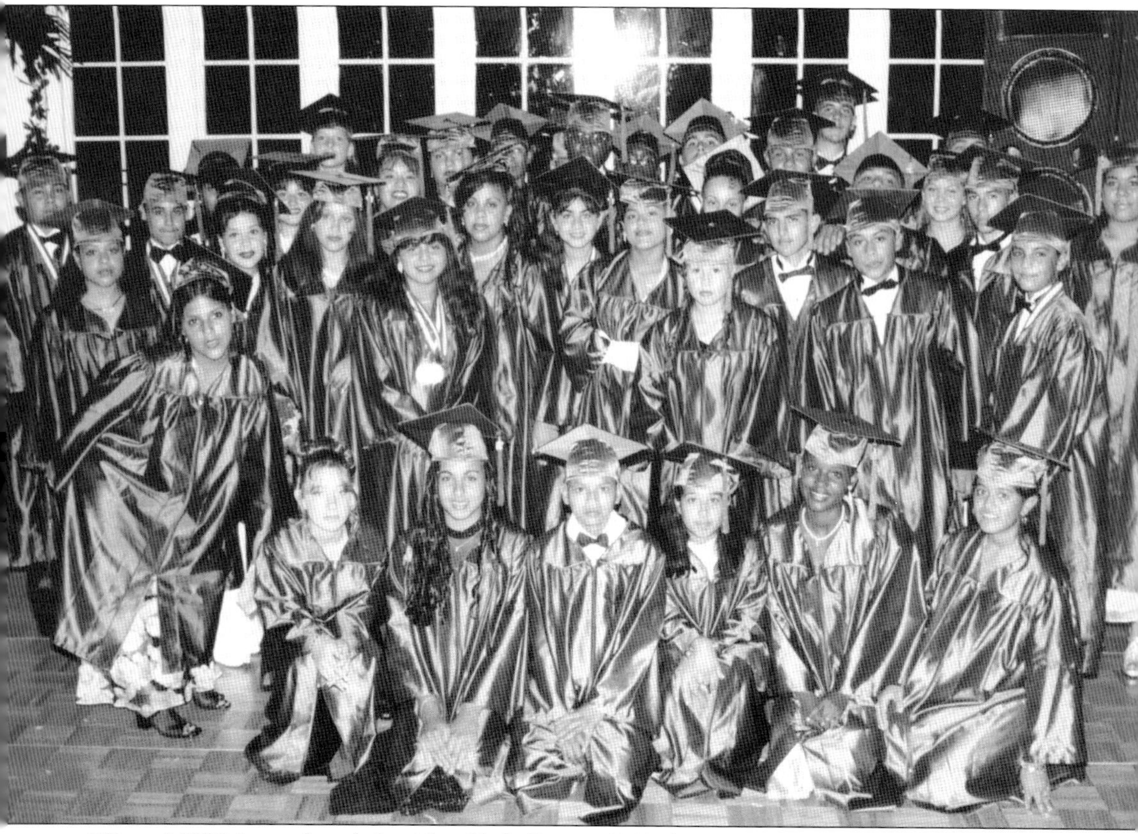

When ASPIRA was founded in New York City in 1961, the great concern among Puerto Ricans like Dr. Antonia Pantoja was the increasing high school dropout rate of Puerto Rican youth, so its mission focused on high schoolers. By the 1980s, the deindustrialization in major cities like Miami, along with drug epidemics, began to affect dropout rates in middle schools as well. ASPIRA of Florida shifted resources to open and run those schools. This is a graduation at the ASPIRA Accolades South Alternative Middle School in 1997. (Courtesy of ASPIRA of Florida.)

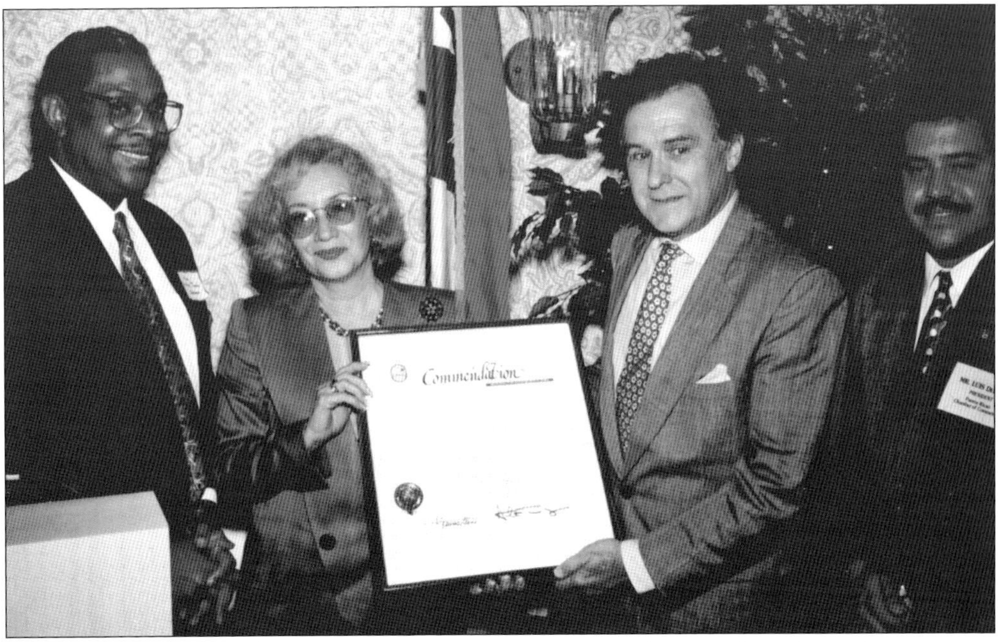

This photograph was taken during a c. 1997 event honoring Marivi Montalvo, a Puerto Rican and journalist for the Miami-based *Diario de la Americas*, a Spanish language newspaper founded in the 1950s. Montalvo was recognized for her writing on Puerto Rican affairs. She is flanked by Miami County commissioners Arthur Teele (left) and Maurice Ferre. (Courtesy of Luis De Rosa.)

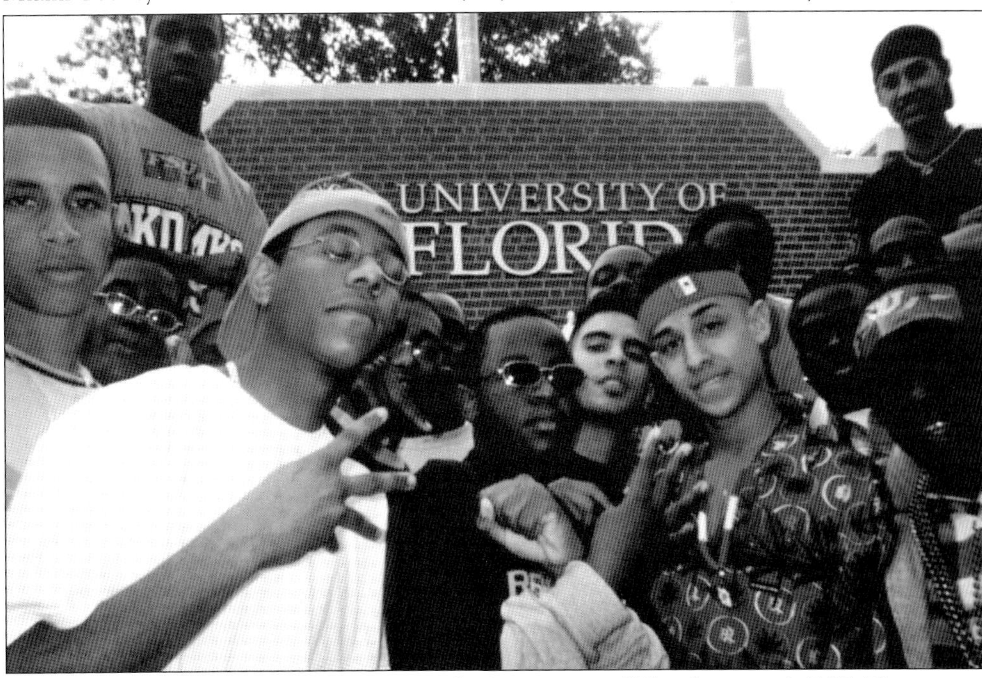

ASPIRA students attend College Day at the University of Florida around 1997. This was an event in which Aspirantes experienced firsthand the many educational opportunities available to them. They were often given a reception, and activities were designed especially for them. (Courtesy of ASPIRA of Florida.)

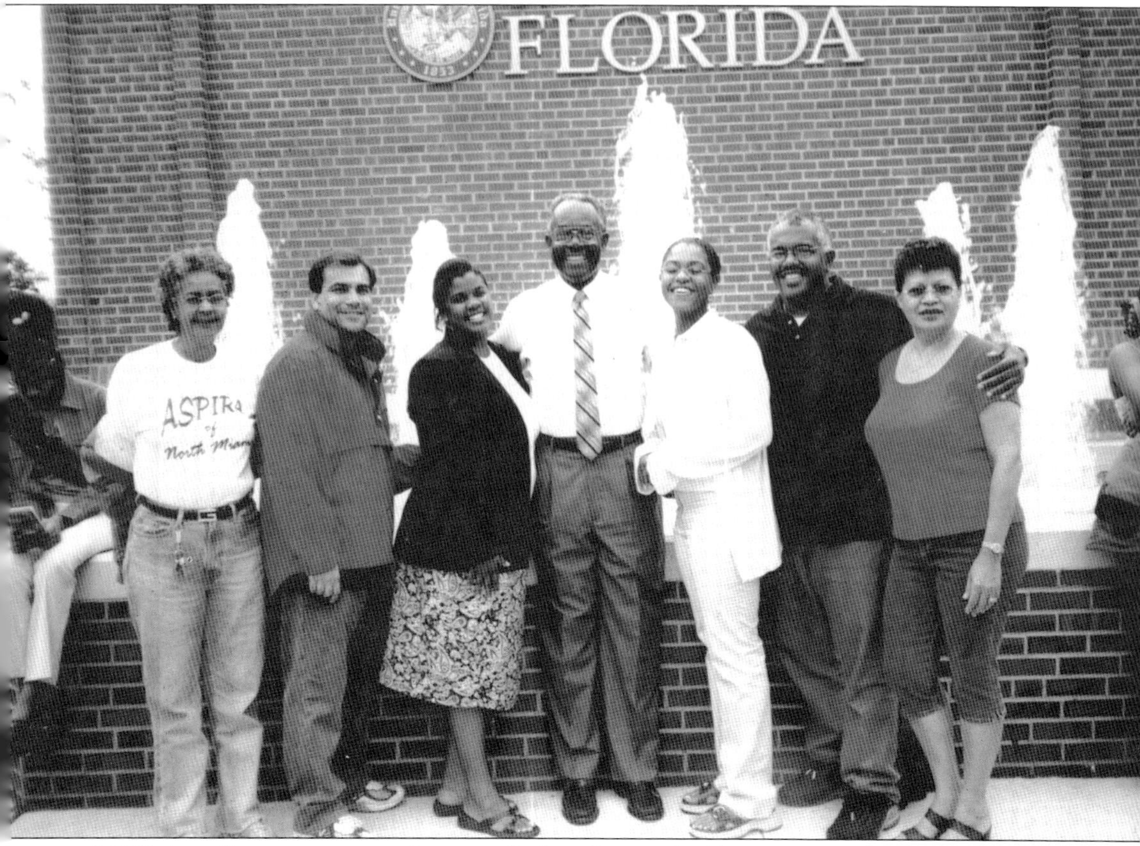

ASPIRA staff accompanies students on College Day at the University of Florida in 1997. From left to right are Iris Corchado, youth advisor; Orlando Espinoza, youth advisor; Ruth Bland, division director; Eugenie Mompremier, recruiter; Blanca Rodriguez, administrative assistant; and two teachers from the ASPIRA Leadership Charter School ASPIRA North. (Courtesy of ASPIRA of Florida.)

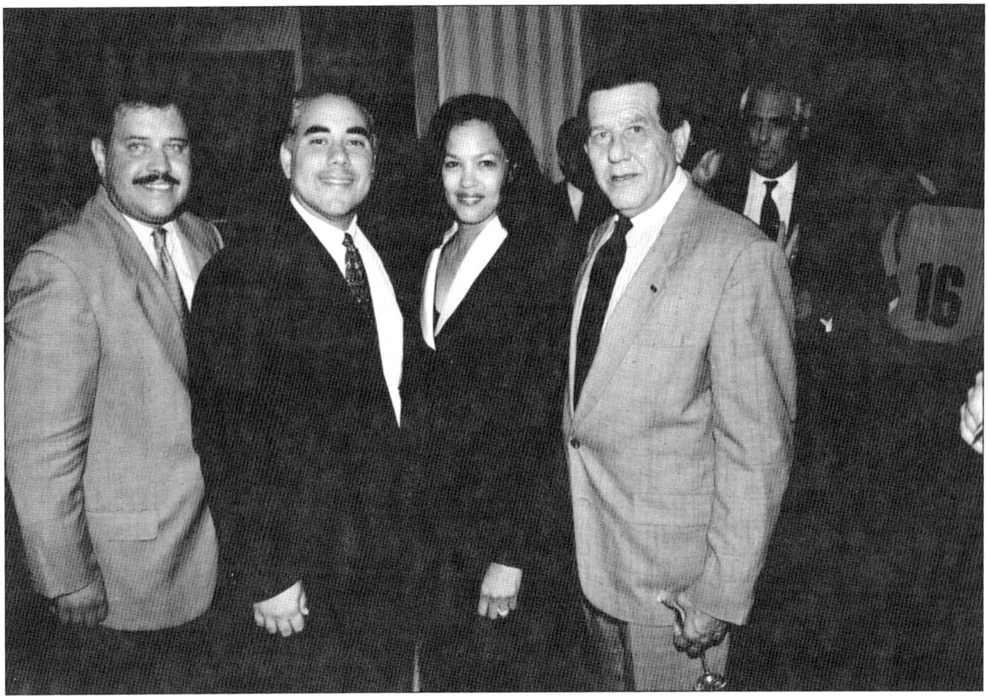

Attending this c. 1998 gala event at Miami City Hall are, from left to right, unidentified; Puerto Rican Miami County commissioner Jimmy Morales; Bobbi Ibarra, Puerto Rican and one-time vice president of Jungle Island; and Melvin "Skip" Chaves, founder and chairman of the board of directors of the Puerto Rican Chamber of Commerce of South Florida. (Courtesy of Luis De Rosa.)

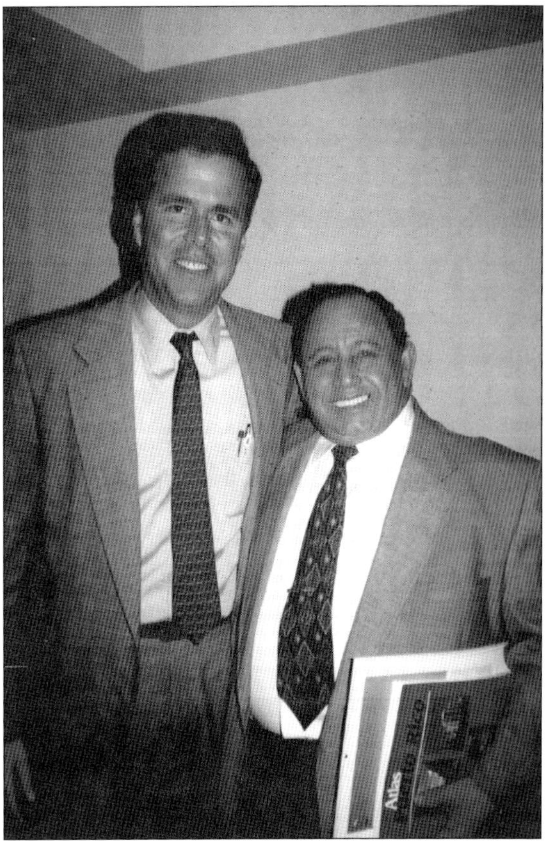

Florida gubernatorial candidate Jeb Bush was the keynote speaker at a Puerto Rican Chamber of Commerce event in 1998. The event was a joint venture with the San Juan Puerto Rico Chamber of Commerce to create mutual opportunities. Along with Bush in the picture is Ramon S. Velez, a South Bronx political chief. The event was held at the Carlton Hotel in Brickell. (Courtesy of Luis De Rosa.)

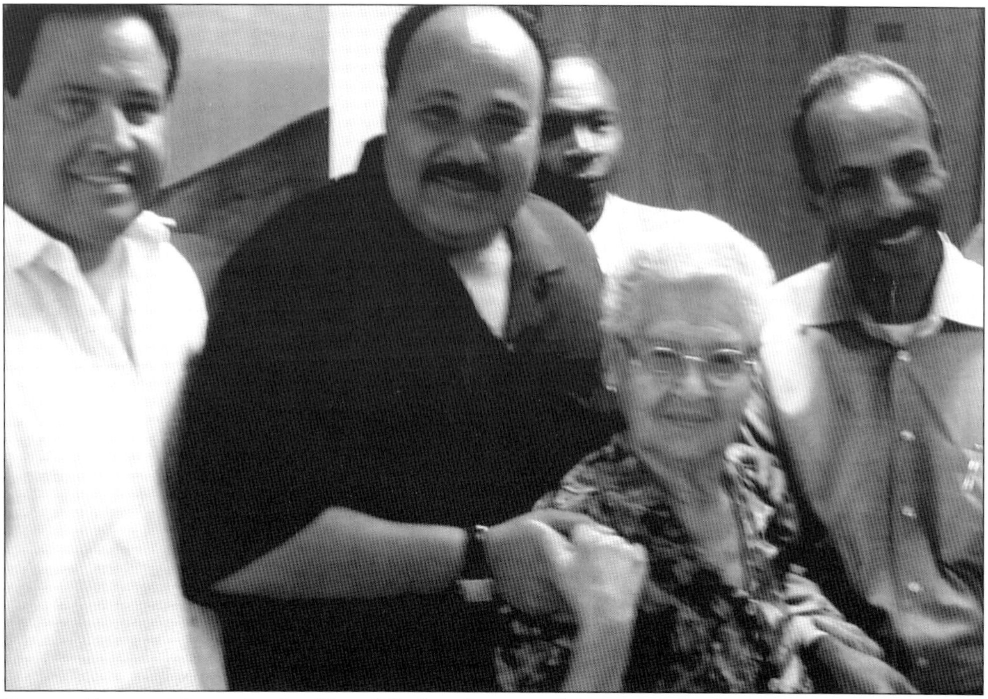

Pictured here is Martin Luther King III when he visited ASPIRA's facilities in Wynwood in 1999. The facilities were on the second floor of the Eugenio Maria de Hostos Senior Citizens Center. Along with King is the legendary Dorothy "Dottie" Quintana, who was celebrating her 90th birthday (she lived to be 101). At the time, Quintana had been living in Wynwood for almost 50 years. At far right is Dorothy's nephew Luis Canales, executive director of the Rafael Hernandez Housing Development Corporation. (Courtesy of ASPIRA of Florida.)

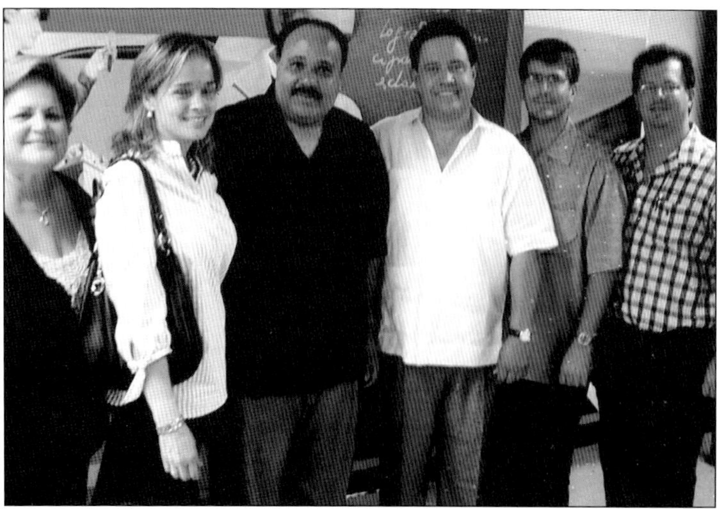

Martin Luther King III is pictured at a meeting at ASPIRA with, on the left, Nora Smith, with the Community Action Program in Wynwood; Suzanne Salich, an ASPIRA of Florida board member and niece of Maurice Ferre; Luis De Rosa; and two co-owners of the San Juan Bautista Clinic, also located in Wynwood. (Courtesy of ASPIRA of Florida.)

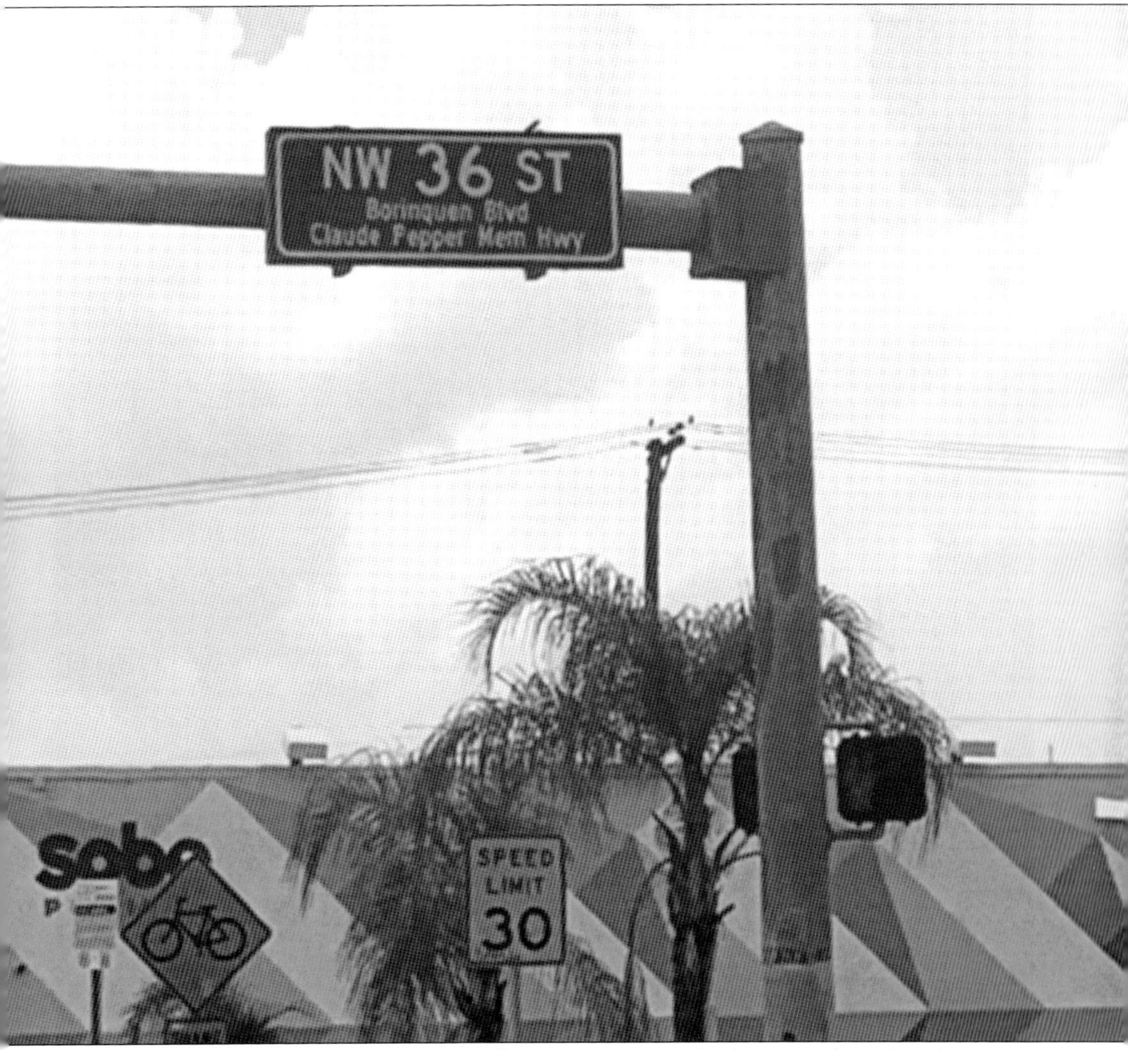

NW Thirty-Sixth Street, which runs east and west in Miami, marks the original northern boundary of the Puerto Rican enclave in Wynwood. The southern border is NW Twenty-Ninth Street. Pictured here is the street sign marking the stretch of NW Thirty-Sixth Street that in 1999 the Florida state legislature designated Borinquen Boulevard in honor of the ancestral name given to the island of Puerto Rico by its original inhabitants. This is where the term "Boricua" comes from, which all Puerto Ricans use to identify themselves. (Courtesy Luz Sofia Vazquez-Hernandez.)

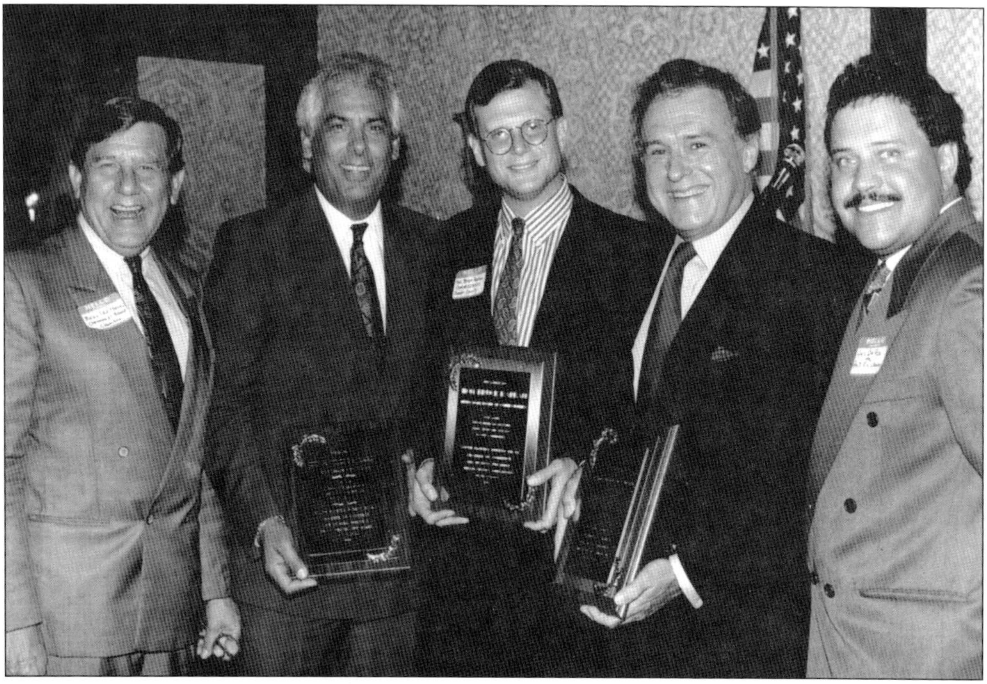

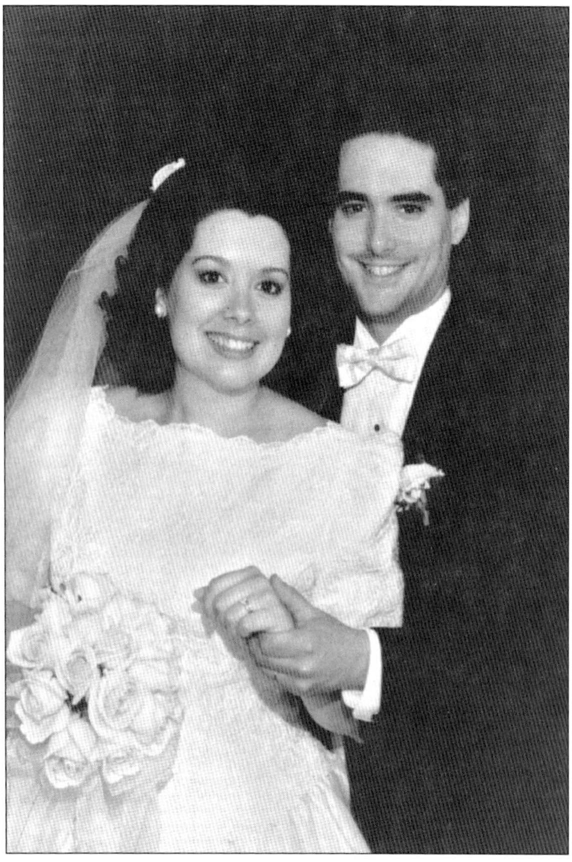

This 1999 event honored Raymond F. Marin, Puerto Rican and city councilman of North Miami Beach from 1989 to 2005. He also served as mayor of North Miami Beach from 2005 to 2009. He is pictured here second from left. He is also related to Luis Munoz Marin, governor of Puerto Rico from 1949 to 1965. To Marin's right is Bruce Kaplan from the Puerto Rico Federal Affairs Office in Miami. (Courtesy of Luis De Rosa.)

Lisa Pedrogo, the youngest daughter of Jose and Carmen Pedrogo, married Kelly Michael Pearsall in November 1995. The wedding took place at Saint David's Church in Davie, Florida. The couple met at Hofstra University in Long Island, New York. They live in New Jersey, where Lisa works as a vice president of operations, and her husband is a staff director for CNN. (Courtesy of Carmen Pedrogo.)

Beginning in 1992, Maribel Melendez organized the Miss Puerto Rico Pageant US in South Florida. The winner became Miss Puerto Rico Queen for the Puerto Rican festivals. The pageant queen received scholarship funds for college. Melendez is pictured here with Carlos Julia (left), one of the organizers of the festival and a cousin of the Puerto Rican actor Raul Julia. (Courtesy of Luis De Rosa.)

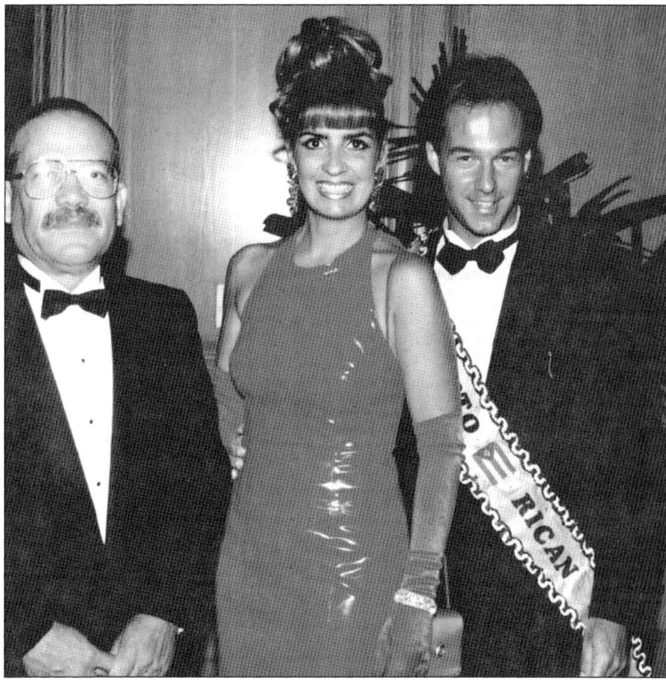

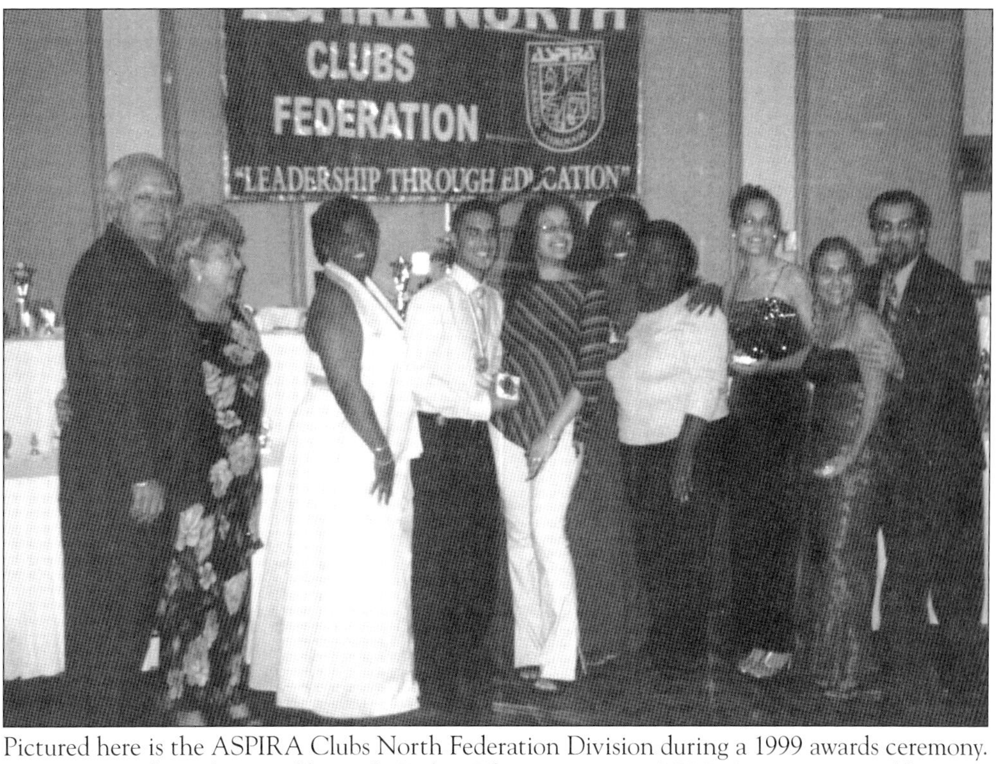

Pictured here is the ASPIRA Clubs North Federation Division during a 1999 awards ceremony. At far left is Julio Balsera and his wife, Esther. They were major ASPIRA supporters and boosters for many years. (Courtesy of ASPIRA of Florida.)

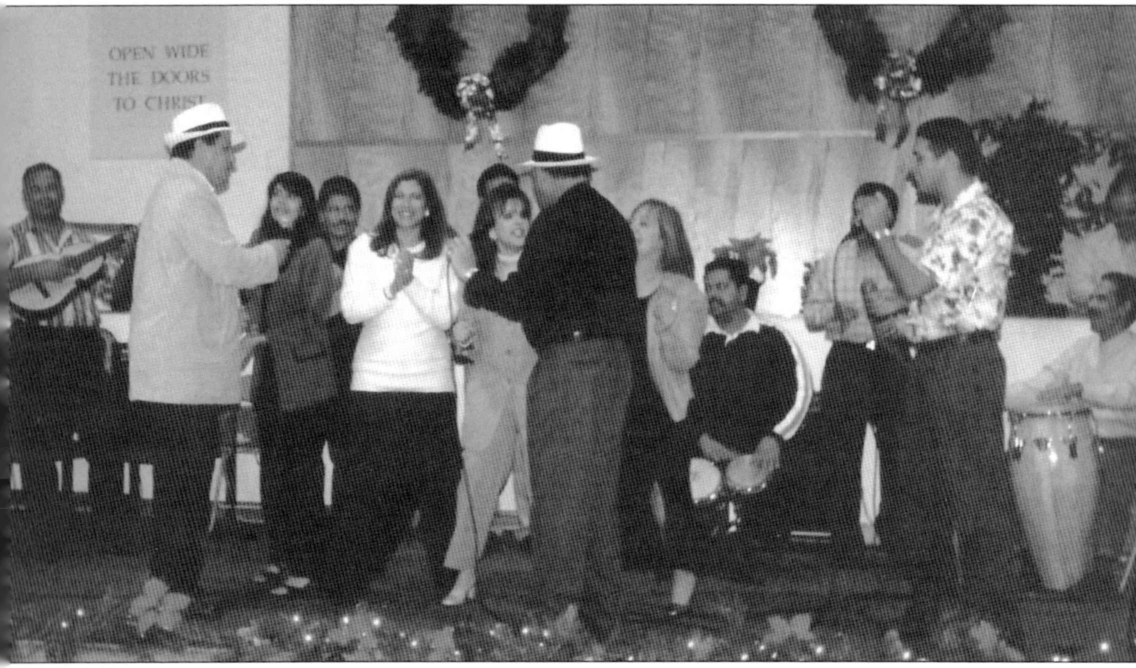

The Centro Cultural Puertorriqueño del Sur del la Florida (Puerto Rican Cultural Center in South Florida) was founded in 1999 by a group of Puerto Rican residents interested in promoting Puerto Rican culture and folklore in South Florida. Based in Miami, the organization held its first activity in Coral Springs in neighboring Broward County on Christmas day 1999. Pictured here are several of the artists who traveled from the island. (Courtesy of Jose Luis Rodriguez.)

Four

Into the New Millennium

Through the end of the 20th century, Puerto Ricans continued an increasing stream of migration to Florida. They came not only from the island directly, but from all points around the United States. There are many reasons why Puerto Ricans continued to see the Sunshine State as a promising place to settle: economic opportunities, connecting with families and friends, and of course, the pleasant weather. However, there are other factors to consider.

During the 1990s, Puerto Rico's economic output began to decline as investment by US corporations, always looking for better tax breaks from the Puerto Rican government, began to run out. The Puerto Rican government sought parity with the states. The US Congress voted to end tax haven corporation breaks, and the decline began. By 2006, the economic decline was in full bloom, and so was the exodus from the island. This time, however, more Puerto Ricans looked away from the traditional Northeast and Midwest areas and turned to states in the South and Southwest. Florida became the primary focus. By 2010, there were more Puerto Ricans living in the United States than on the island.

The island's economy continued to decline, and then came Hurricane Maria. On September 20, 2017, Maria, a category 4 hurricane, flattened the island. Puerto Ricans in Miami mobilized as they did around the country and sent millions of dollars in help. A significant part of the help came from Puerto Rican organizations. The community also received assistance from every group in the city, spanning all ethnicities and races in Miami.

As soon as air travel became available, many refugees began to arrive in Miami and other points in the United States and Florida. Most people do not consider Puerto Ricans as refugees because they are US citizens, but for the tens of thousands who lost everything on the island, the word feels apropos.

As the 2020 US Census approaches its release, the full scope of the population increase will be clear. It will no doubt reveal an immense increase of Puerto Ricans living in Miami and the surrounding counties.

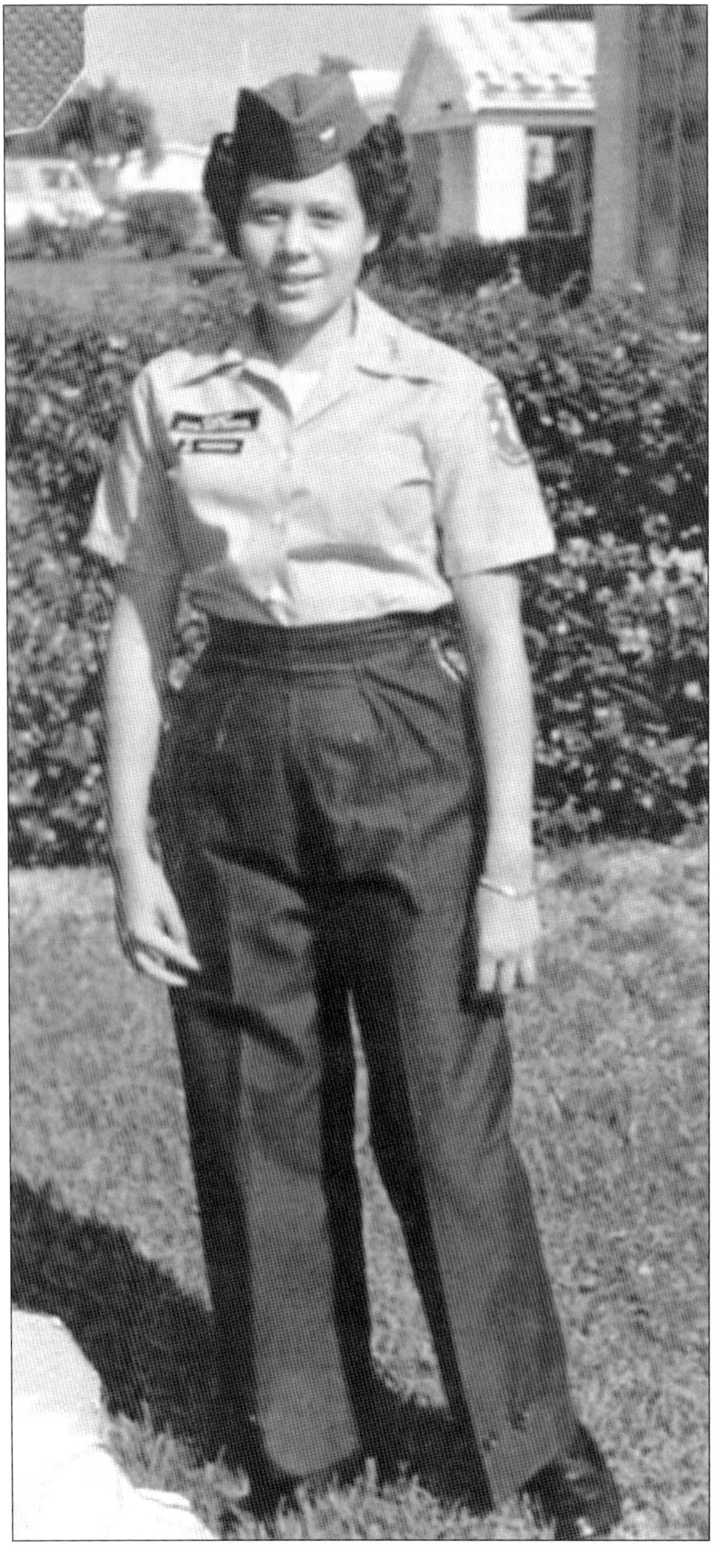

In this photograph from the 1970s is Carmen Pedrogo, daughter of Jose and Carmen Pedrogo, who brought their family from Puerto Rico to live in Miami in 1956. Carmen appears in the uniform of the Civilian Air Patrol, an auxiliary organization of the US Air Force. She belonged to this group from junior high school through her first year of college at the University of Miami. The group met at the National Guard Armory in North Miami. (Courtesy of Carmen Pedrogo.)

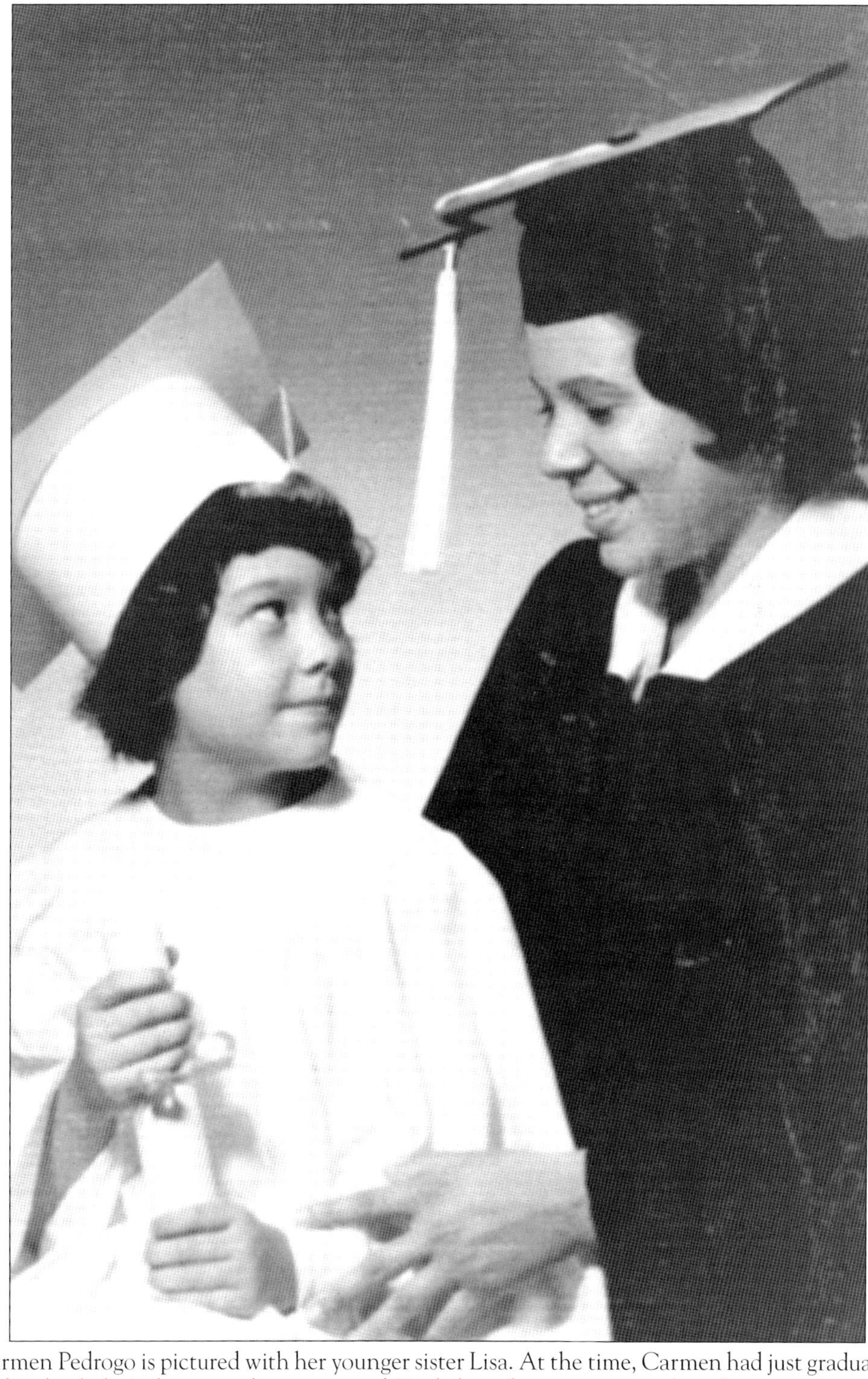

Carmen Pedrogo is pictured with her younger sister Lisa. At the time, Carmen had just graduated with a bachelor's degree in literature and English with a minor in political science from the University of Miami in 1973, and Lisa had just completed kindergarten. (Courtesy of Carmen Pedrogo.)

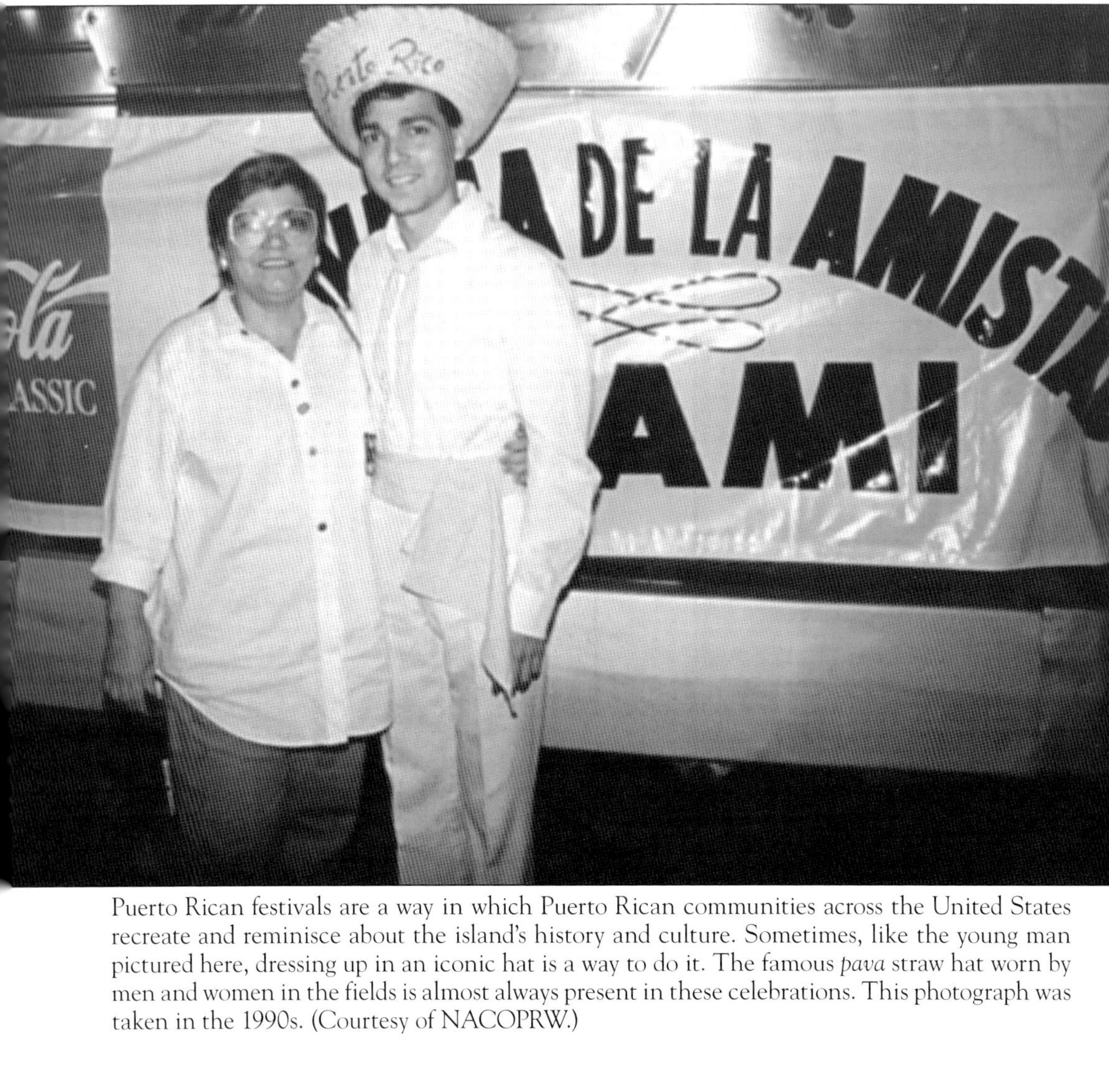

Puerto Rican festivals are a way in which Puerto Rican communities across the United States recreate and reminisce about the island's history and culture. Sometimes, like the young man pictured here, dressing up in an iconic hat is a way to do it. The famous *pava* straw hat worn by men and women in the fields is almost always present in these celebrations. This photograph was taken in the 1990s. (Courtesy of NACOPRW.)

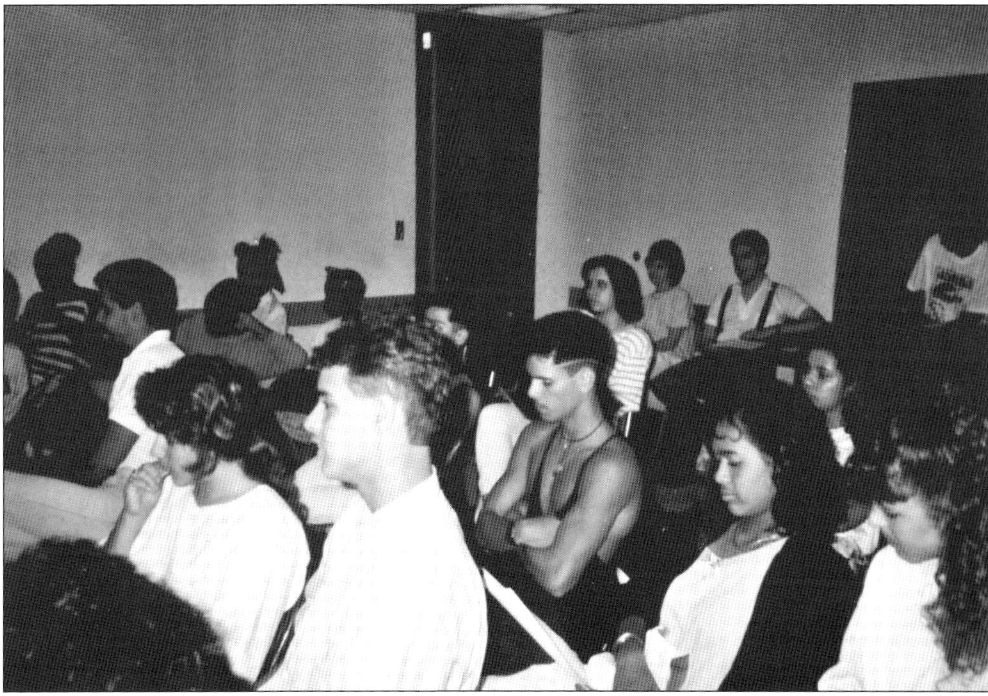

The youth clubs of ASPIRA are the principal means by which students receive support from the organization. The leadership development and history courses are taken at group meetings like the one pictured here in the 1990s. Each club belongs to an ASPIRA Club Federation. (Courtesy of ASPIRA of Florida.)

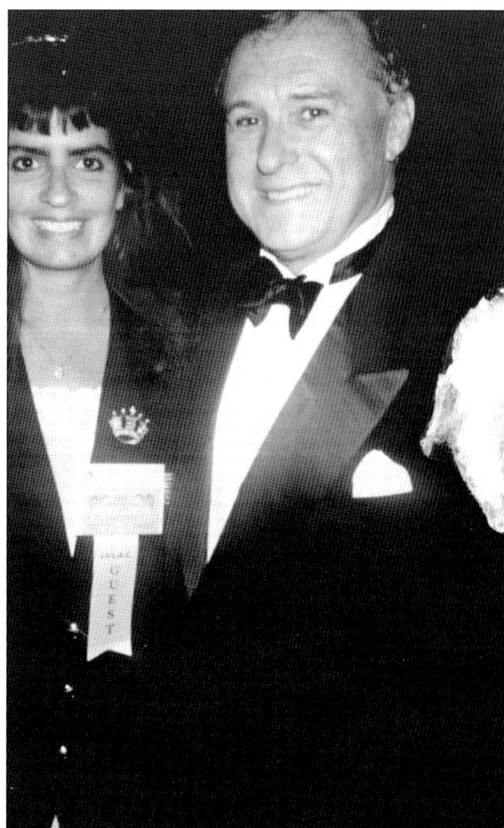

Pictured here are Maribel Melendez and former mayor Maurice Ferre at a gala event kicking off the Puerto Rican Festival in the late 1990s. The gala was the ceremony at which the pageant contestant winner was announced. The recipient would receive her scholarship; most of the participants were college students. (Courtesy of Luis De Rosa.)

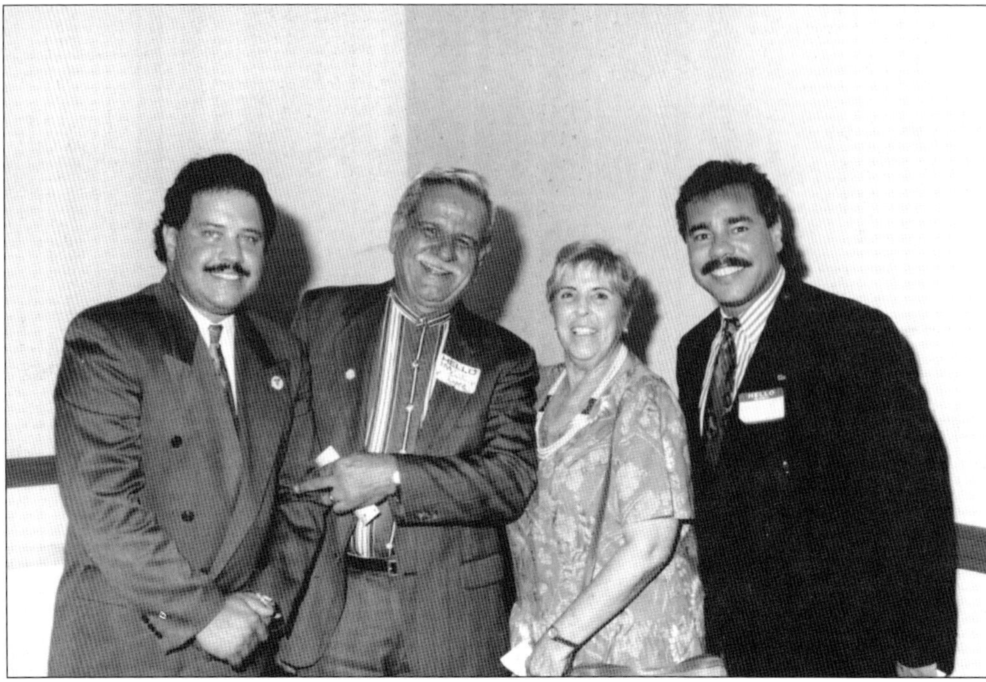

This 2000 event honored Emilio Lopez (second from left) for lifetime achievement and commitment to the Puerto Rican community in Wynwood. Lopez is the founder and CEO of Borinquen Health Clinic in Wynwood. Honoring Lopez are, from left to right, Luis De Rosa, president of the Puerto Rican Chamber of Commerce; Dr. Ivette Morgan, Puerto Rican Community Action Center, Wynwood District; and Henry Mojica, US Navy veteran and head of the Puerto Rican festival. (Courtesy of Luis De Rosa.)

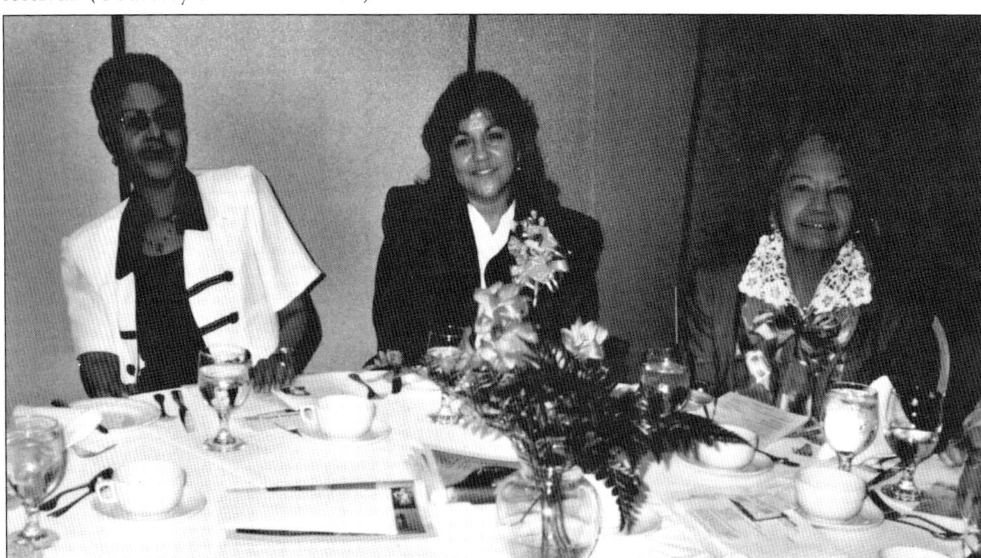

Pictured here at the NACOPRW annual meeting in 2000 is Dr. Teresa Albizu, that year's recipient of the Dr. Alicia Baro Award for commitment to her community. Albizu is seated at center. To her right is Dr. Baro, and to her left is longtime ASPIRA youth advisor Iris Corchado. (Courtesy of NACOPRW.)

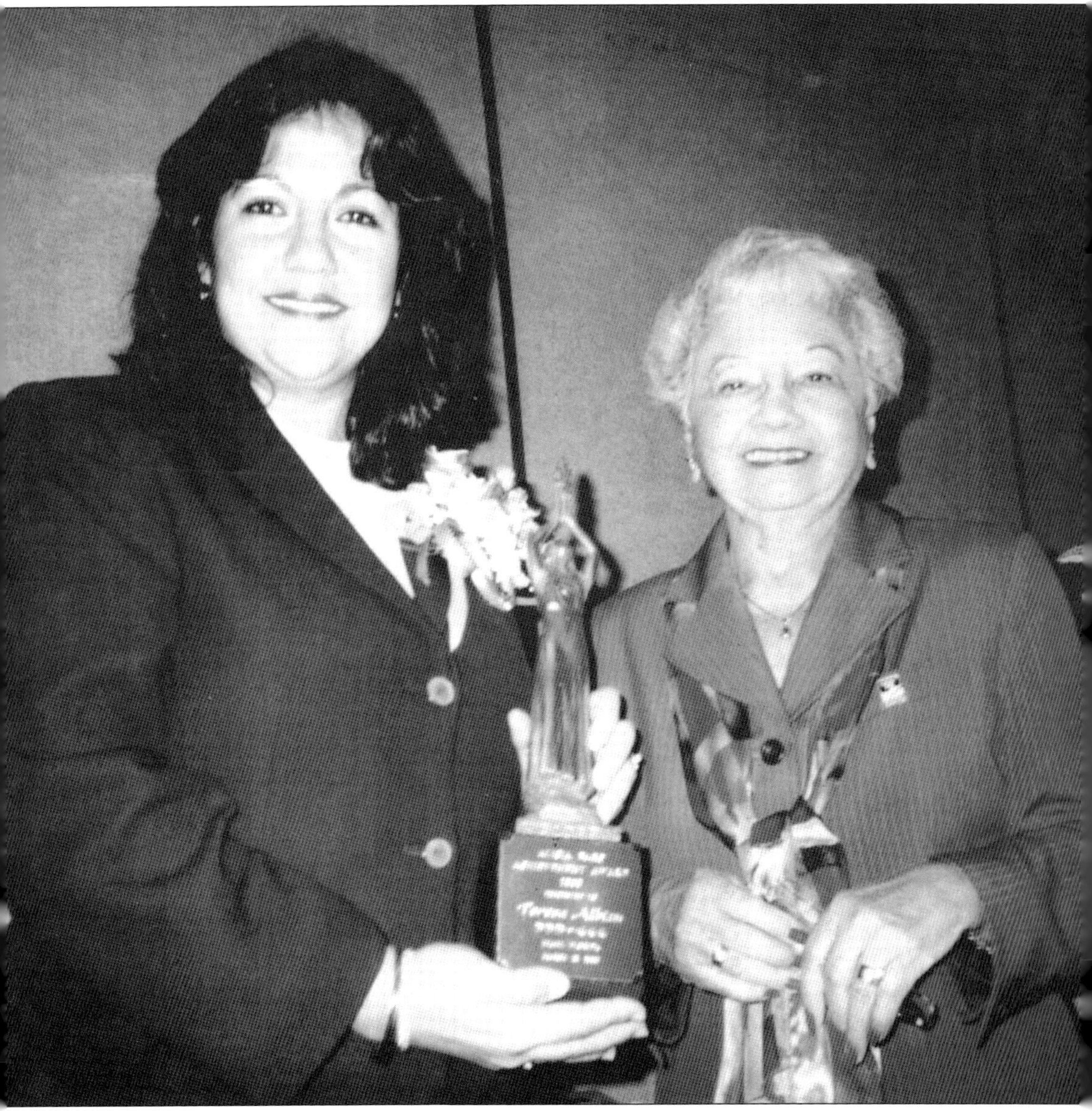

In 1994, NACOPRW–Miami Chapter created the Dr. Alicia Baro Achievement Award to recognize Puerto Rican women who demonstrate qualities as role models, contribute to the general well-being of the community, and reflect dedication and service for the betterment of women. In 2000, when this photograph was taken, the recipient of the award was Dr. Teresa Albizu, daughter of Dr. Carlos Albizu, founder of the Miami International Institute. Upon his passing, it was renamed Carlos Albizu University. Presenting her the award is Dr. Alicia Baro herself. (Courtesy of NACOPRW.)

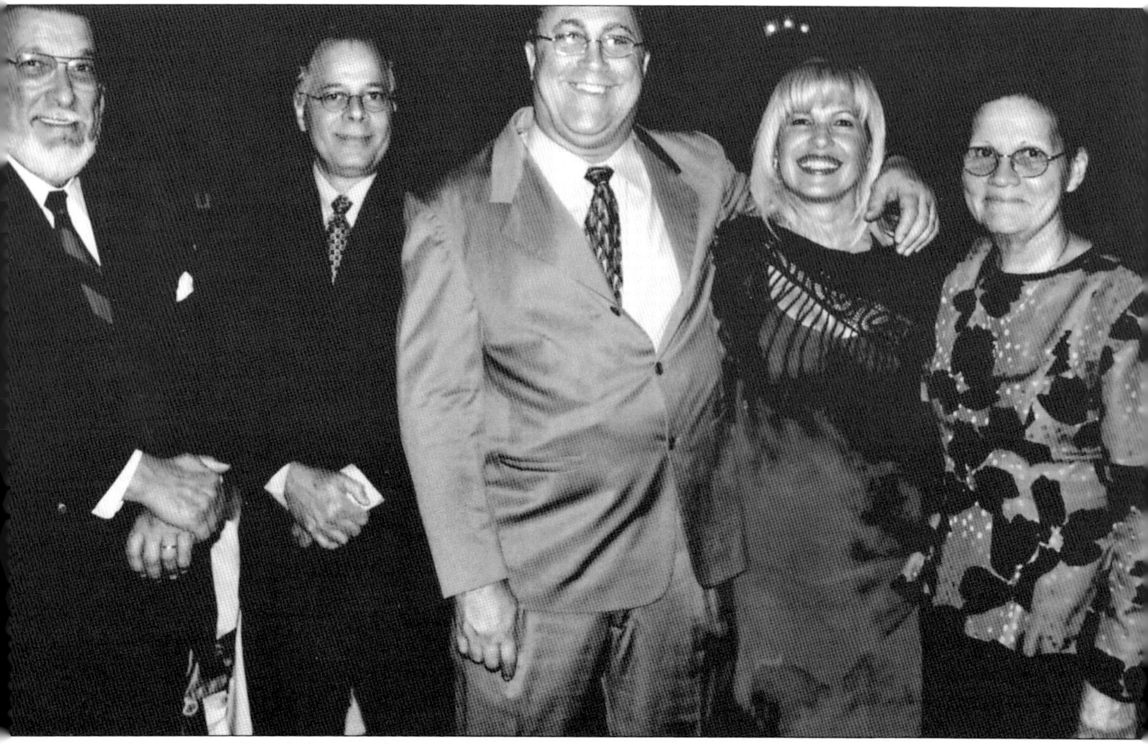

This 2004 gala celebration honored Borinquen Health Center. In the center, with his arm around his wife, Ivette Velez, is Paul Velez, CEO of Borinquen. His father was among the many military personnel who came to Miami during World War II and stayed. On his left is Manuel Benitez, a Rums of Puerto Rico representative in South Florida. Also pictured is Eva Perez, chair of the Borinquen board of directors. (Courtesy of Luis De Rosa.)

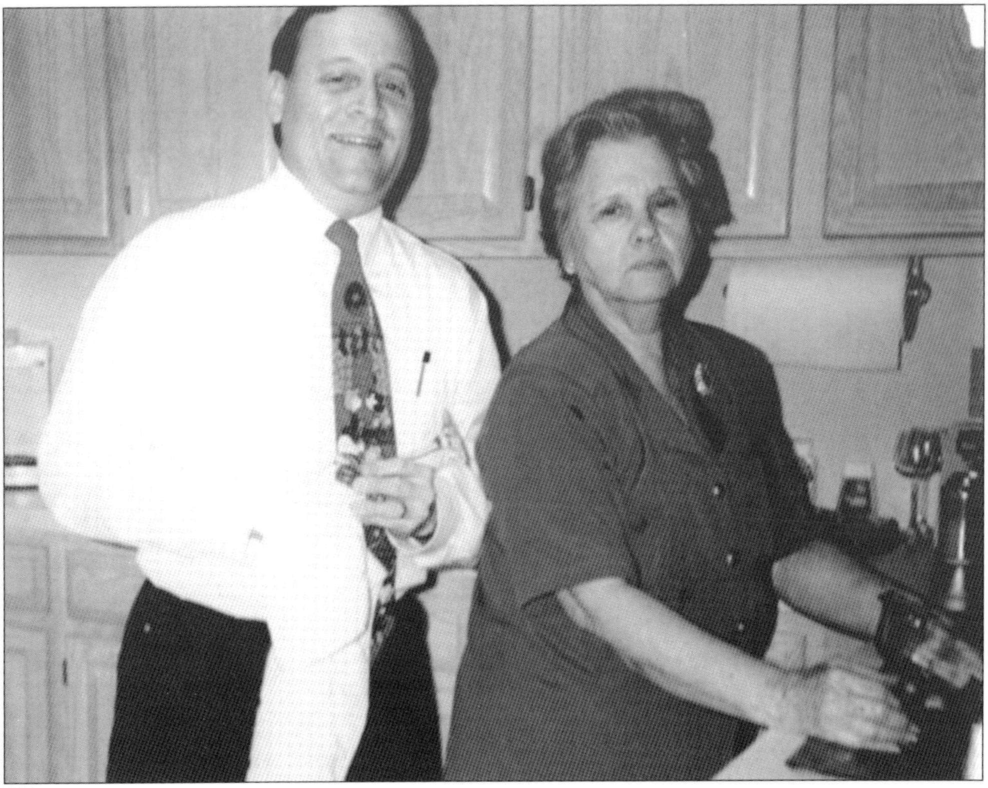

Pictured here is Jose Carlos and his mother, Carmen, doing the dishes after a Christmas dinner. The Pedrogo home in North Miami was where the family gathered for these events. They brought their wives, children, aunts, uncles, and in-laws for a typical Puerto Rican celebration. (Courtesy of Carmen Pedrogo.)

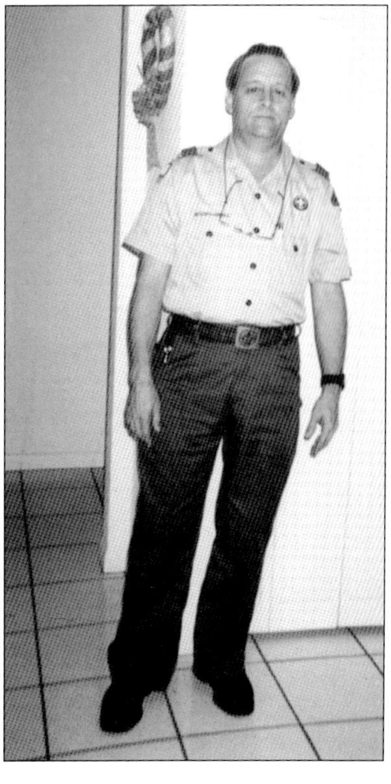

Jose Carlos Pedrogo is pictured here in his Cubmaster uniform, where he serves at St. David's Church in Davie. Pedrogo, who had been a Boy Scout in his youth, continues to serve youth through Scouting. The Scouting program is strong, with over 50 Eagle Scouts coming out of it. Pedrogo's nephew is now in Cub Scouts. (Courtesy of Carmen Pedrogo.)

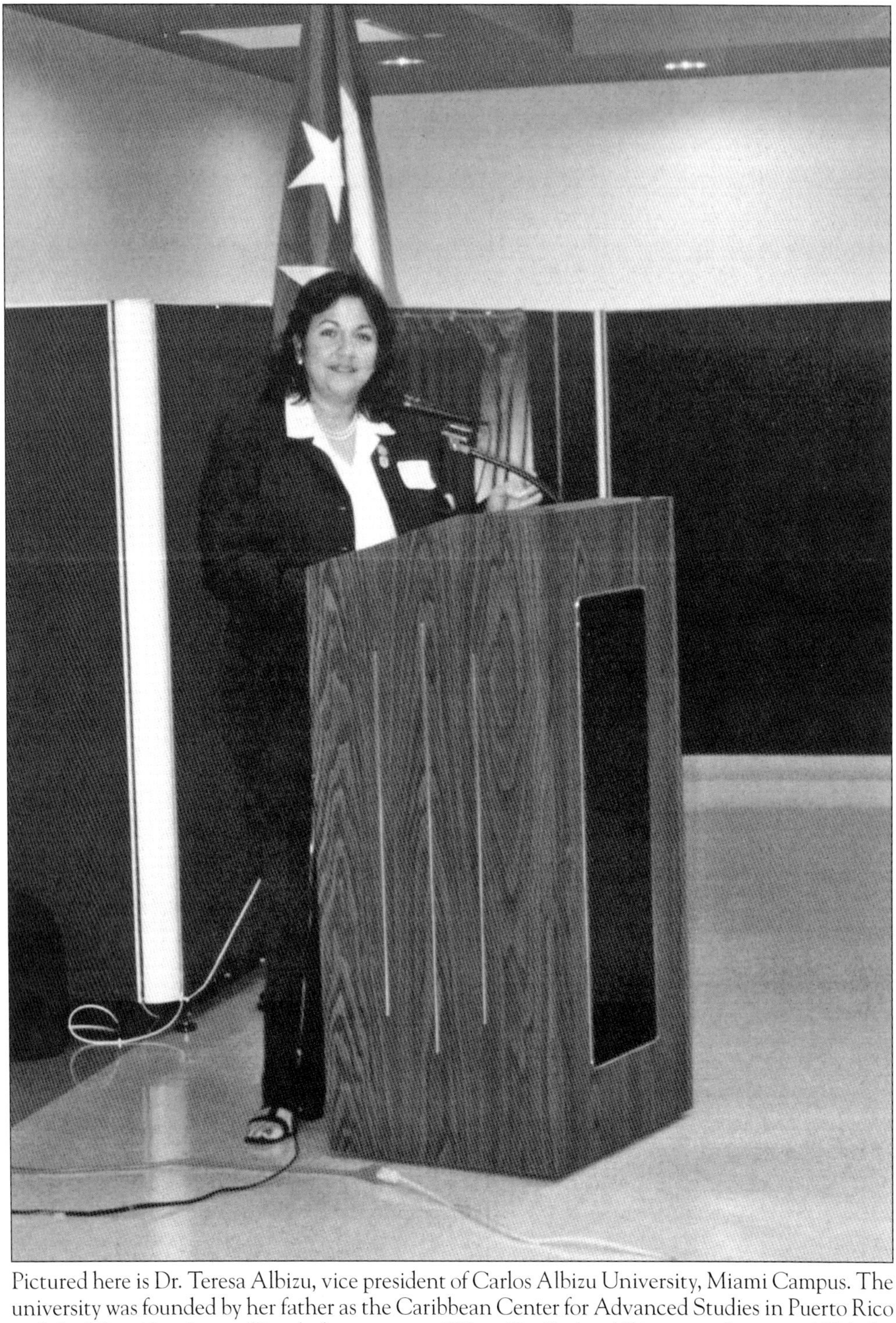

Pictured here is Dr. Teresa Albizu, vice president of Carlos Albizu University, Miami Campus. The university was founded by her father as the Caribbean Center for Advanced Studies in Puerto Rico and the Miami Institute of Psychology campus. When Dr. Carlos Albizu passed away in 1984, the board of the center changed the name of the institution to honor him. In this photograph, Dr. Teresa Albizu welcomes a meeting of NACOPRW to the university. (Courtesy of NACOPRW.)

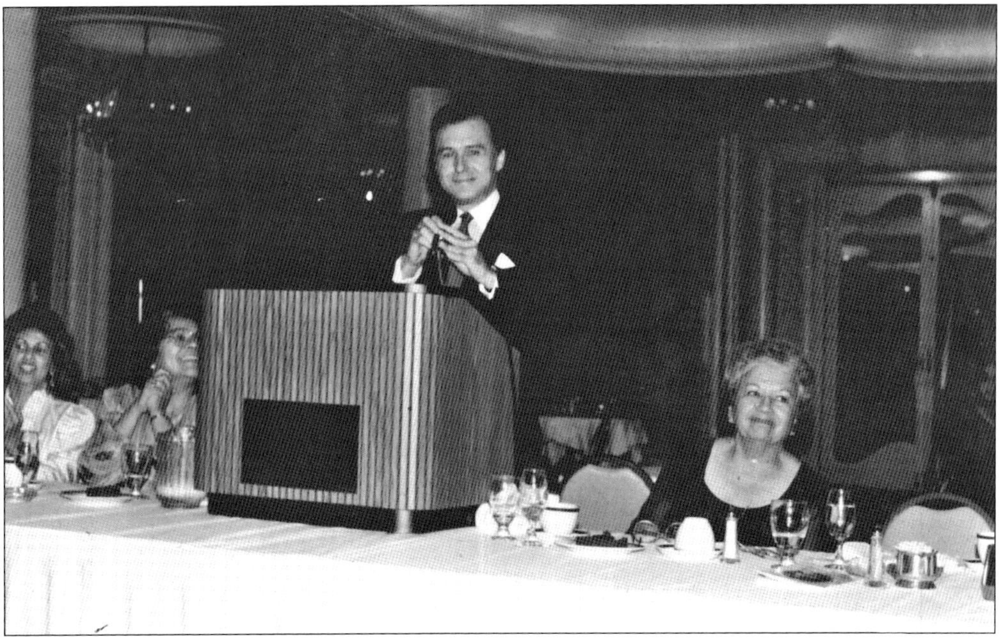

Pictured here is Mayor Maurice Ferre, who is often a featured speaker at events. His support helped raise funds for the annual scholarships that NACOPRW gave high school Puerto Rican women for college each year. The scholarships were generally paid directly to the college or university the women attended. (Courtesy of NACOPRW.)

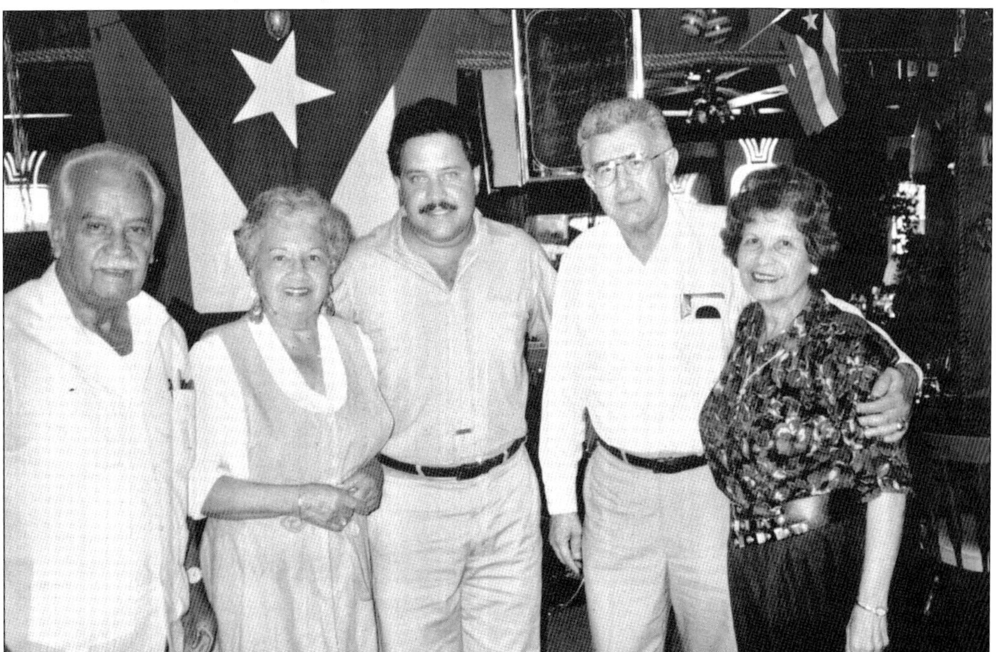

Pictured here are members of the Puerto Rican Democratic Organization after one of their meetings. From left to right are Jose Baro, Dr. Alicia S. Baro, Luis De Rosa, and Robert Camacho and his wife. These meetings were held for planning voter registration and Get Out the Vote drives in Puerto Rican neighborhoods. (Courtesy of Luis De Rosa.)

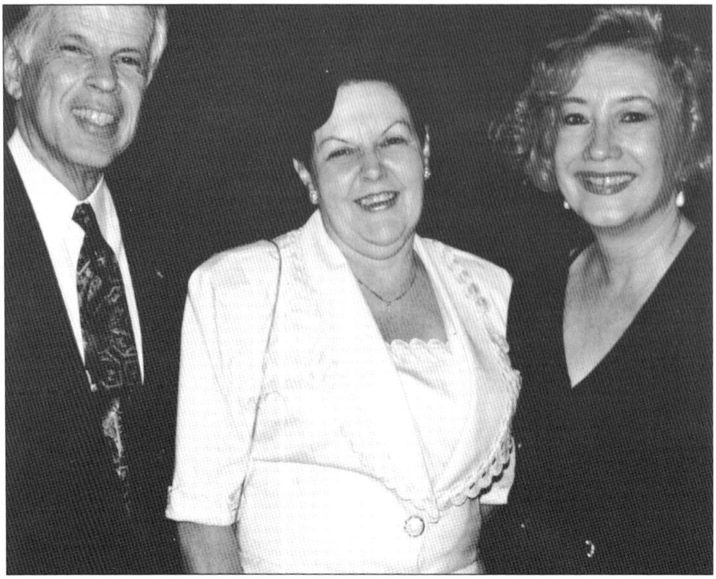

Pictured here are Puerto Rican journalist Marivi Montalvo (right), with Nicholas Álvarez and his wife, Carmen. Montalvo worked for El Diario de la Americas. Alvarez was the Goya Foods representative assigned to work directly with the Puerto Rican community in Miami in the 1990s. This was an event organized by NACOPRW. (Courtesy of Luis De Rosa.)

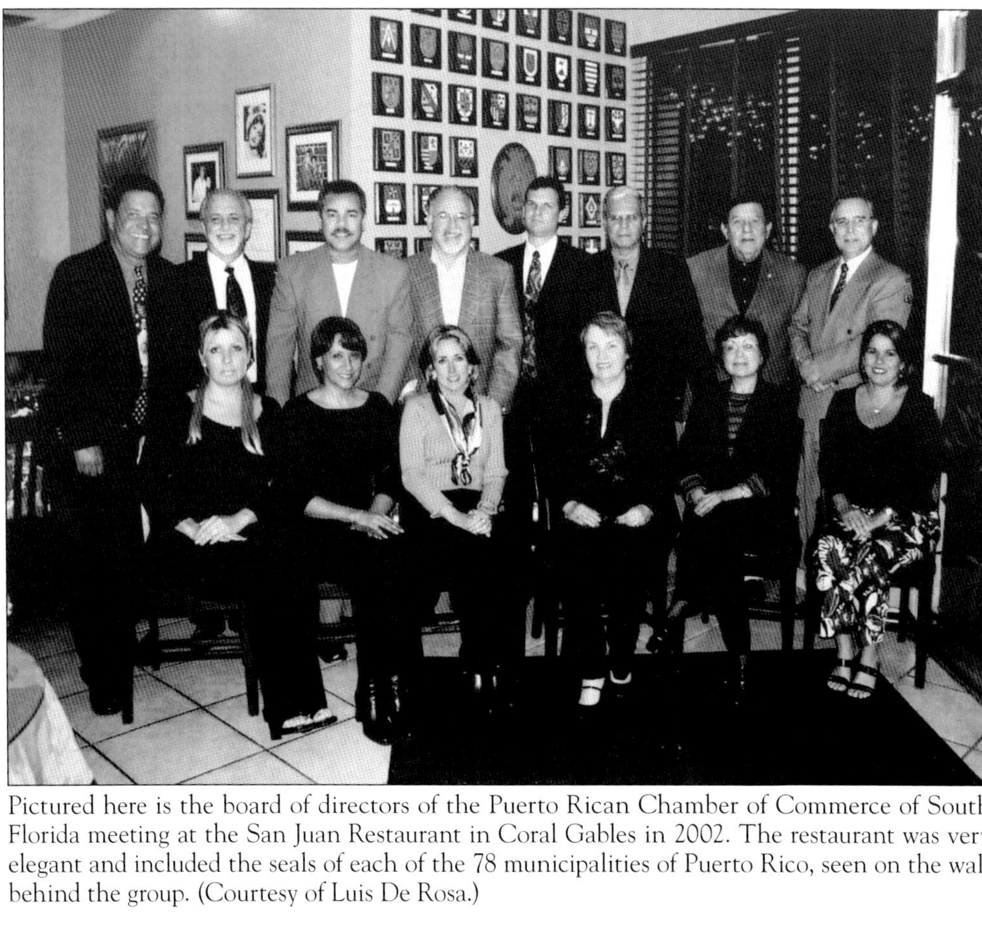

Pictured here is the board of directors of the Puerto Rican Chamber of Commerce of South Florida meeting at the San Juan Restaurant in Coral Gables in 2002. The restaurant was very elegant and included the seals of each of the 78 municipalities of Puerto Rico, seen on the wall behind the group. (Courtesy of Luis De Rosa.)

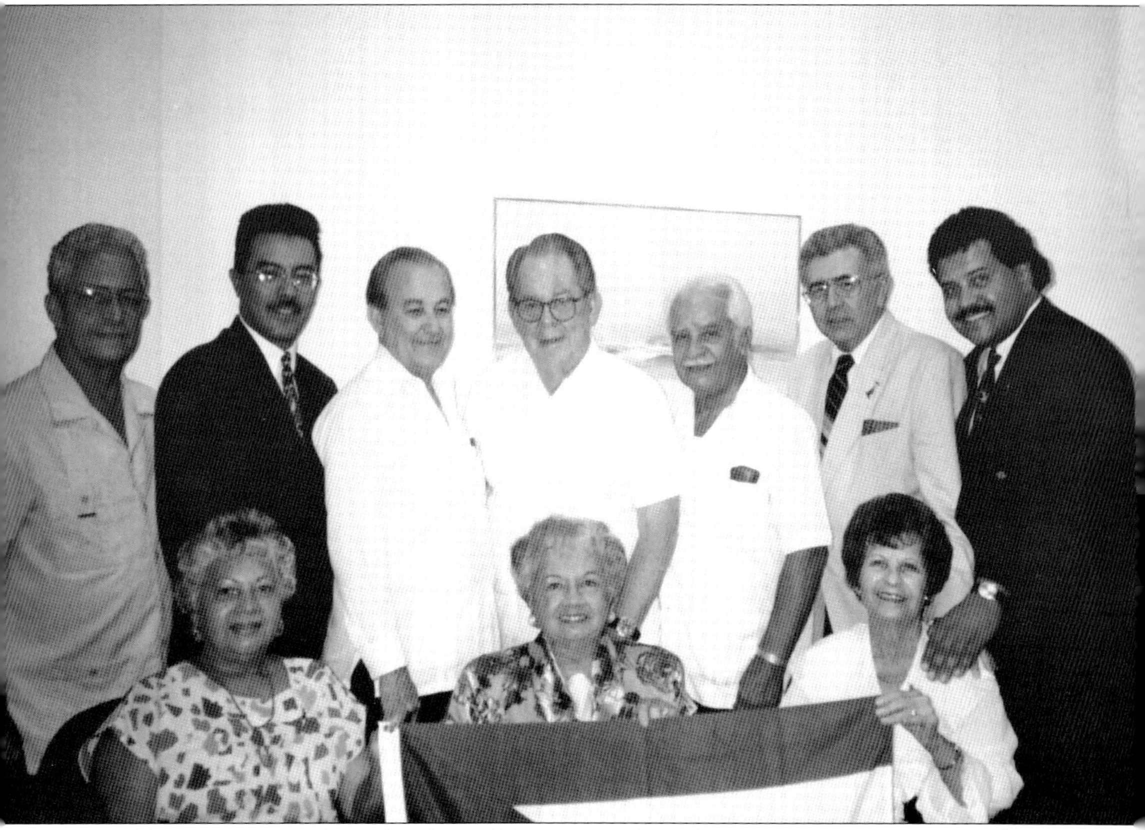

Pictured here are some of the founders of the Puerto Rican Democratic Organization. They include Jose Baro (standing third from right) and Al Bermejo (standing at center). Also pictured are Robert Camacho (standing second from right), Alicia Baro (seated at center), and Eva Perez (seated at right). For more than five decades, the group fought for equality for Puerto Ricans and other Latino immigrant groups, including Cubans. (Courtesy of Luis De Rosa.)

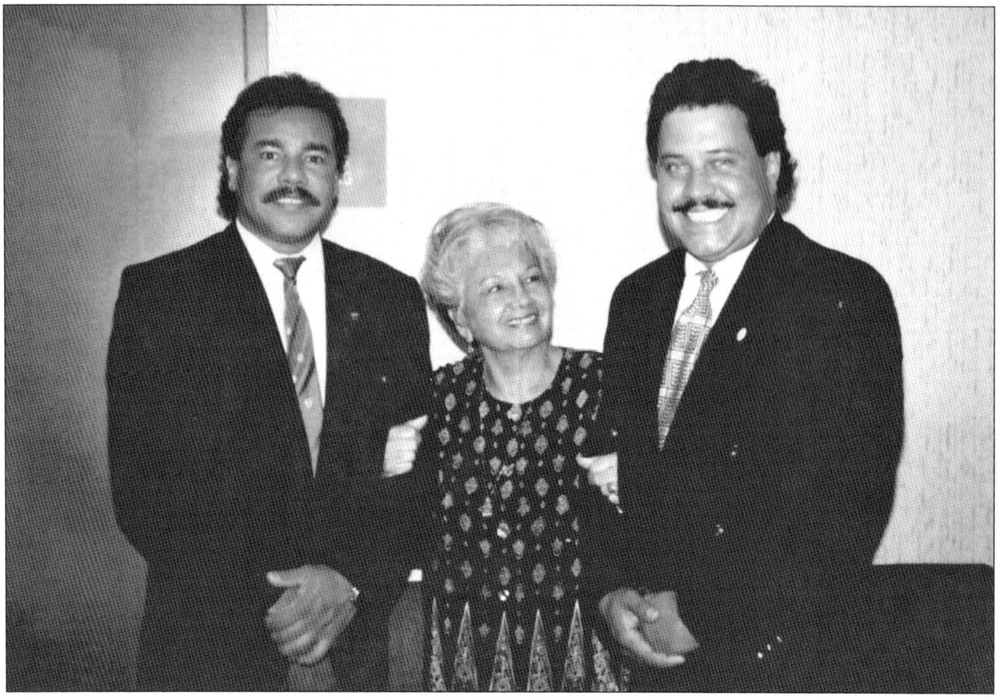

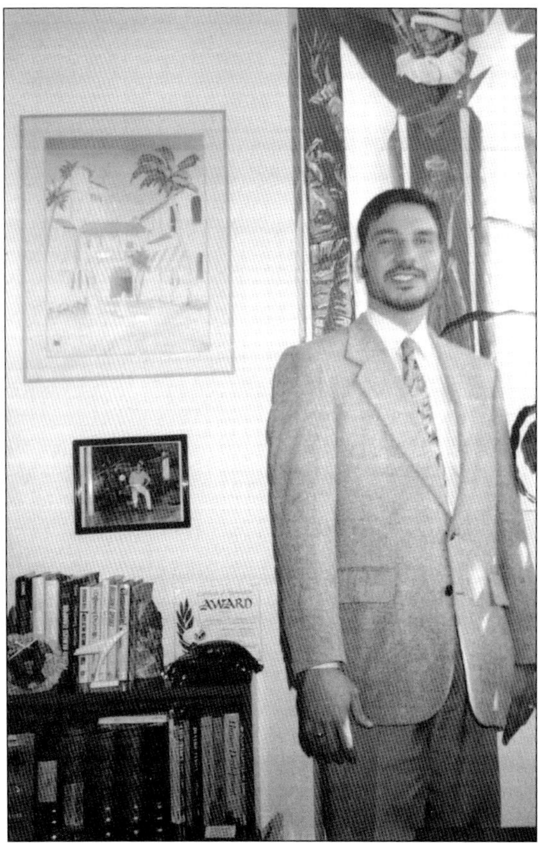

Dr. Alicia Baro was honored in 2000 for her 45 years of service in promoting and protecting the voting rights of Puerto Ricans and other minorities through the Puerto Rican Democratic Organization, a group she helped found in 1955 to address the mistreatment that Puerto Rican farmworkers faced in Homestead. (Courtesy of Luis De Rosa.)

Raul A. Martinez, pictured here in his office in the Wynwood, led ASPIRA for more than 25 years. He turned a small operation into a tri-county organization serving thousands of Puerto Rican and other minority youth in some of the toughest and poorest communities. He was highly respected by politicians and ordinary people, with whom he never lost touch. (Courtesy of ASPIRA of Florida.)

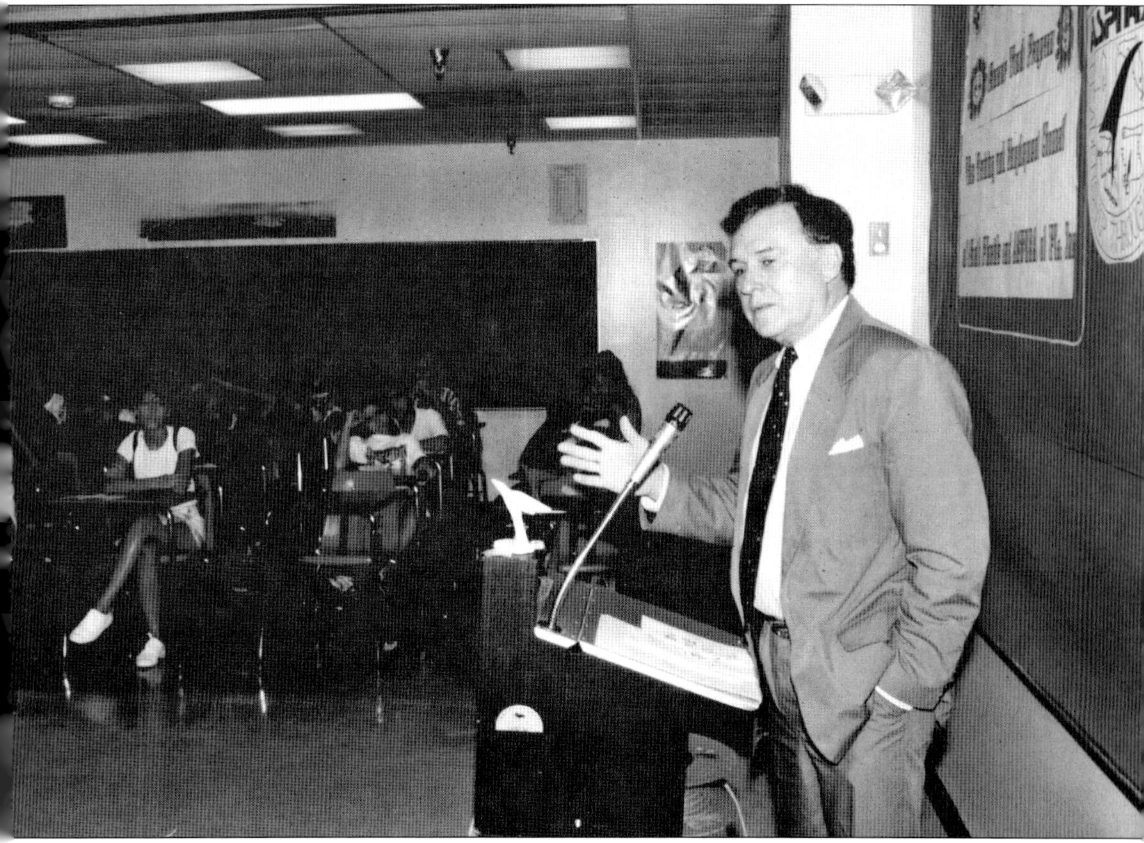

Mayor Maurice Ferre rarely missed an opportunity to speak in public. He was a gifted orator who could touch on the classics, philosophy, political science, scriptures, math, and engineering in one speech. He had a passion for young people and always encouraged and nurtured them to reach higher, and that is why ASPIRA, whose name comes from the Spanish for "aspire," was a natural venue for him to speak, as he does here before a group of students. (Courtesy of ASPIRA of Florida.)

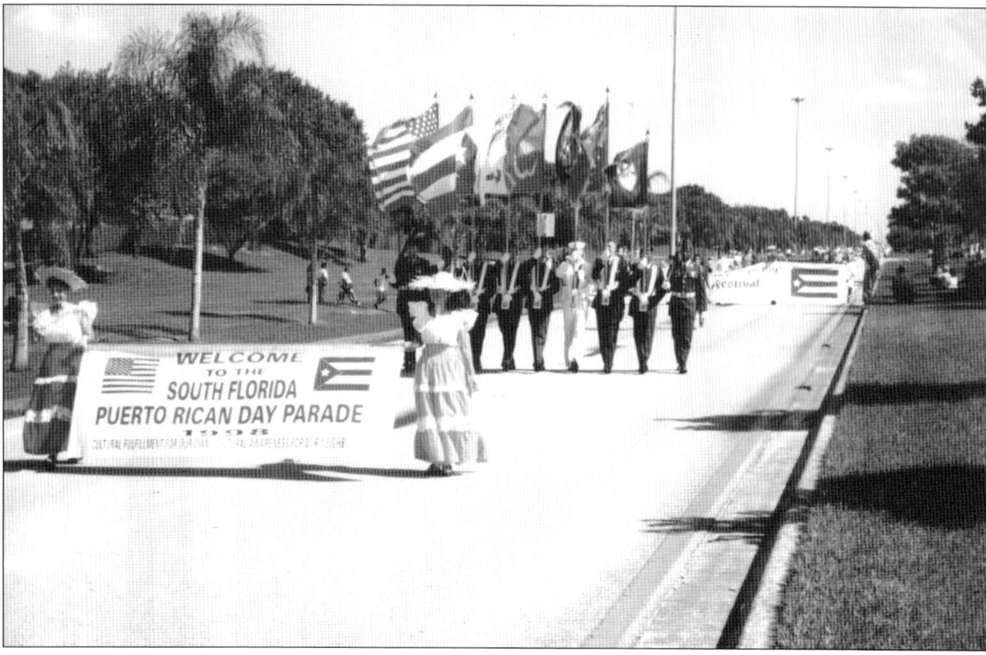

By the end of the 1990s and the beginning of the new millennium, the numbers of Puerto Ricans began to grow exponentially, particularly in Miami-Dade and Broward Counties. This growth was demonstrated in the organization of the first Puerto Rican Day Parade of South Florida, pictured here in 1998. The organizers attempted to bring together Puerto Ricans from Pembroke Pines in Florida. They invited those from across the county line to join them, and many did. (Courtesy of NACOPRW.)

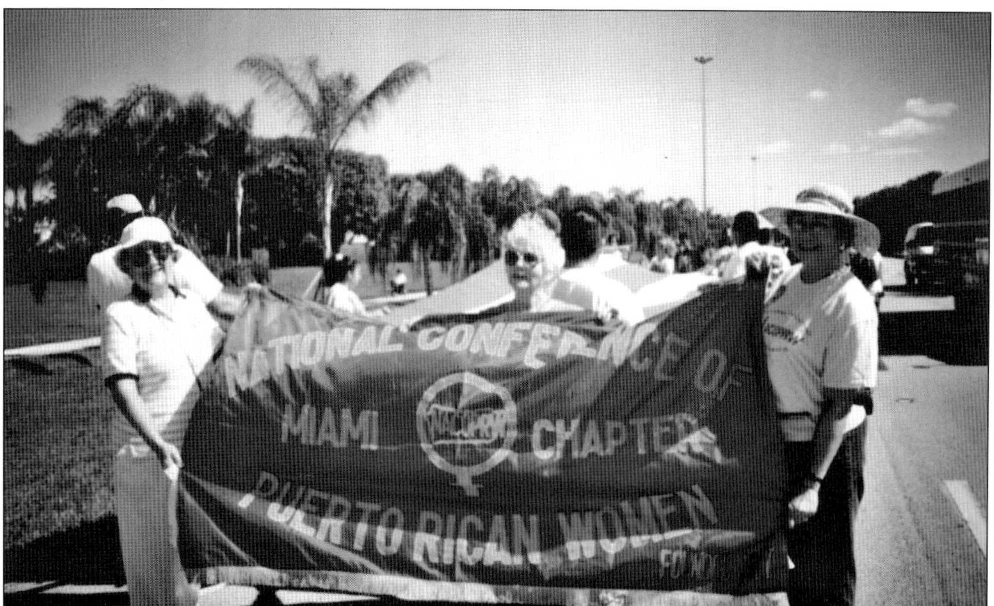

One of the first organizations to answer the call from the organizers of the first Puerto Rican Day Parade in South Florida in 1998 was NACOPRW. Pictured here is a group of women members of NACOPRW preparing to head down the parade route. (Courtesy of NACOPRW.)

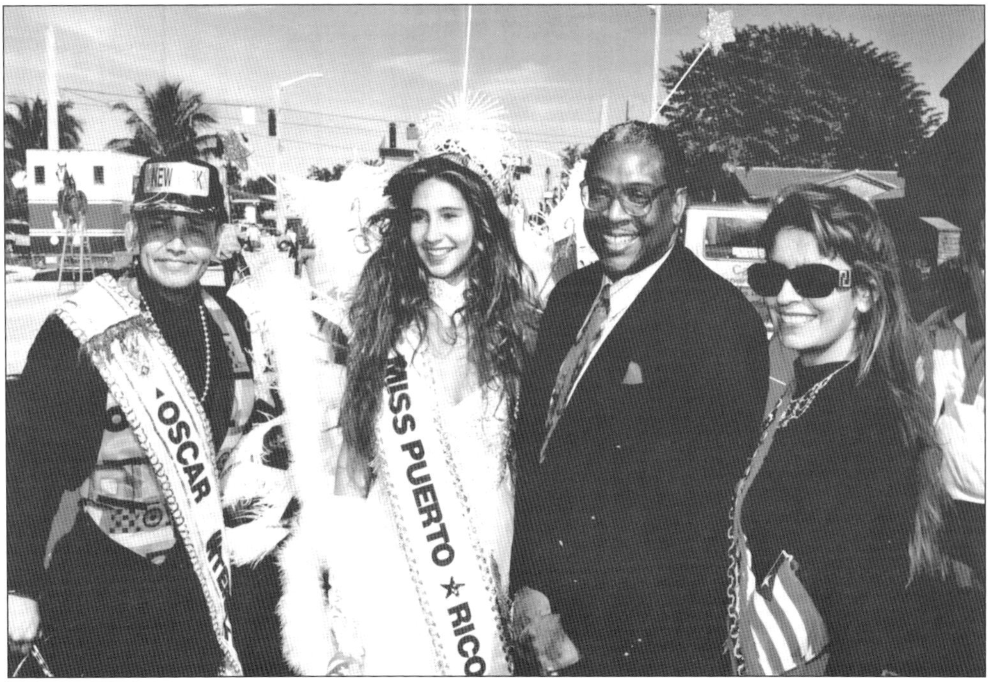

Pictured here is Syndia Grafals, Miss Puerto Rico, as the Puerto Rican Day Parade heads down Calle Ocho. To the left is Miami City commissioner Arthur Teele. Grafals participated in the pageant, organized by the Puerto Rican Festival of the Puerto Rican Chamber of Commerce and coordinated by Maribel Melendez. (Courtesy of Luis De Rosa.)

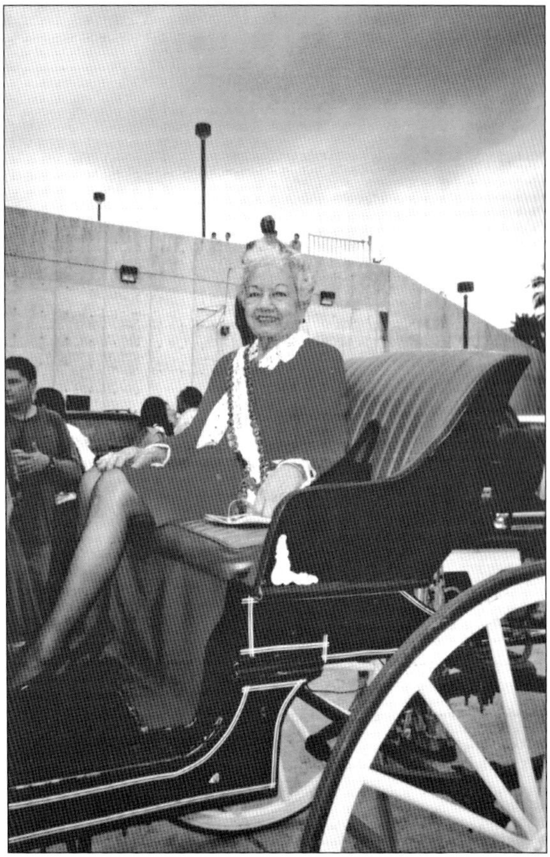

For more than two decades, different Puerto Rican cultural organizations have been celebrating the Festival of the Plantain/Festival del Platano. It is a recognition of how important this type of banana is to Puerto Rican cuisine. In addition, it has a special association with Puerto Rican agriculture, and hence a cultural connection with farming communities. Pictured here is Dr. Alicia Baro, a special guest at one of the festivals. (Courtesy of NACOPRW.)

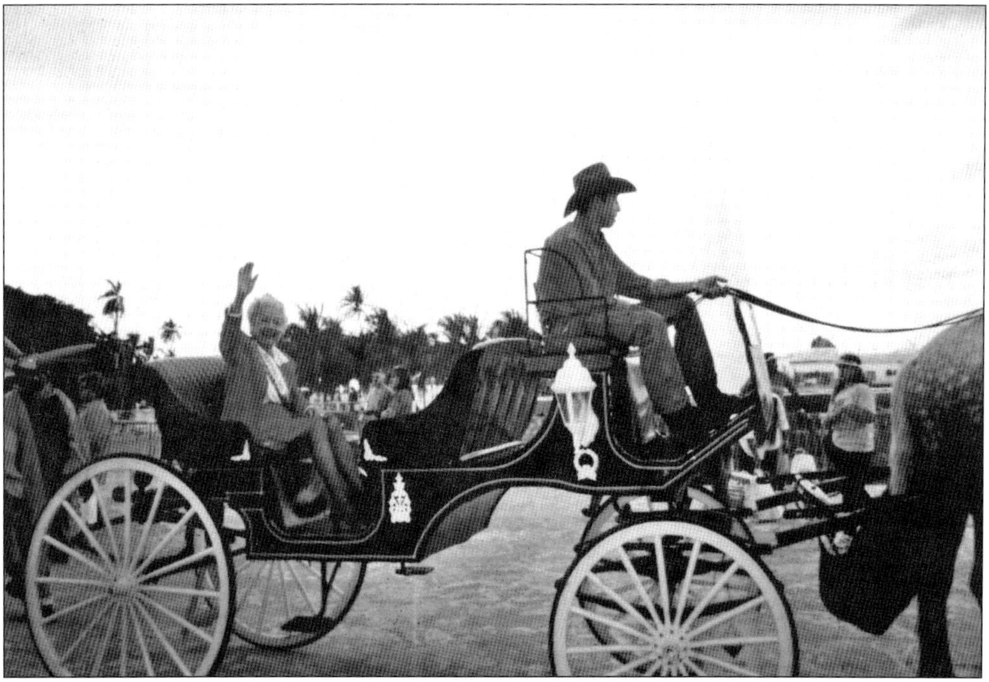

This is another view of Dr. Baro being brought to the Festival de Platano in a horse-drawn coach. The events in Miami are typically held in the southern part of Miami–Dade County in the farming communities of the Redlands in Homestead. Some organizations have bought land or have members who own land, and this is typically where the festival is held. (Courtesy of NACOPRW.)

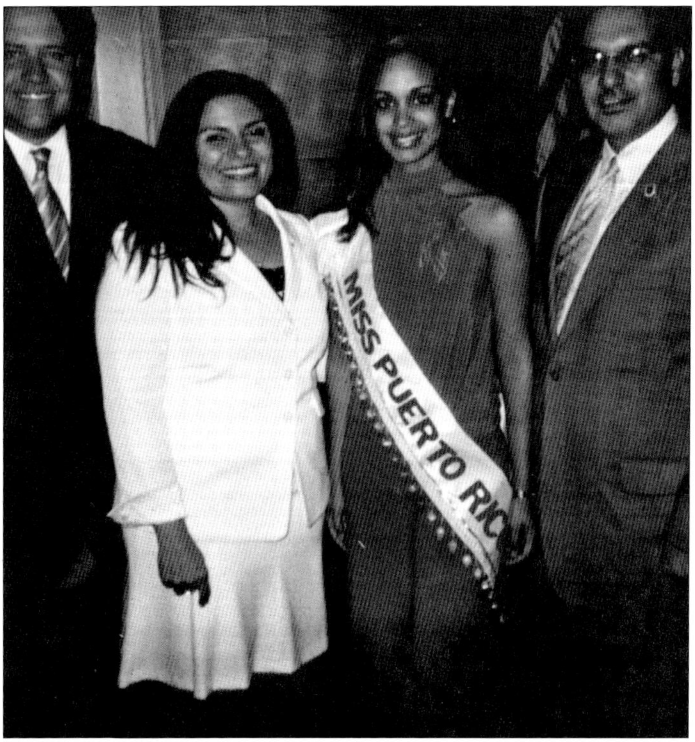

This was a celebration of ASPIRA's 35th anniversary in 2006. From left to right are Luis De Rosa, Puerto Rican Chamber of Commerce; Miream Sierra, chair, ASPIRA board; Ivette Rosa, Miss Puerto Rico; and Raul Martinez, ASPIRA CEO. Sierra, who had been in ASPIRA in New York, was well versed in the programs and became very active when she moved to Florida. She was instrumental in bringing the programming to Broward County. (Courtesy of ASPIRA of Florida.)

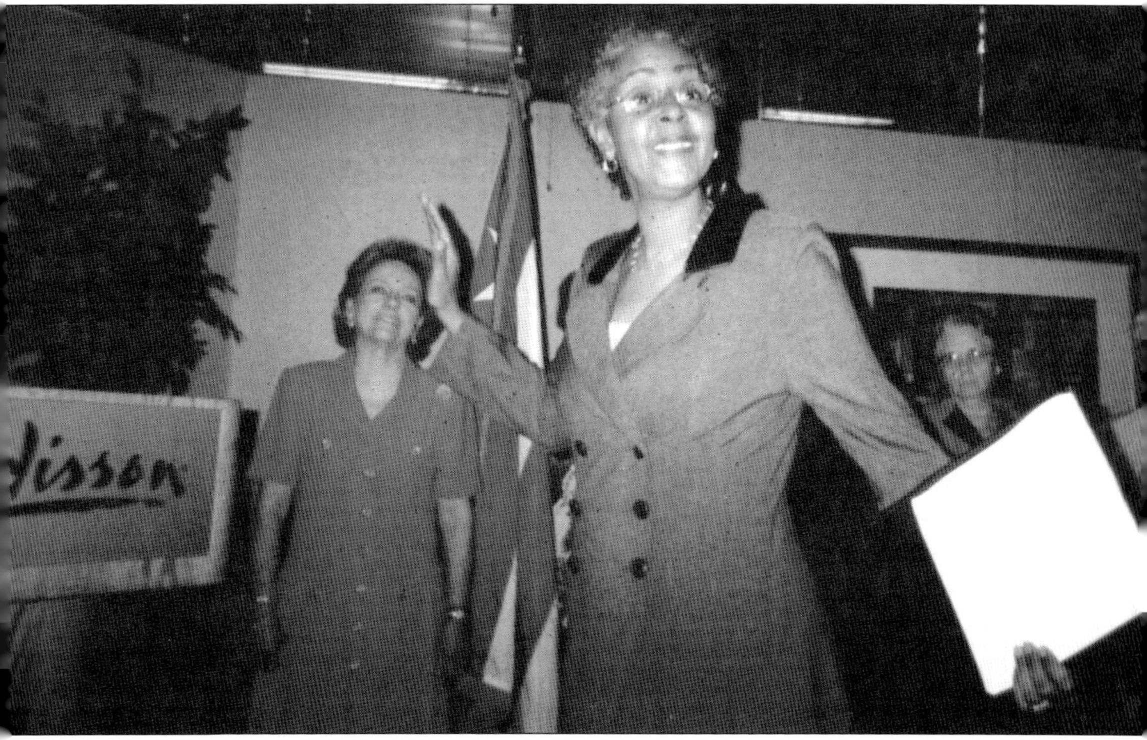

Iris Corchado was a lifelong member of the ASPIRA family since her days in Puerto Rico. She was a youth advisor for ASPIRA of Florida, but also embodied the type of community values instilled by the organization. She worked for ASPIRA for 40 years. For decades, she not only served youth, but also volunteered in many of the Puerto Rican organizations, including NACOPRW and the Puerto Rican Cultural Center. (Courtesy of ASPIRA of Florida.)

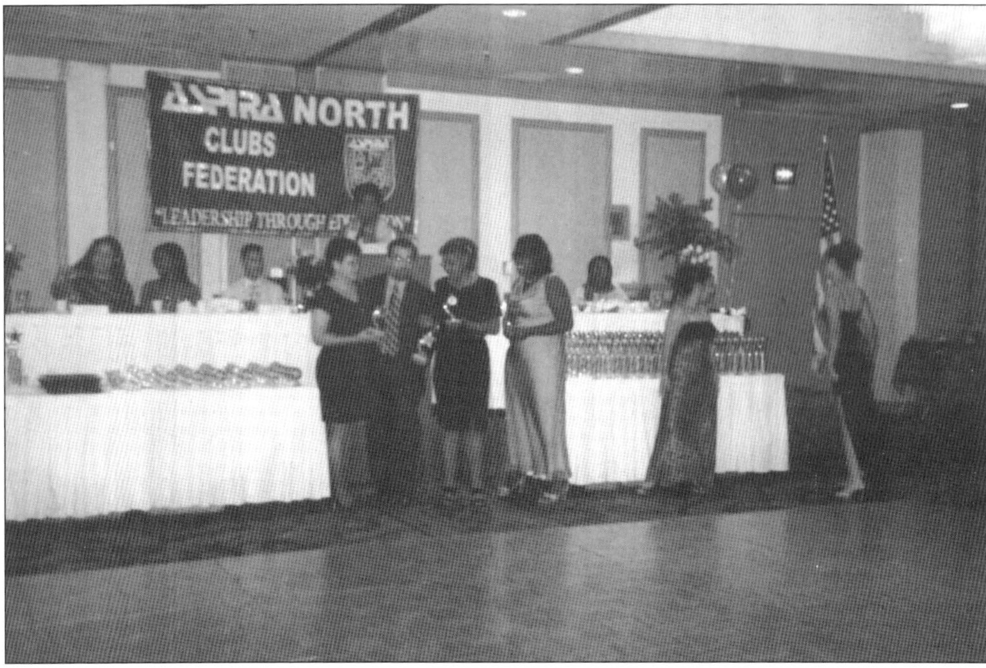

ASPIRA Clubs Federation award ceremonies are very significant for ASPIRA, like the one pictured here in 1999. An ASPIRA club is the foundational, base structure of the leadership program. Though the clubs have staff support in the schools and from ASPIRA, they are wholly run by the students. The students learn organizational skills, conflict resolution, and many other skills. (Courtesy of ASPIRA of Florida.)

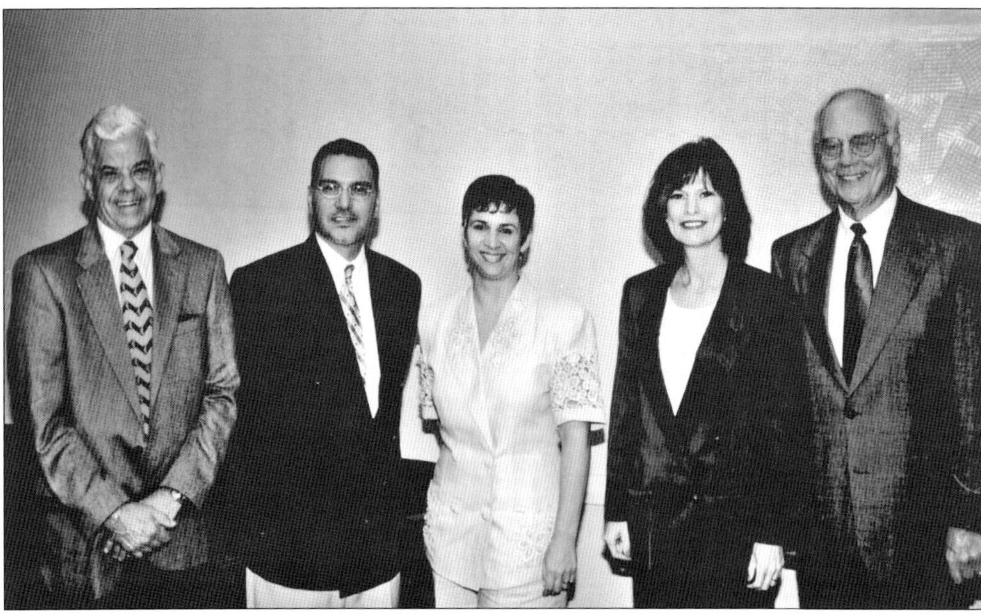

ASPIRA board members were always encouraged to attend not only events of ASPIRA, but also visit the facilities, schools, and other outlets. Pictured here from left to right are an unidentified board member, ASPIRA CEO Raul Martinez, ASPIRA COO Aymet Chaples, and two other board members visiting ASPIRA North. (Courtesy of ASPIRA of Florida.)

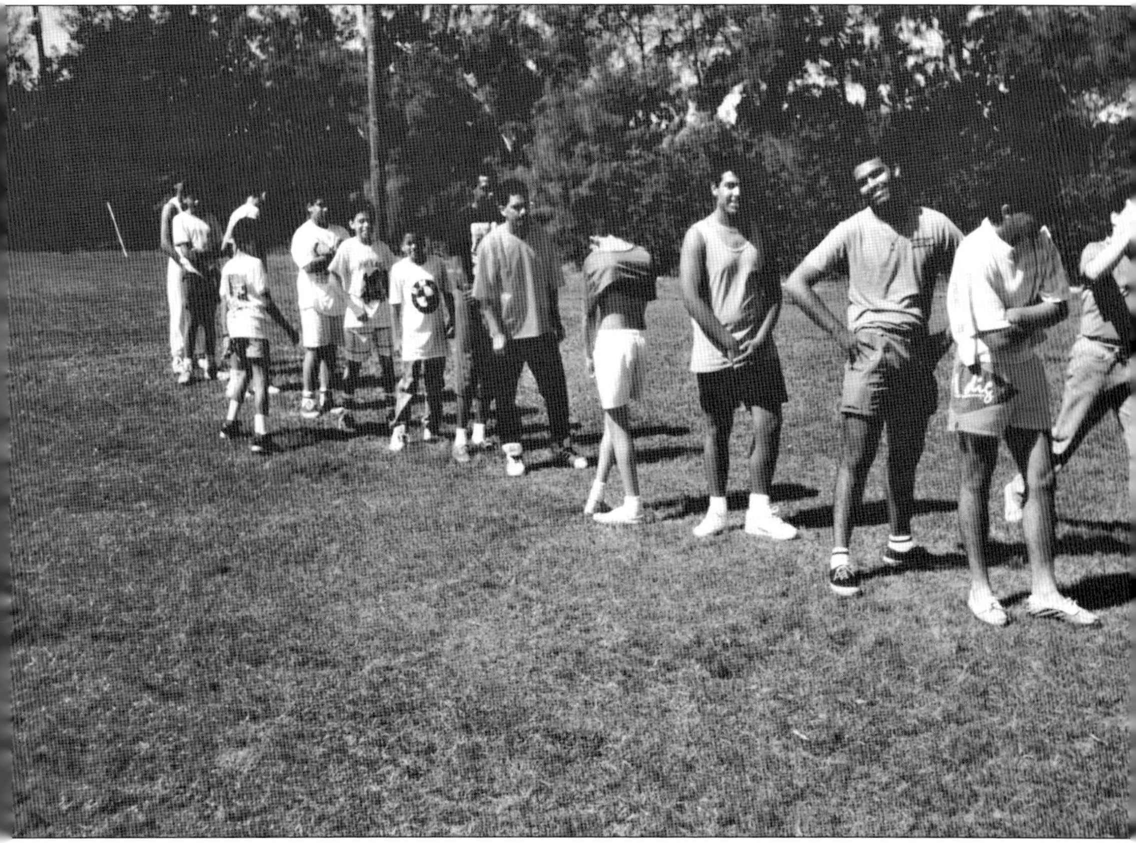

Aspirantes' team-building activities often involved physical events outdoors, like the one pictured here, to build leadership skills. Teamwork very often depends on confidence in the individuals one works with. Confidence building comes from being put in a situation of trust. A popular exercise of this type among Aspirantes is to have a youth stand on a chair or table and lean back to be caught by the group. (Courtesy of ASPIRA of Florida.)

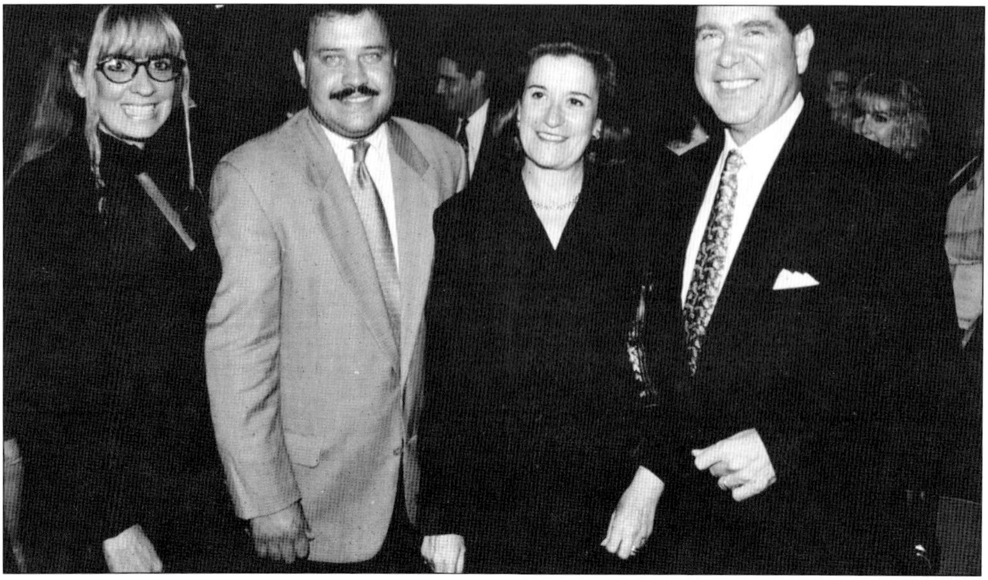

Pictured here from left to right are Maribel Melendez and her husband, Luis De Rosa, president of the Puerto Rican Chamber of Commerce, along with Alberto Ibargüen, chairman of the John S. and James L. Knight Foundation and his wife, Susana. Ibargüen, from Ponce, Puerto Rico, of Puerto Rican and Cuban descent, was for many years the president of the *Miami Herald* and *El Nuevo Herald*. (Courtesy of Luis De Rosa.)

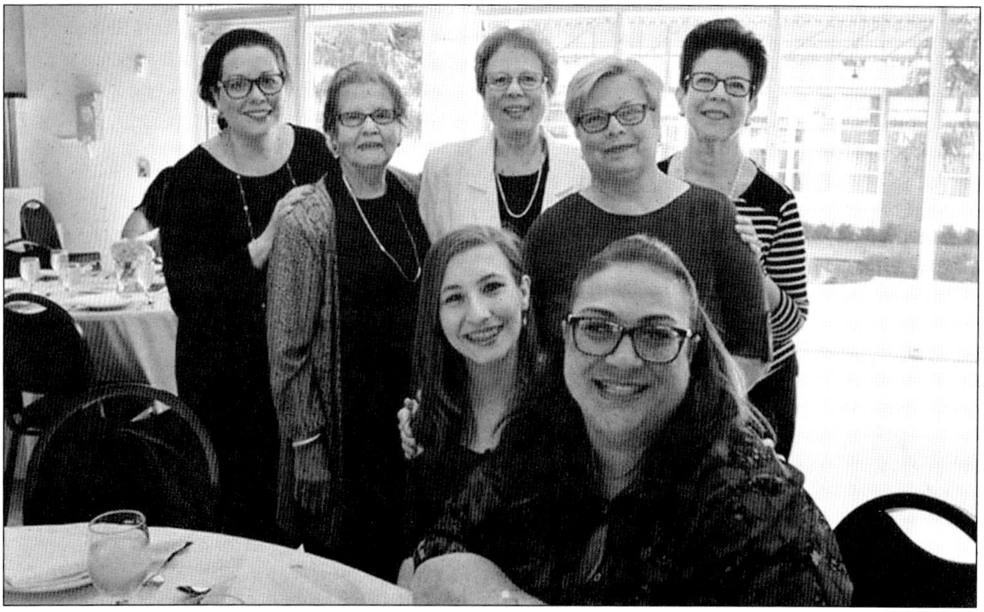

Pictured here are women of the Pedrogo extended family at the Madonna Academy Legacy Brunch in 2017. Madonna Academy, in Hollywood, Florida, was run by the Sisters of Notre Dame. Chaminade High School was the boys' college prep high school run by the Order of Marianists Brothers. In 1988, they merged into the Madonna-Chaminade School. Every year, the women meet for brunch. From left to right are (seated) Hannah Carswell and Sylvia Carswell; (standing) Lisa Pedrogo Pearsall, Carmen Pedrogo, Carmen Pedrogo, Louis Carswell, and Jane Padewah. (Courtesy of Carmen Pedrogo.)

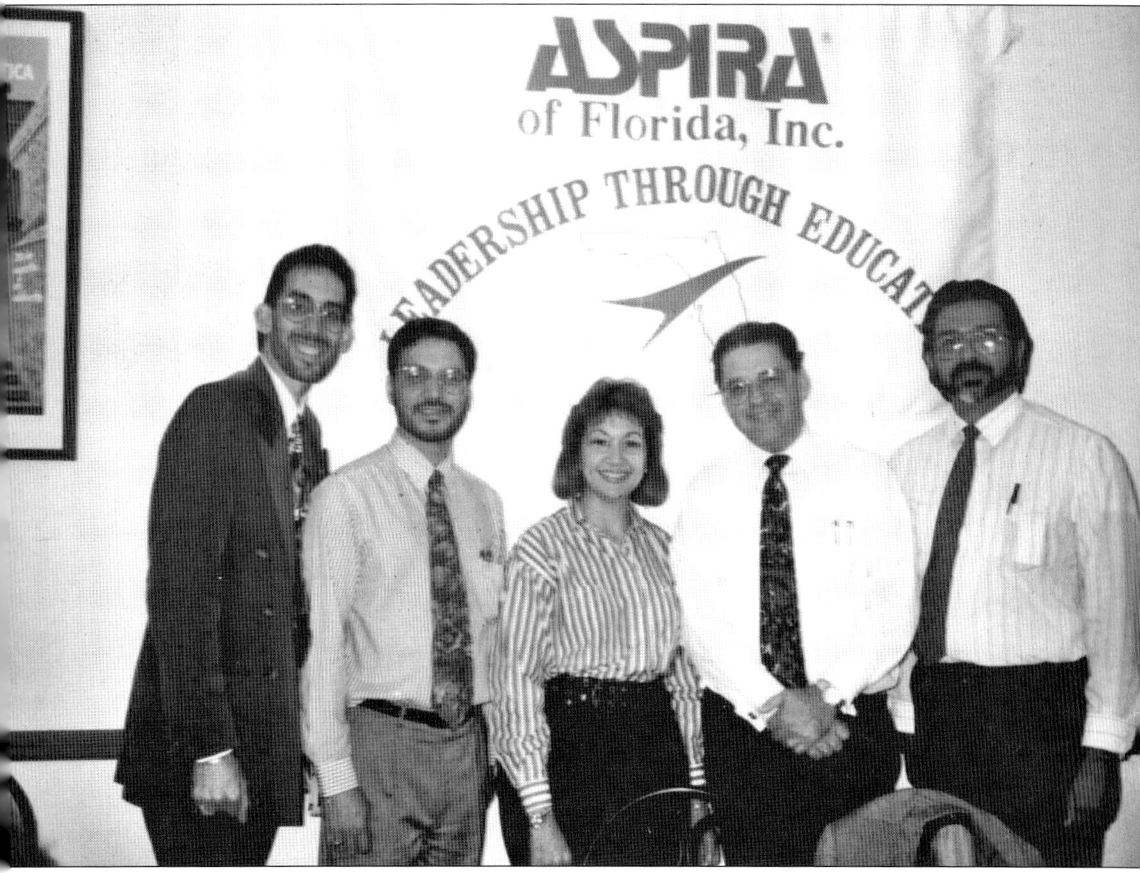

Community leaders were always welcome to visit the ASPIRA office and schools. Pictured here are CEO Raul Martinez and assistant director Willie Ramos, along with youth advisor Tomas Cintron (far right) and community leaders. Not only were community leaders welcome, but the ASPIRA facilities were often used for community meetings. This was a tradition at all ASPIRA operations around the United States. (Courtesy of ASPIRA of Florida.)

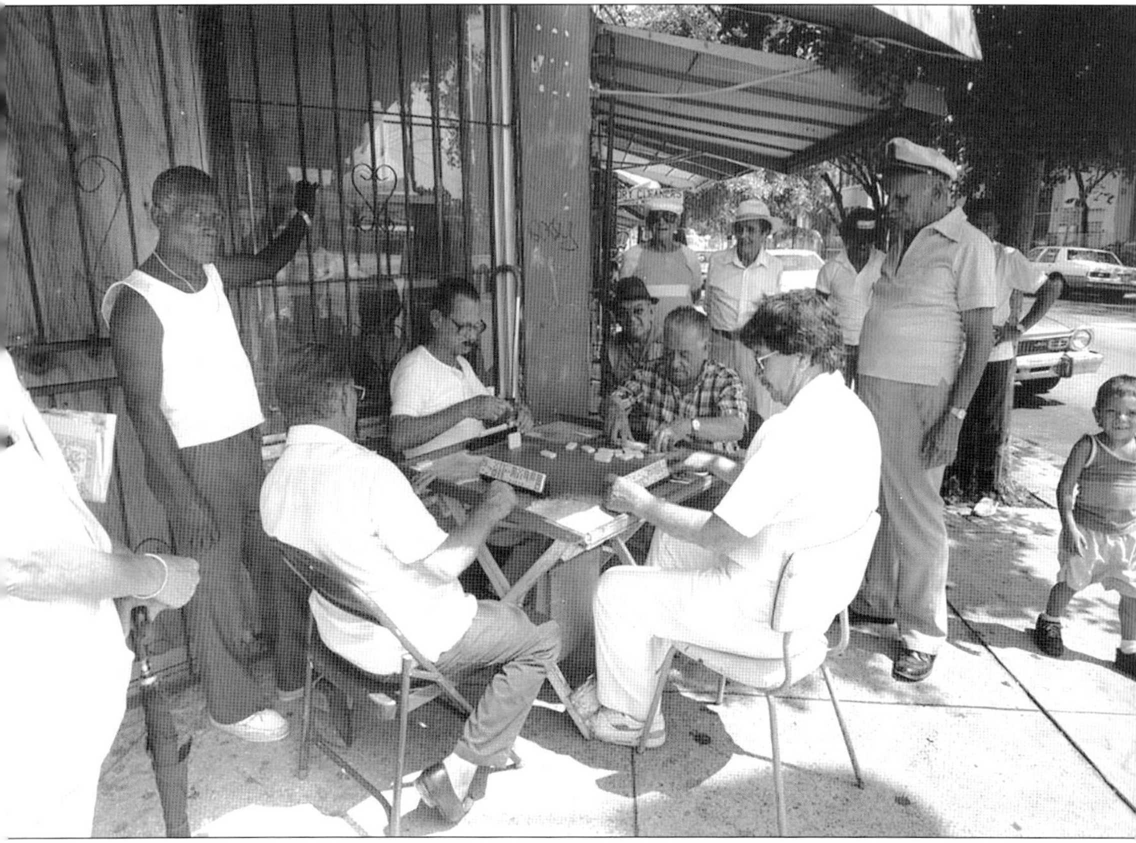

Typical in many Puerto Rican barrios, and also true in Wynwood, are men playing dominoes like those pictured here on the corner of NW Second Avenue in the 1990s. This group is using Cuban-style dominoes, which provide nine pieces for each player; the Puerto Rican style uses seven pieces per player. After the Mariel Boatlift, Wynwood attracted a fair number of Cuban refugees. Courtesy of Casey Piket.)

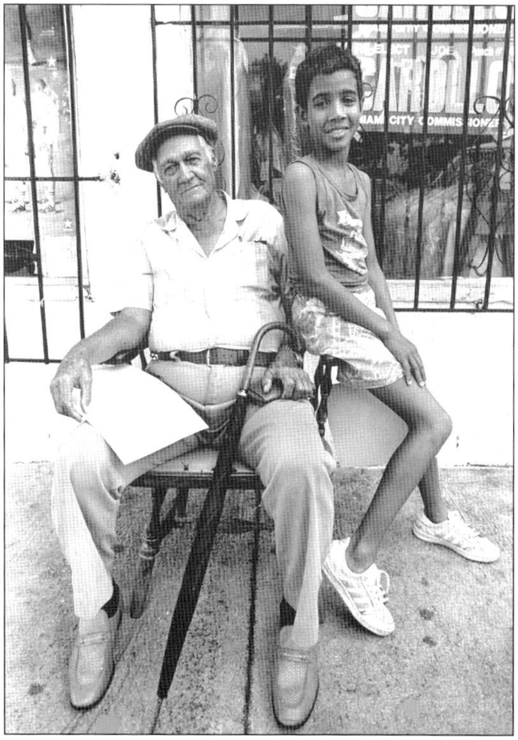

Two generations and two cultures are seen here in Wynwood in the 1990s. Cuban American Elio Ramirez, 71 years old, and Puerto Rican John Slaughter, 14, seem to be enjoying some company. Puerto Ricans tended to welcome Cuban refugees into their communities. There is a long history of solidarity between them. This was not only true in Wynwood, but in New York, Philadelphia, and New Jersey. The historical connection between the islands dates to the colonial period and the struggles of both to free themselves from Spanish control. (Courtesy of Casey Piket.)

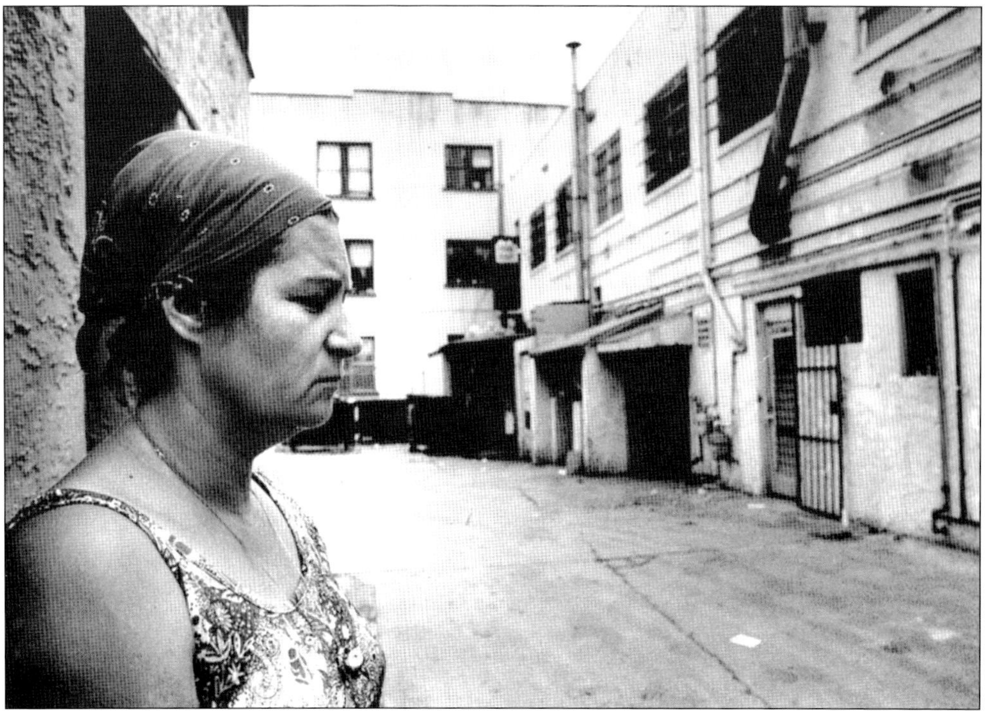

Throughout the 1980s and beyond, Wynwood began to experience a significant economic downturn and an equal rise in illegal drug use. Pictured here around 1979 is a young woman in Wynwood in one of the alleyways behind the small businesses in the community. (Courtesy of Casey Piket.)

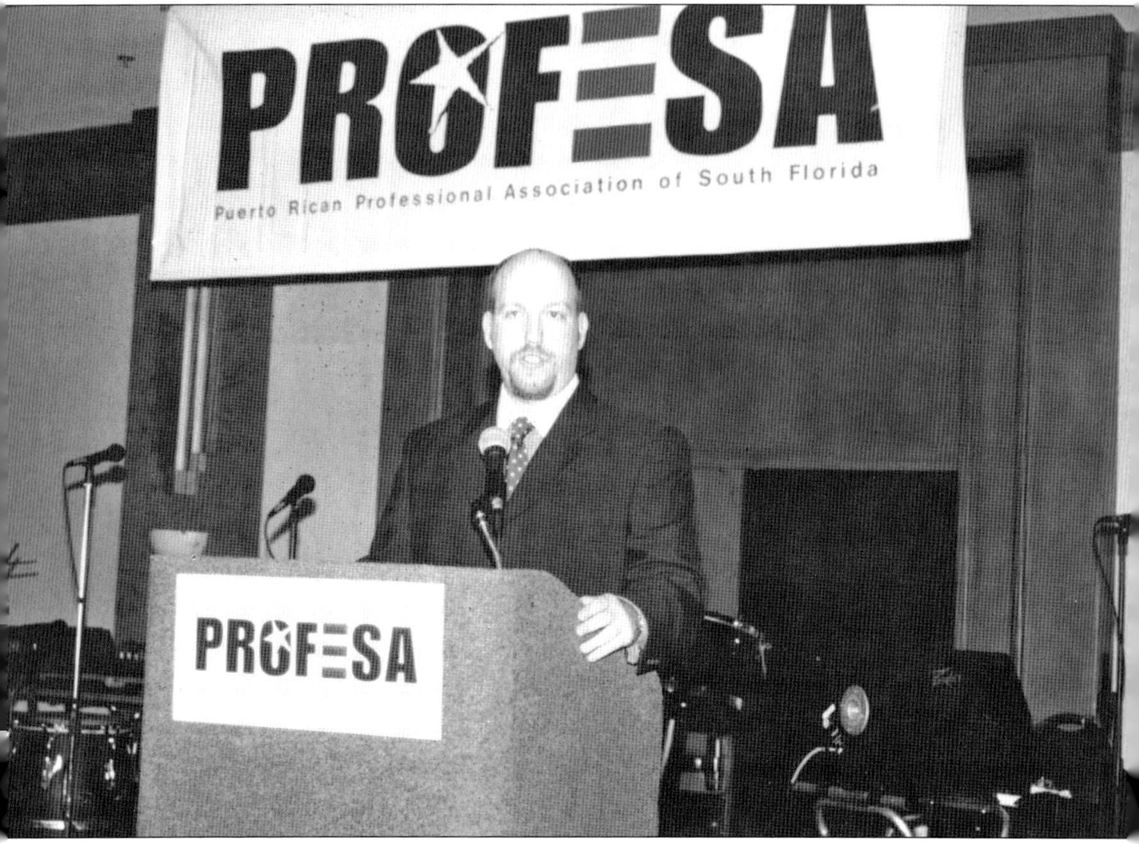

In April 1999, a group of Puerto Rican professionals came together to form the Puerto Rican Professional Association (PROFESA). They inaugurated the group at the Ricky Martin Casa Salsa Restaurant in South Beach. The platform of PROFESA was to unite Puerto Rican professionals around three main concepts: culture, network, and empowerment, along with service to the community. Pictured here is Raul Duany, the first president of the group. (Courtesy of Raul Duany.)

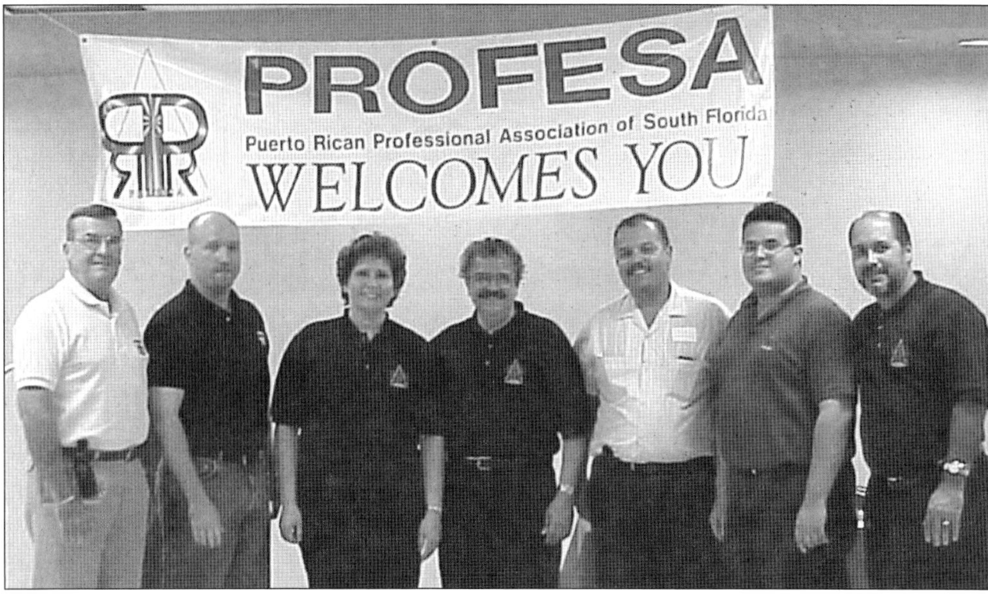

Pictured here is the first PROFESA board of directors in January 2000. From left to right are Luis Torres, Raul Duany, Agnes Rodriguez, Manny Mirabal, unidentified guest, Dr. Edwin Cordero (president of the National Puerto Rican Coalition), and Dr. Geraldo Rodriguez, chancellor of Carlos Albizu University, where the event was held. (Courtesy of Raul Duany.)

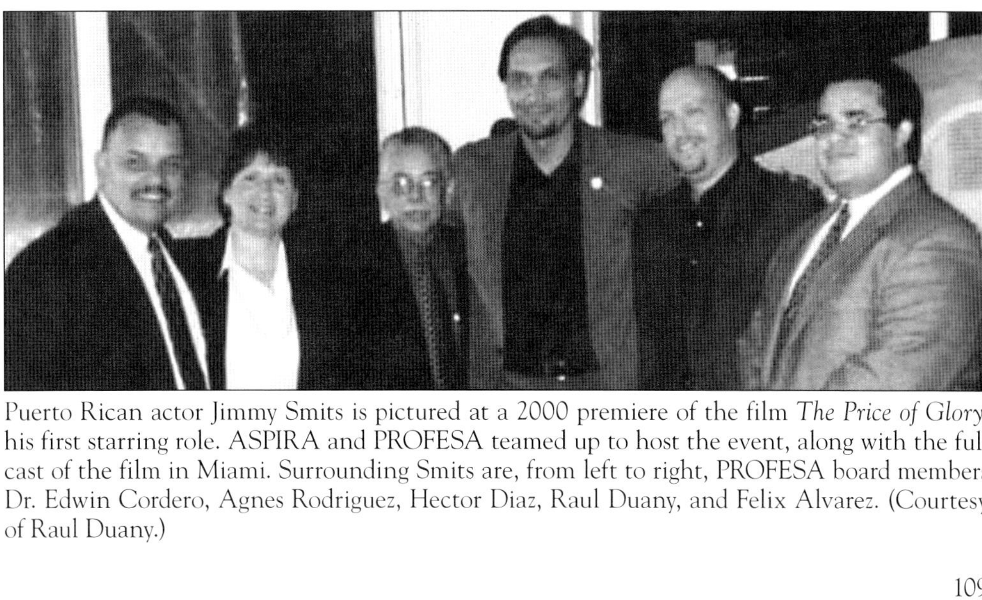

Puerto Rican actor Jimmy Smits is pictured at a 2000 premiere of the film *The Price of Glory*, his first starring role. ASPIRA and PROFESA teamed up to host the event, along with the full cast of the film in Miami. Surrounding Smits are, from left to right, PROFESA board members Dr. Edwin Cordero, Agnes Rodriguez, Hector Diaz, Raul Duany, and Felix Alvarez. (Courtesy of Raul Duany.)

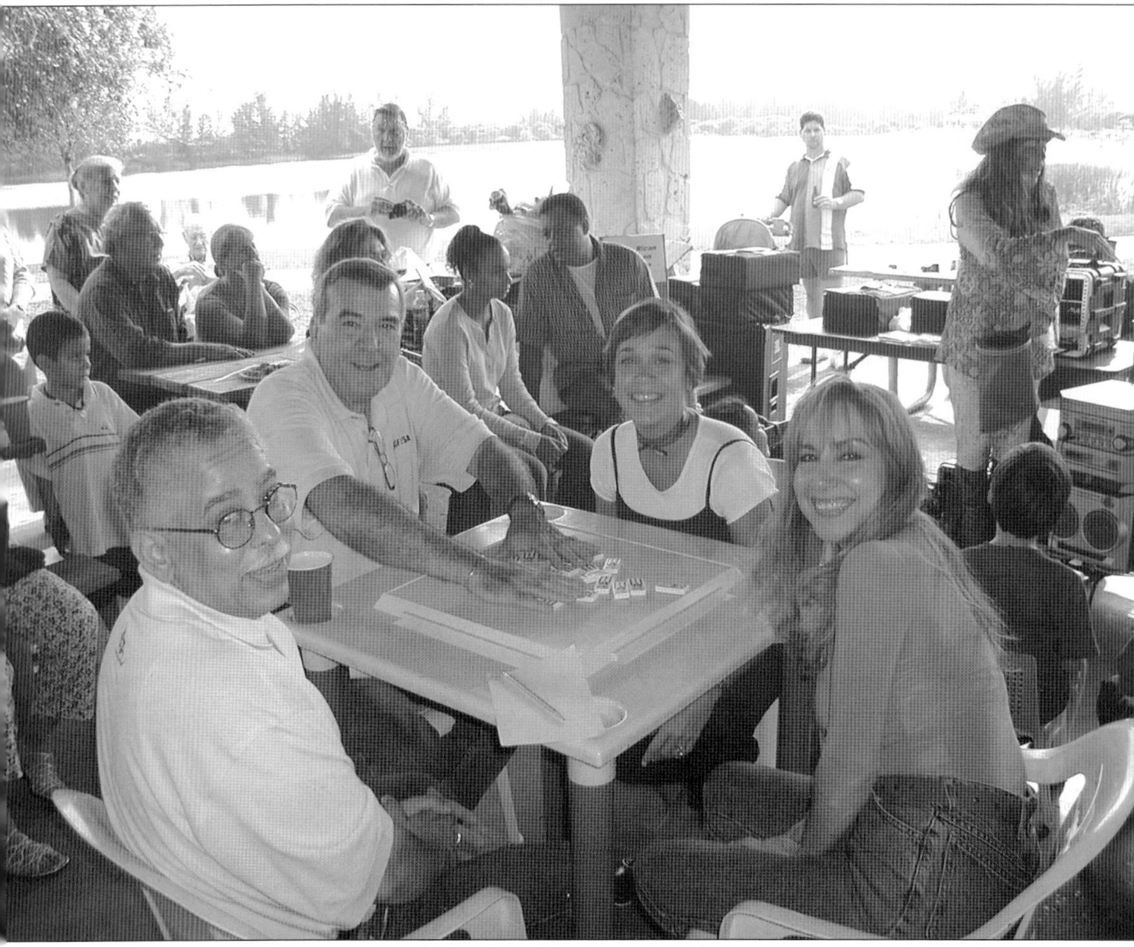

At PROFESA's Christmas family picnic in 2001 are, from left to right, founders Hector Diaz and Luis Torres, unidentified, and Sandra Rosa. The event was celebrated at Tropical Park in southwest Dade County and included a toy collection for needy children, to be distributed through the Open Door Medical Clinic in Homestead. (Courtesy of Raul Duany.)

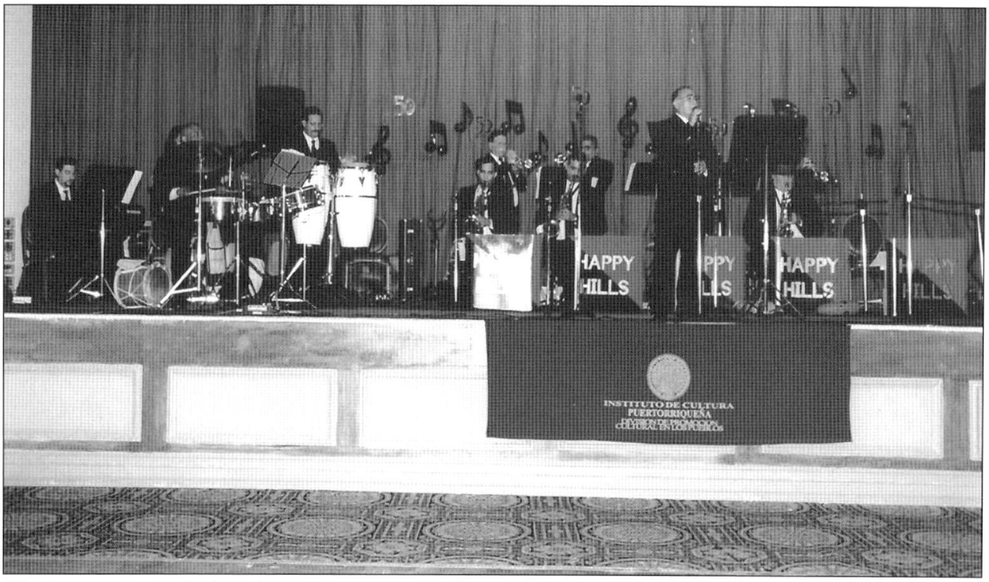

The Puerto Rico Cultural Center in South Florida held an event in 2002 to honor Puerto Rican high-fashion designer Carlota Alfaro. The event was held at the Diplomat Hotel and featured the Happy Hills Orchestra from San German, Puerto Rico. (Courtesy of Jose Luis Rodriguez.)

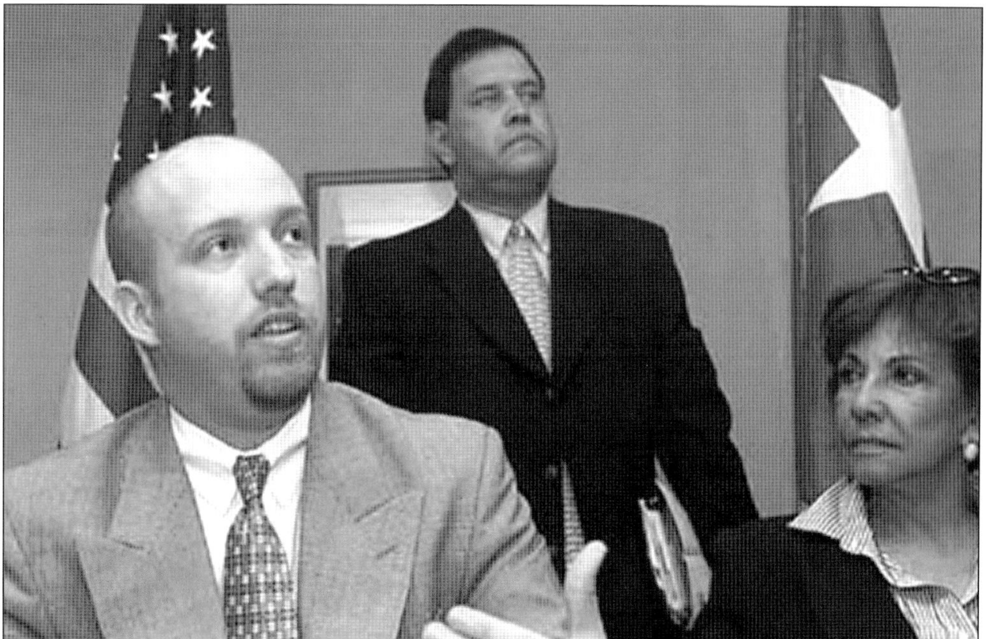

Pictured here is a press conference called by Puerto Rican leaders in Miami to reject the findings of a Center for Disease Control and Prevention (CDC) report that suggested Puerto Ricans are less healthy and spend more time at the doctors' than Mexicans, Cubans, and other Latino groups. The speakers pointed to inconsistencies in the data and claimed that the report was biased. The 2002 conference, held at the Office of the Government of Puerto Rico in Miami, was led by, from left to right, Raul Duany, PROFESA; Luis De Rosa, Puerto Rican Chamber of Commerce; and Gladys Colon, NACOPRW. (Courtesy of Raul Duany.)

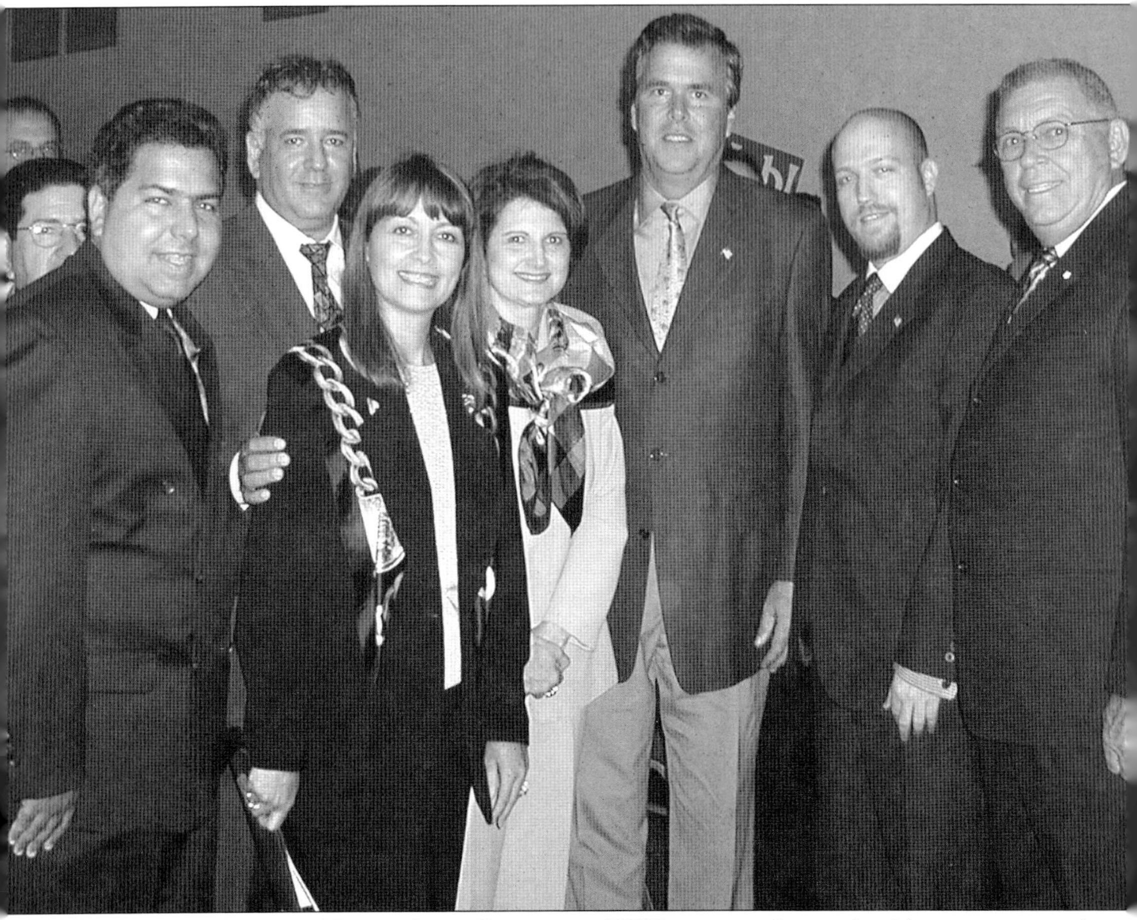

The Organization of Puerto Rican Democrats (ODP) sponsored several public events around Florida gubernatorial races in 2002. In this picture is Republican governor Jeb Bush, who was running for reelection. Even though the ODP was a Democratic group, members felt compelled to invite candidates from both major parties. They found it to be a good policy for Puerto Ricans to see both candidates up close. Among those pictured here are Judge Lilliana Torreh-Bayouth, Governor Bush, Raul Duany, and Conrado Lopez. (Courtesy of Raul Duany.)

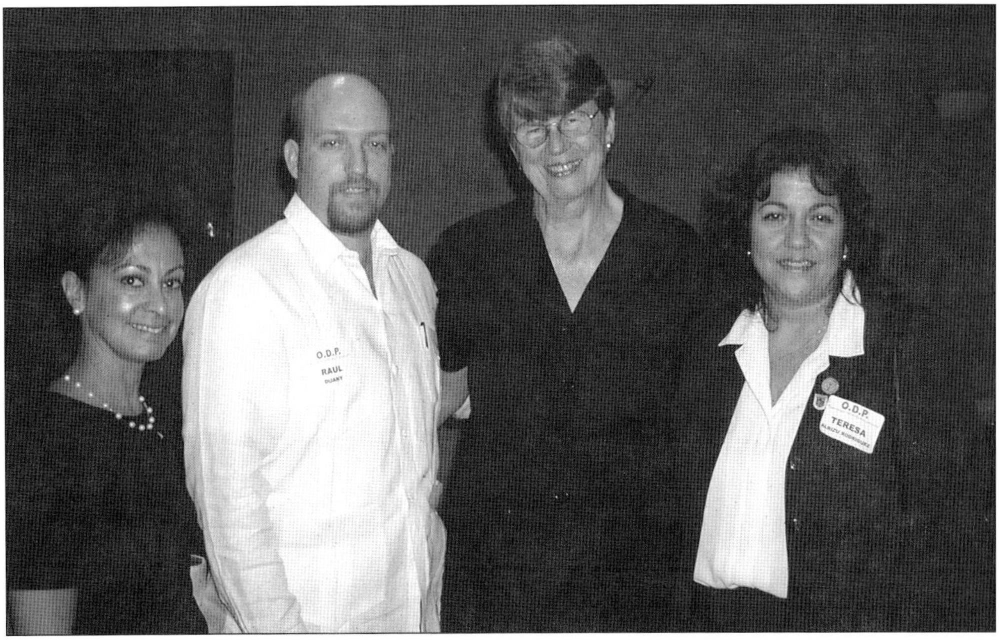

Former Clinton administration US attorney general and Miami native Janet Reno ran for governor of Florida in 2002. The ODP sponsored this forum with Reno before the Democratic primary. From left to right are unidentified, Raul Duany, Reno, and Dr. Teresa Albizu. Reno lost the primary to Bill McBride, who went on to lose to Jeb Bush. (Courtesy of Raul Duany.)

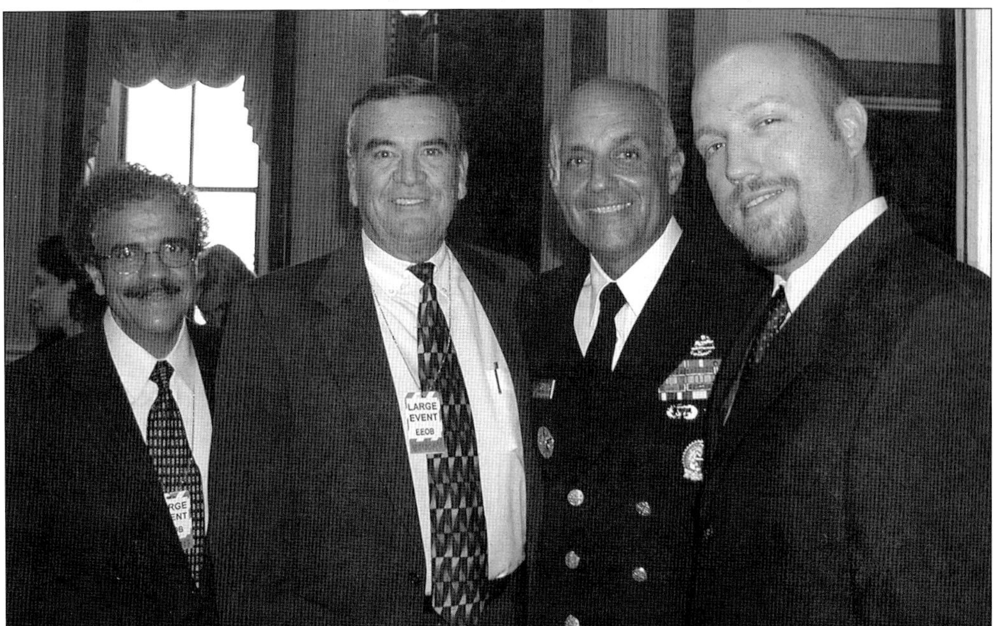

In 2002, Pres. George W. Bush nominated Dr. Richard Carmona to be the surgeon general of the United States. Carmona, born in New York to Puerto Rican parents, was approved by the US Senate. In this picture taken in Washington, DC, at his inauguration are, from left to right, Manny Mirabal, president, National Puerto Rican Coalition; Luis Torres, PROFESA; Dr. Carmona, and Raul Duany, PROFESA. (Courtesy of Raul Duany.)

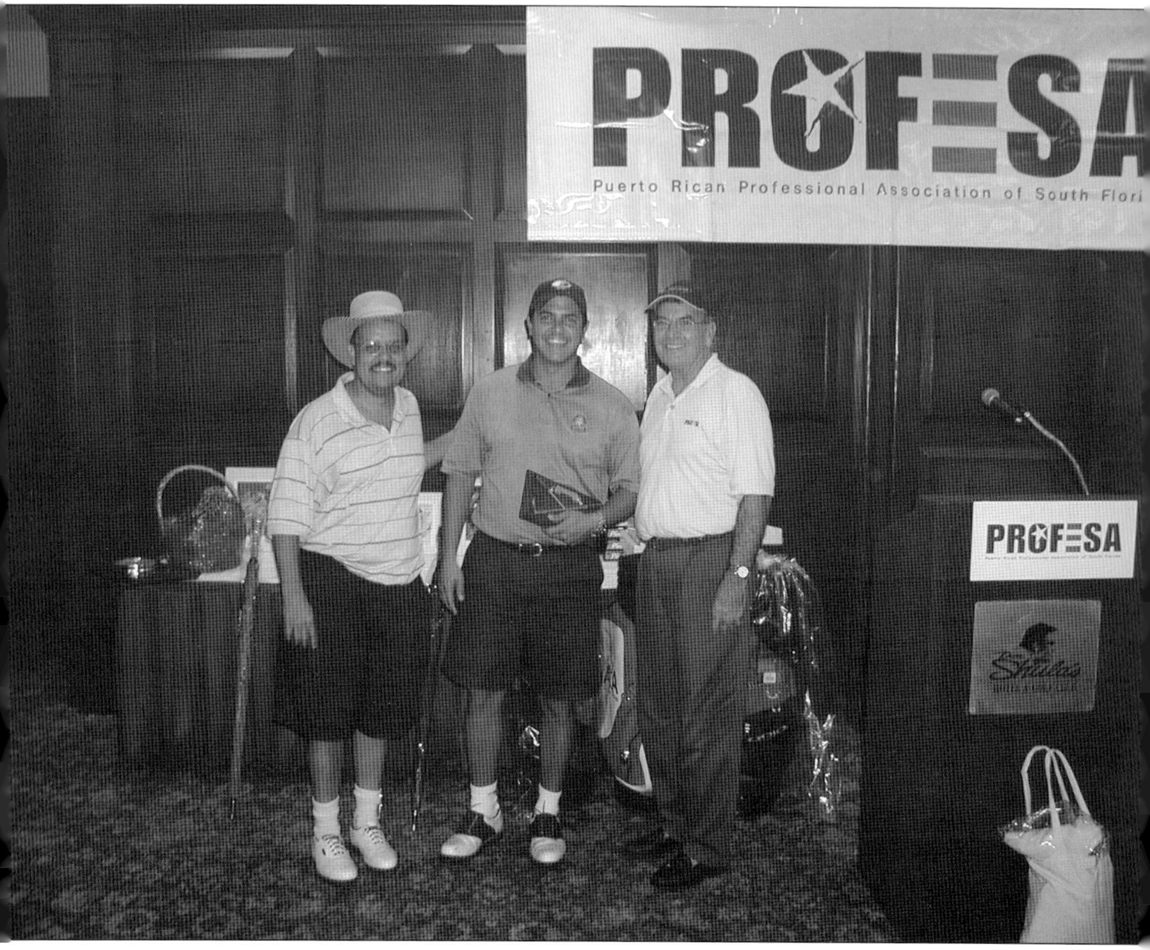

In 2002, PROFESA celebrated its second annual golf tournament at the Don Shula Hotel and Golf Club in Miami Lakes. It raised $7,000, and several entities received donations, including the Open Door Health Clinic in Homestead, which provides quality medical care for the poor. Pictured here are the two organizers of the event, Dr. Hector Cordero, board member of PROFESA (left), and Luis Torres, vice president of PROFESA (right), along with one of the players in the tournament. (Courtesy of Raul Duany.)

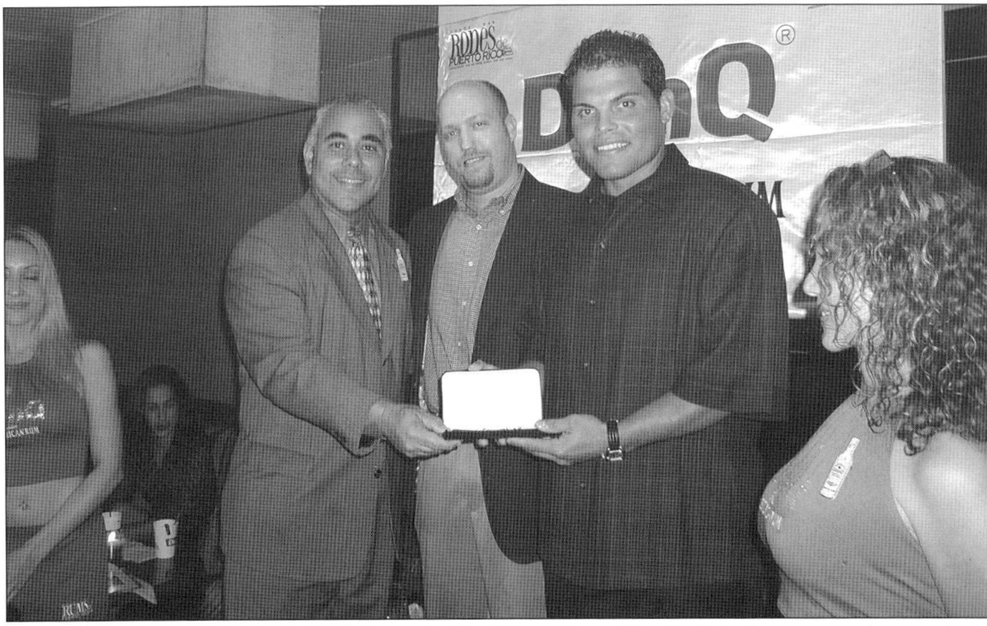

Puerto Rican all-star catcher and future hall of famer Ivan "Pudge" Rodriguez was honored at a community welcome event in 2003 when he signed a contract to play for the Florida Marlins. The event was hosted by PROFESA and held at the Rumi Lounge and Restaurant in South Beach. Pictured here with Rodriguez are Puerto Rican Miami–Dade County commissioner Jimmy Morales, who presented Rodriguez with the key to the county, along with Raul Duany, president of PROFESA. (Courtesy of Raul Duany.)

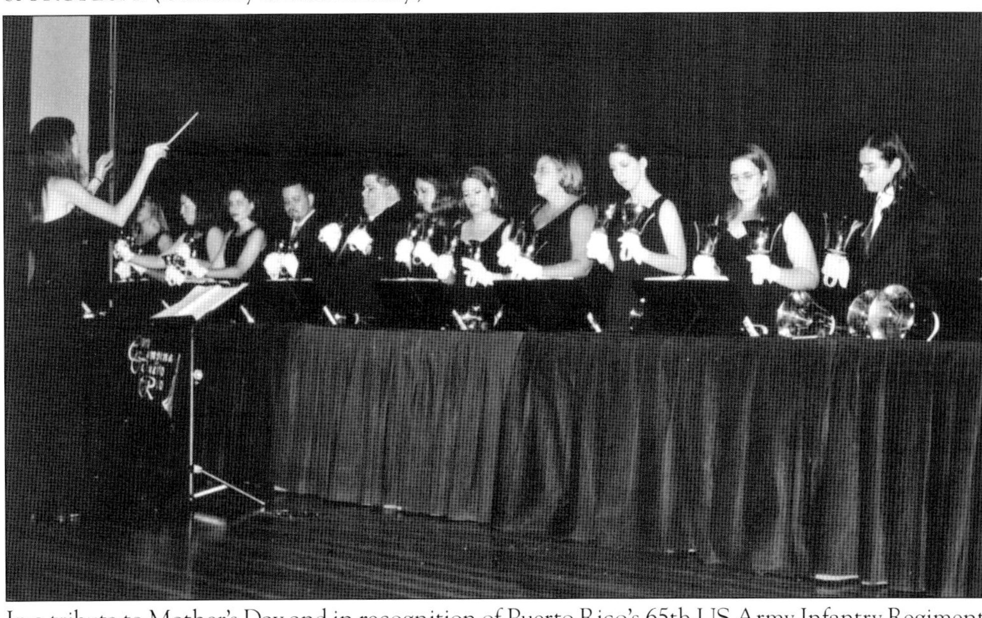

In a tribute to Mother's Day and in recognition of Puerto Rico's 65th US Army Infantry Regiment, PROFESA invited Puerto Rico's handbell choir to perform in 2003. The event was held at the Miami Hyatt Regency Arthur Ashe Auditorium. There was also a reception and art exhibition by distinguished Florida Puerto Rican artists Elizabeth Baez, Obed Gomez, Elias Lopez, Gerardo Oyola, Armando Rivera, and Marcos Serrano. (Courtesy of Raul Duany.)

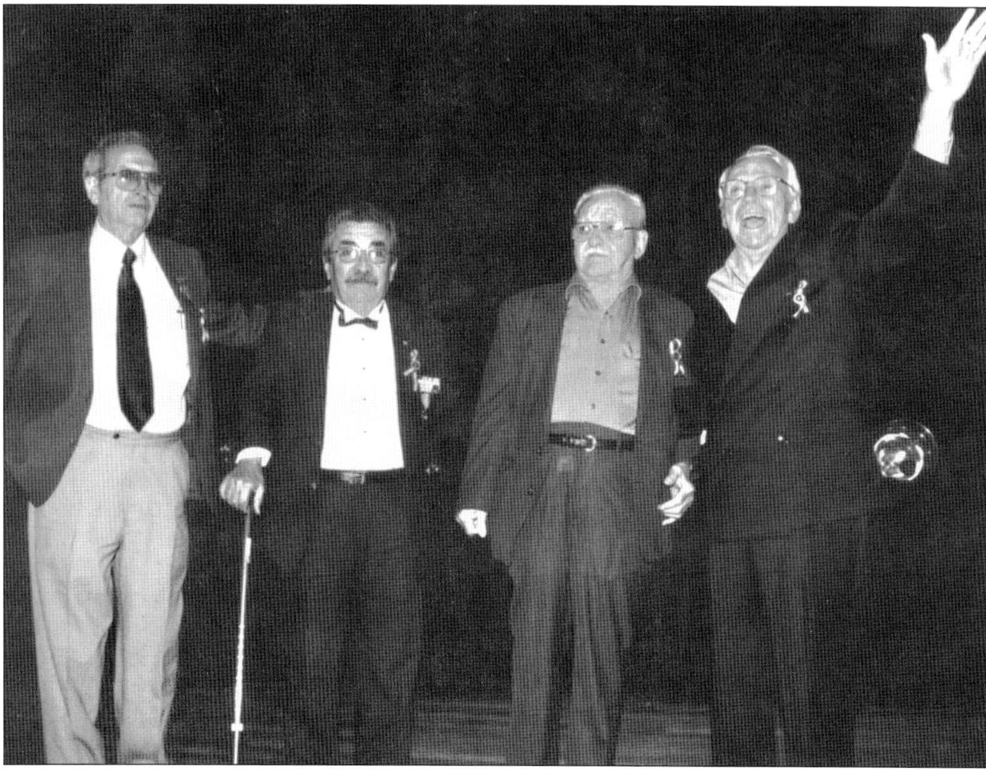

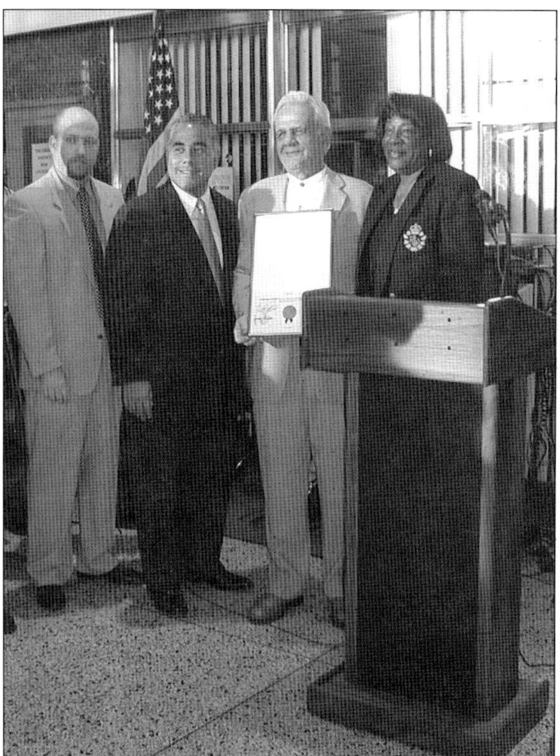

Pictured here are four veterans of the 65th Infantry Regiment, the only Puerto Rican segregated unit, receiving a standing ovation at a musical concert in 2003. The event raised funds for the documentary *The Puerto Rican Soldier* (a work in progress) by producers Noemi Figueroa Soulet and Raquel Ortiz, which documents the harrowing experiences of the 65th during the Korean War. (Courtesy of Raul Duany.)

In 2003, PROFESA held one of its signature networking events in the lobby of the *Miami Herald* building. The events provide an opportunity for Puerto Rican professionals to meet others and make connections. In this event, PROFESA honored Puerto Rican legend Emilio Lopez for his more than 30 years of community service to Wynwood. From left to right are Raul Duany, PROFESA; county commissioner Jimmy Morales, Lopez, and county commissioner Barbara Carey Schuler. (Courtesy of Raul Duany.)

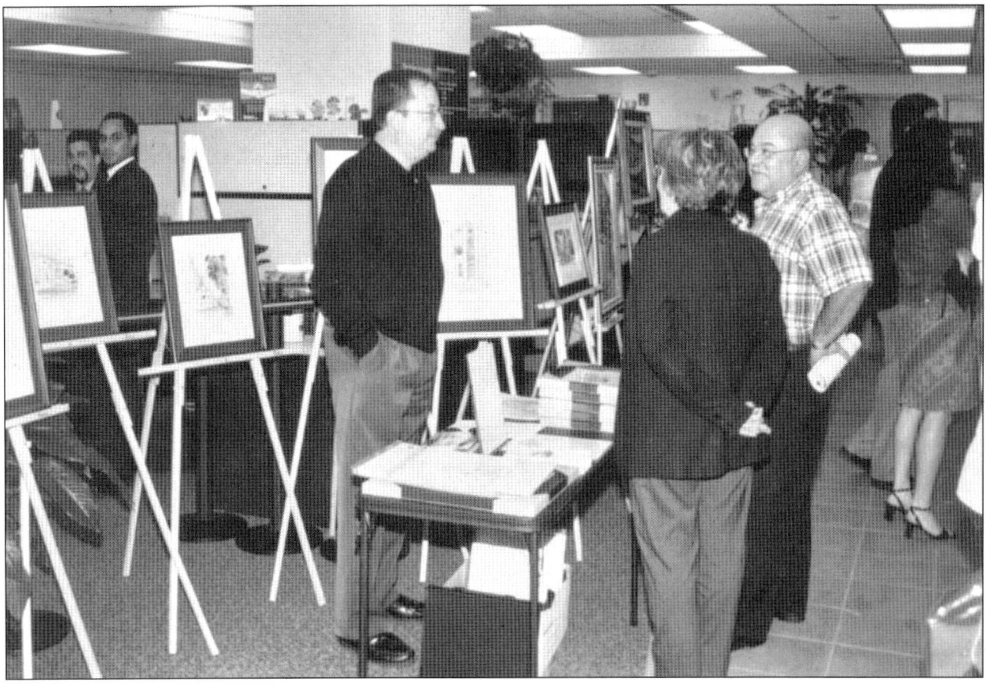

As part of the work of PROFESA to promote and enhance Puerto Rican culture, during the event at the *Miami Herald* building where Emilio Lopez was honored, artists were invited to promote and sell paintings and other artwork. Pictured here is one of several artists who attended the event. (Courtesy of Raul Duany.)

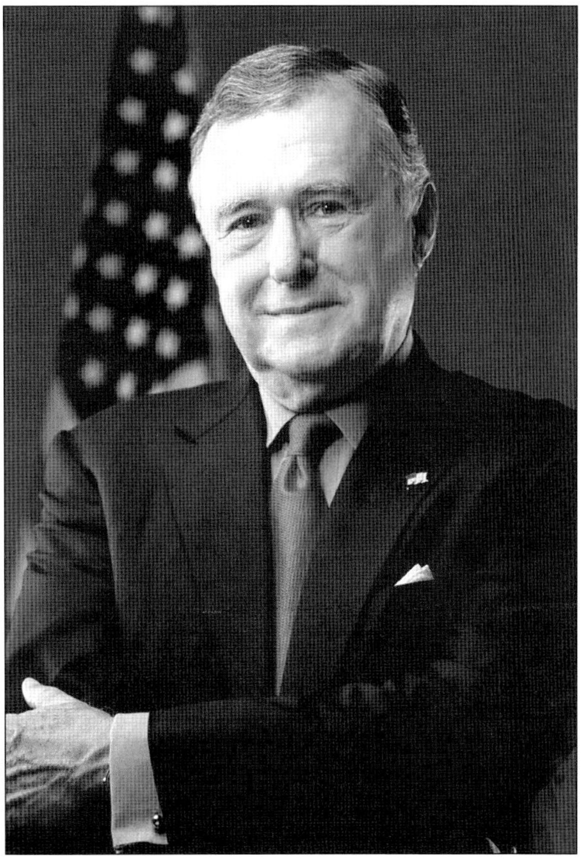

In 2010, Maurice Ferre ran for the US Senate in the Democratic primary, his last political campaign. He ran for the open US Senate seat from Florida, which became vacant when Republican senator Mel Martinez decided not to run again. Ferre lost in the primary. (Courtesy of Meme Ferre.)

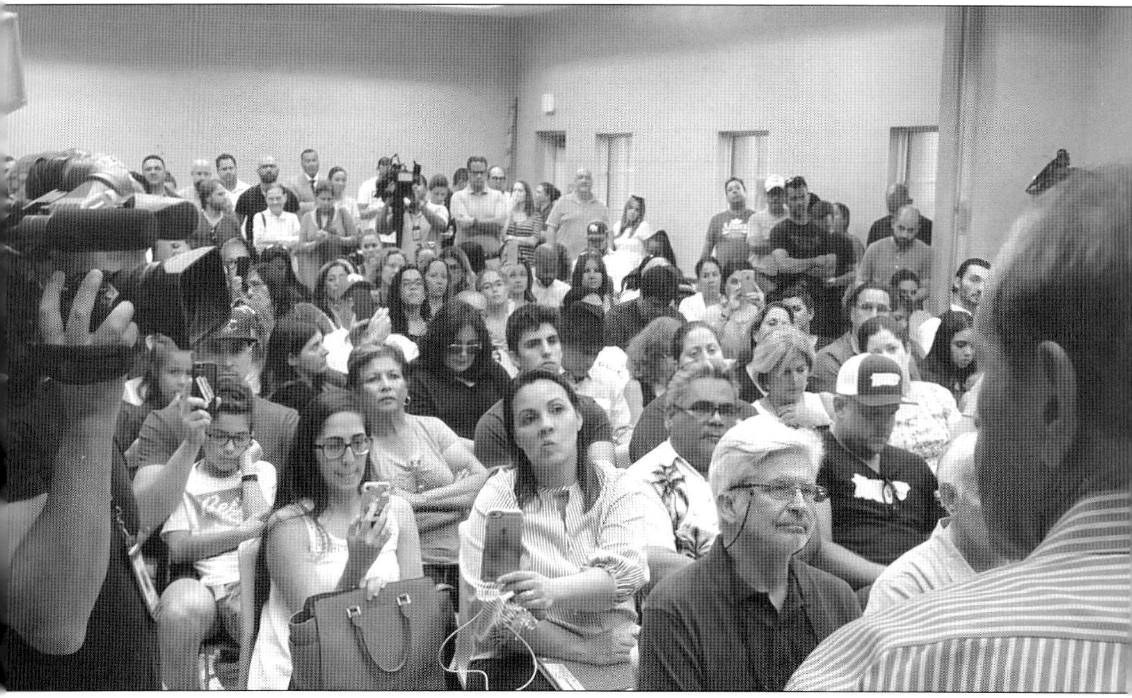

On September 20, 2017, a massive category 4 storm hit Puerto Rico, leaving the island without electricity and many missing or dead. A community meeting was called a few days later at the Dorothy Quintana Center in Wynwood to discuss and coordinate relief for the island. Several centers for the collection of needed materials were established throughout the county. Sitting in front with white hair and glasses is Dr. Hector Collazo, leader of the organization Puerto Ricans Organized Overseas in Florida (PROOF). (Courtesy of Natascha Otero Santiago.)

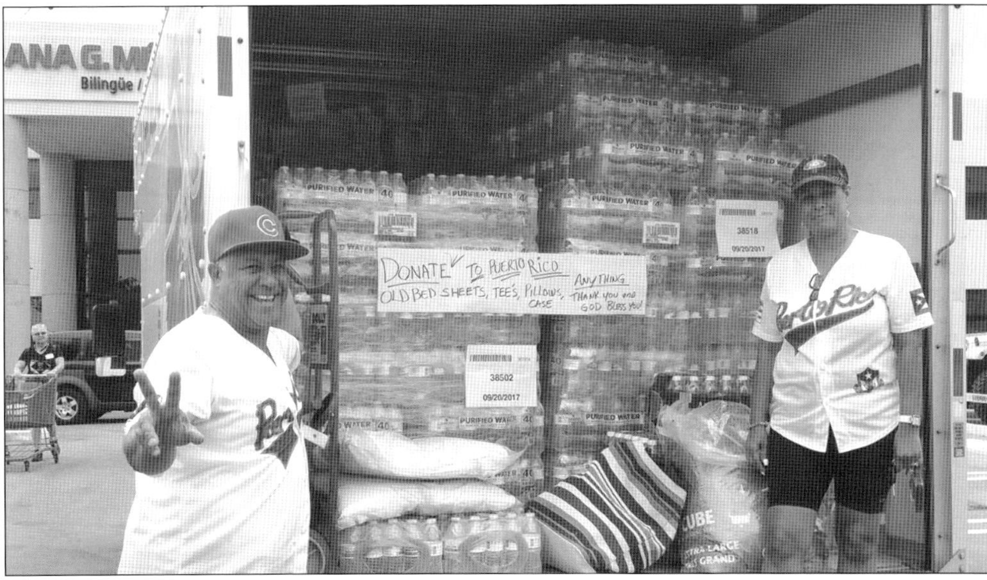

Post-hurricane relief efforts for Puerto Rico were mobilized across Miami by the community. Here, two volunteers fill truckloads of food and water on the campus of Ana G. Mendez University in Miami Lakes, one of several collection centers in Miami. (Courtesy of Natascha Otero Santiago.)

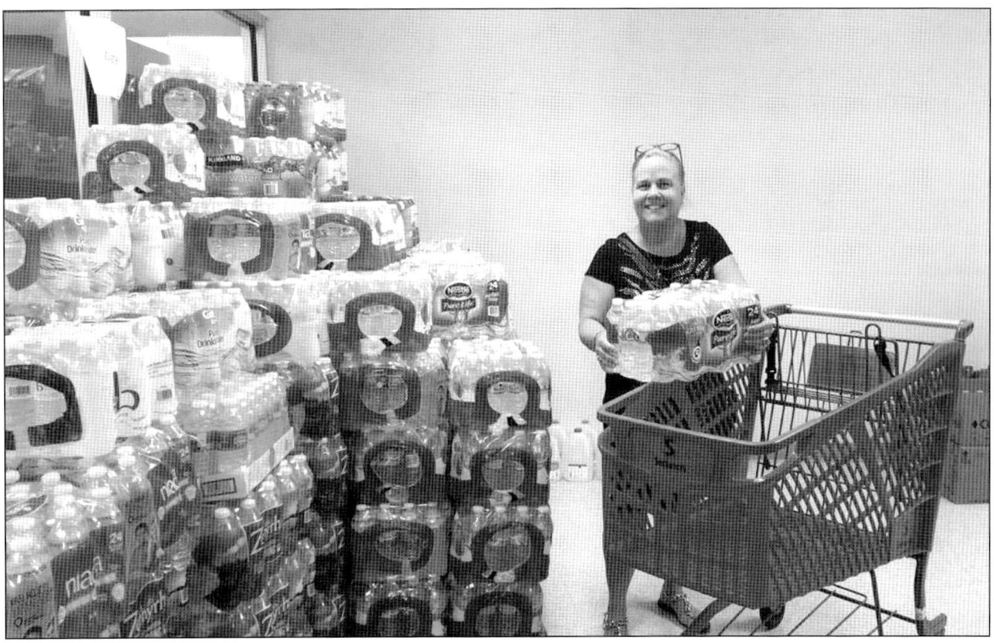

Through the massive efforts of volunteers, more than two million pounds of food, water, and medical supplies were collected in the Miami area. Another collection point was established by Puerto Rican restaurant owner Rafael Acosta in front of his business, where more than 10,000 pounds of supplies were collected by volunteers like Carlos Gill, Daly Linares, and Adriana Vargas Hernandez, the Boricuas Realengos, and PROFESA. (Courtesy of Natascha Otero Santiago.)

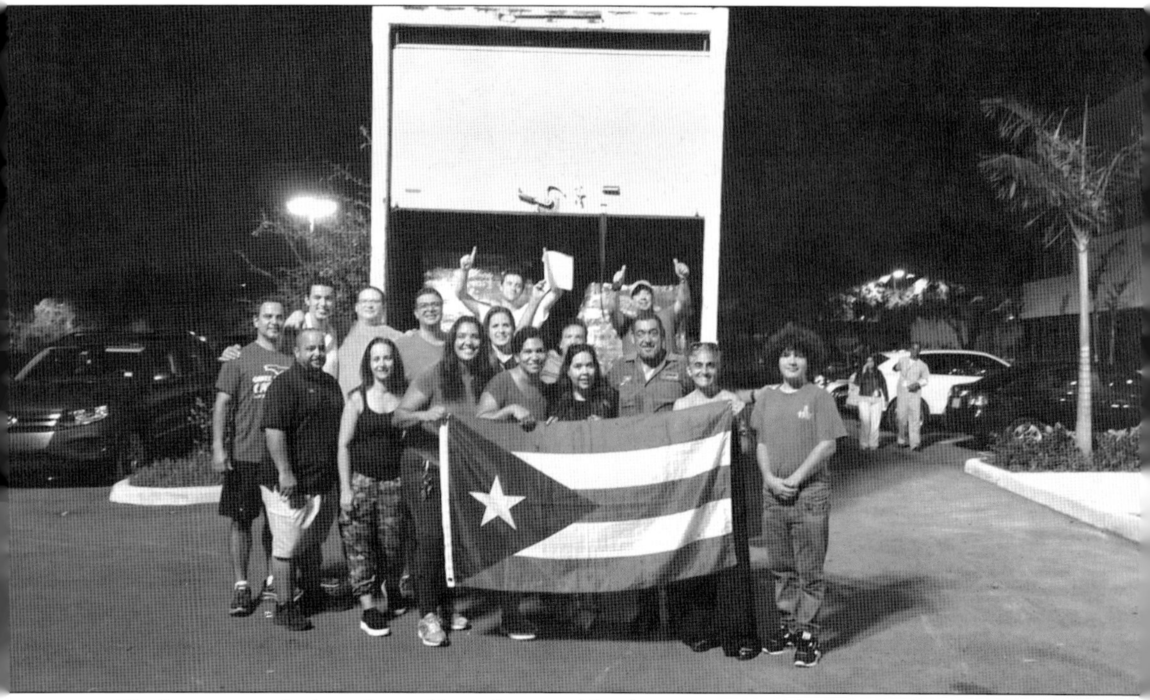

The hurricane relief supplies collected at sites like the one pictured here were then transported to a massive packing center in Wynwood, Mana Enterprises. This was the staging ground for sending the material to Puerto Rico. Robert Asencio, the only Puerto Rican serving in the Florida House of Representatives from Miami at the time, played a major role in getting all the collected material to the island and distributed. In the end, it is estimated that $10 million worth of supplies were collected in Miami. (Courtesy of Natascha Otero Santiago.)

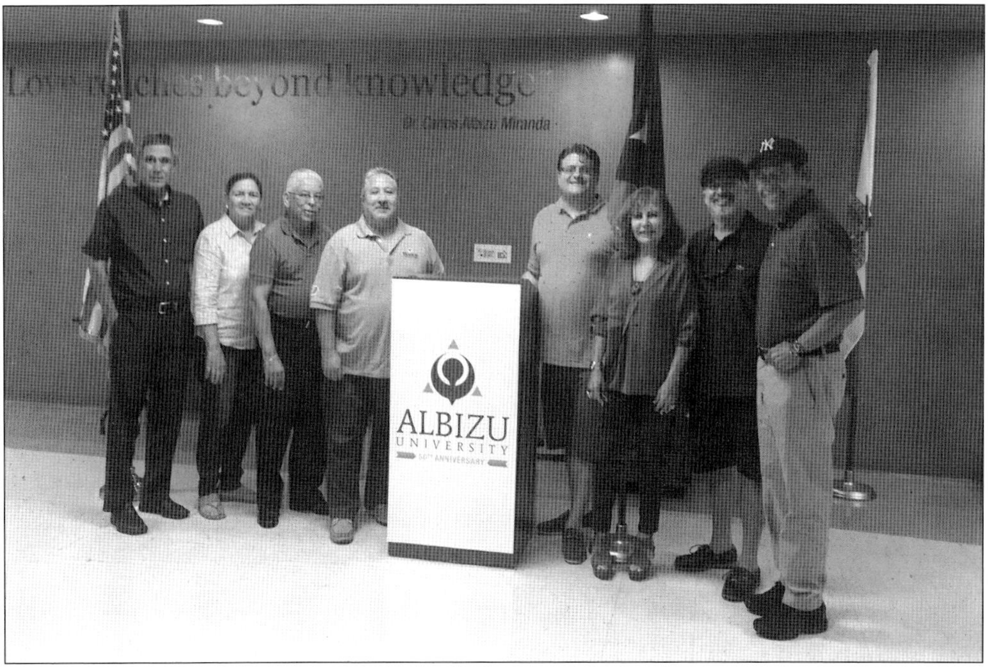

The Puerto Rican Leadership Council of South Florida (PRLCSF) is a coalition of Puerto Rican groups. At the end of its 2016 meeting, the newly elected executive board posed for this photograph. From left to right are Victor L. Ortiz, president of the Puerto Rico Cultural Center of South Florida, elected treasurer; his wife, Susana; Hector Diaz, president, PROFESA, elected vice president; Dr. Victor Vazquez, elected president; Nicholas G. Rossoletti, Puerto Rican Bar; Dr. Nydia Cabrera, president, NACOPRW, elected secretary; Dr. Hector Collazo, PROOF; and Luis DeRosa, president, Puerto Rican Chamber of Commerce. (Author photograph.)

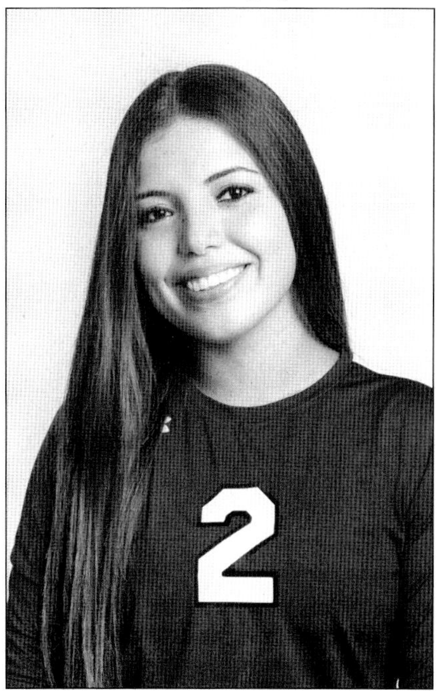

Valeria Santos was one of the thousands of Puerto Ricans who fled the island after Hurricane Maria in 2017. She had just begun her second year at the University of Puerto Rico, Mayagüez Campus, on the west coast of the island, where she attended on a volleyball scholarship. She accepted a scholarship to play for Miami Dade College. She currently plays for the Florida International University volleyball team. (Courtesy of Miami Dade College.)

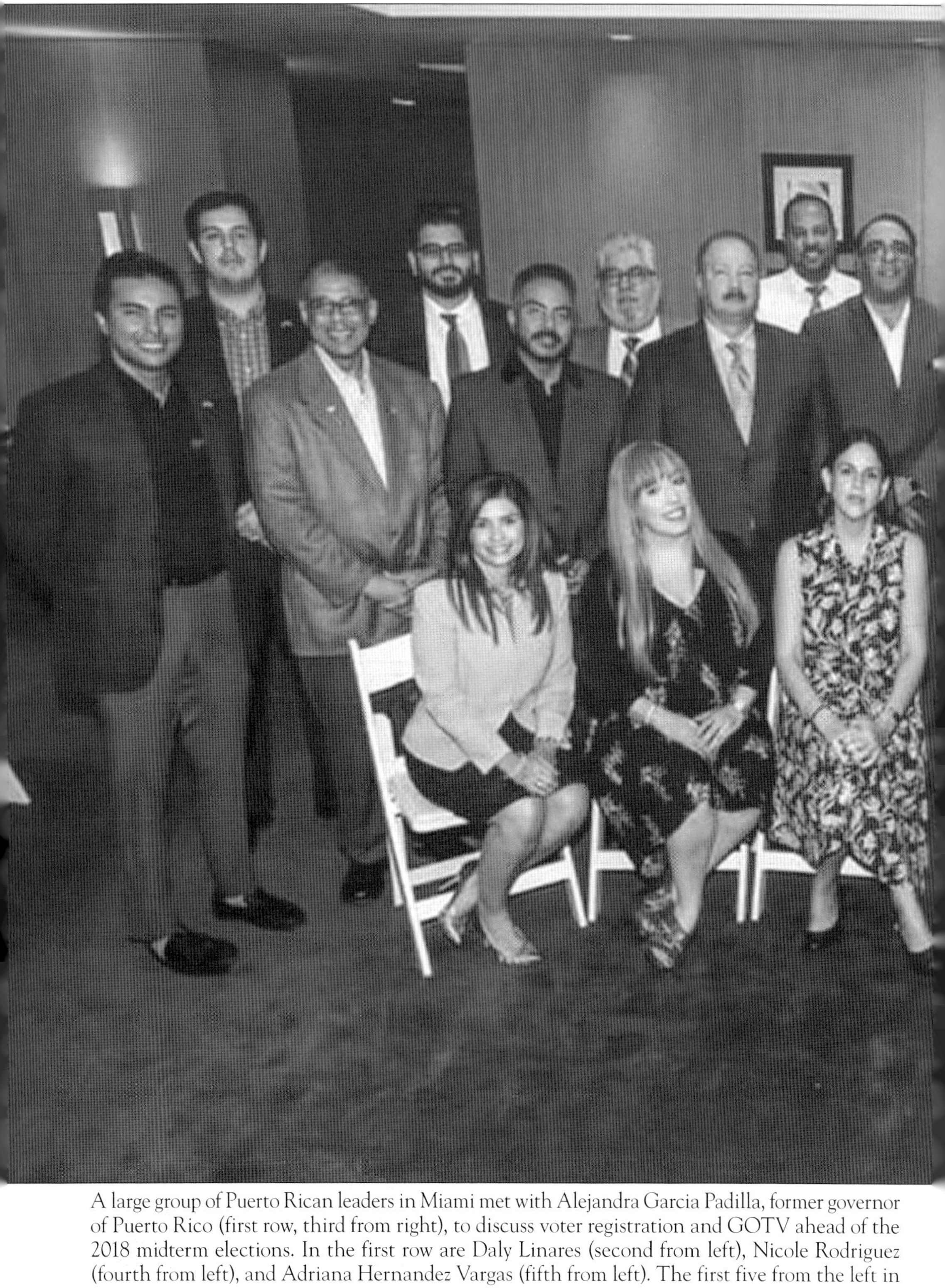

A large group of Puerto Rican leaders in Miami met with Alejandra Garcia Padilla, former governor of Puerto Rico (first row, third from right), to discuss voter registration and GOTV ahead of the 2018 midterm elections. In the first row are Daly Linares (second from left), Nicole Rodriguez (fourth from left), and Adriana Hernandez Vargas (fifth from left). The first five from the left in

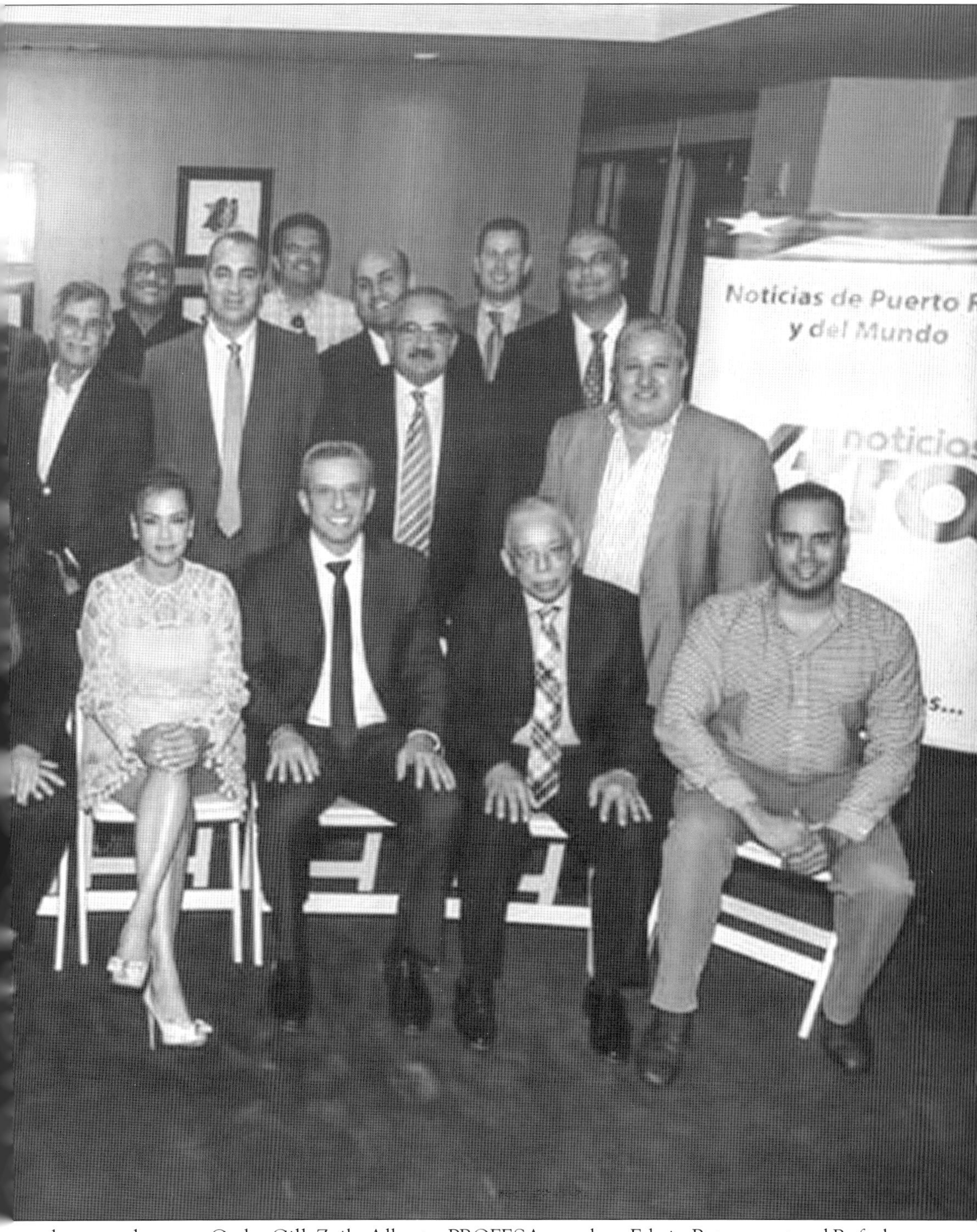

the second row are Carlos Gill, Zoilo Alberto, PROFESA members Edwin Betancourt and Rafael Gonzalez, and Dr. Thomas Agrait. The meeting was organized by Jose Julio Aparicio (third row, second from right). (Author photograph.)

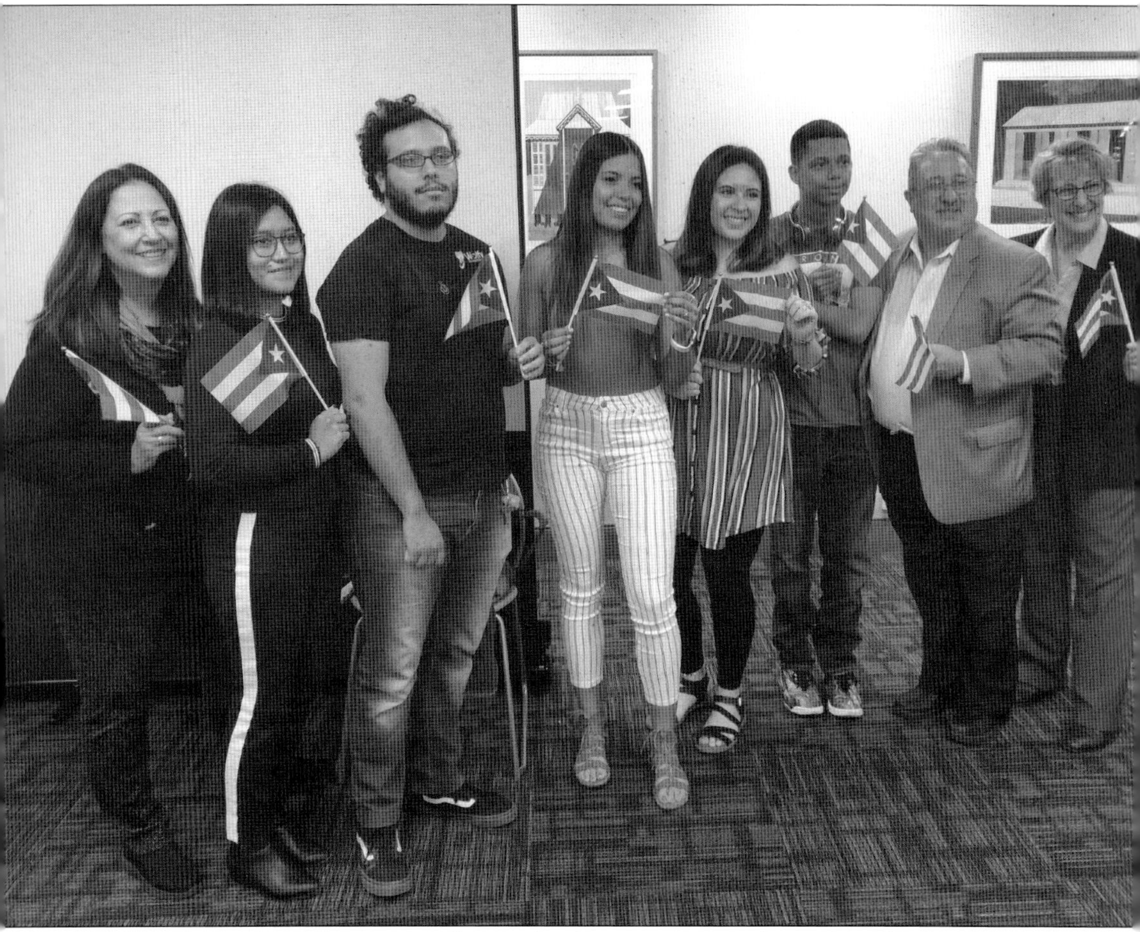

After Hurricane Maria in 2017, thousands of Puerto Ricans relocated to Florida. Among them were some 200 students who came to Miami Dade College. Several of them participated in a documentary project about their experiences after the storm. From left to right are Professor Magdalena Lamarre, filmmakers Merlina Ramirez and Daniel Ponce, Valeria Santos, Christina Perez, Esteban Soler, and Professors Victor Vazquez and Susan Lichtman. (Author photograph.)

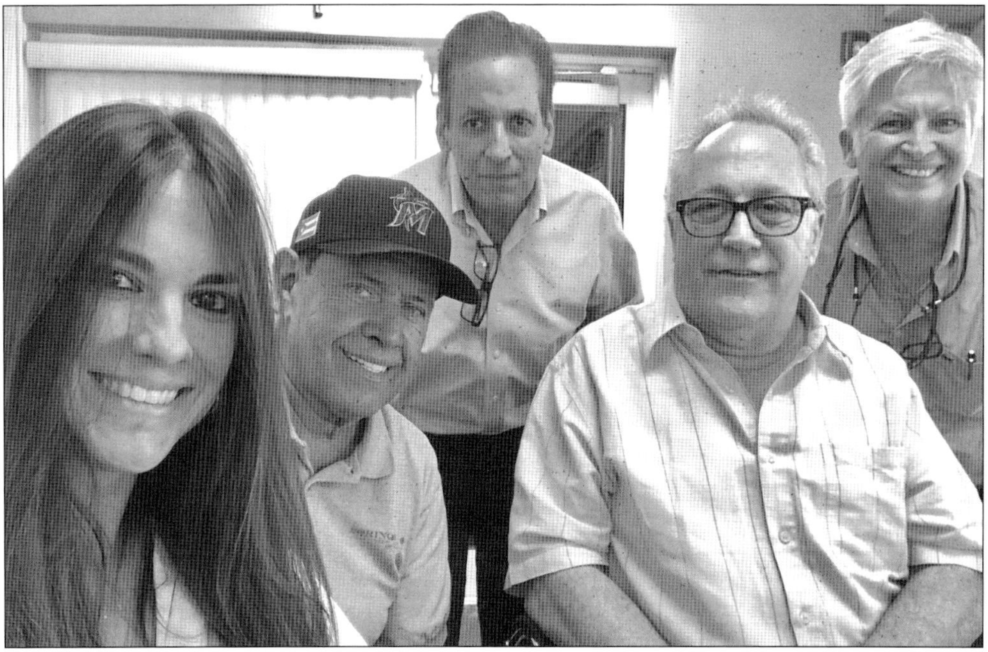

Pictured here are members of the Puerto Rican Leadership Council Luis De Rosa (baseball cap); Paul Velez, CEO of Borinquen Health (wearing glasses); and Dr. Hector Collazo, PROOF (far right) meeting with Elizabeth Rodriguez and an unidentified man to form the Puerto Rican Health Professionals Association. (Courtesy of Luis De Rosa.)

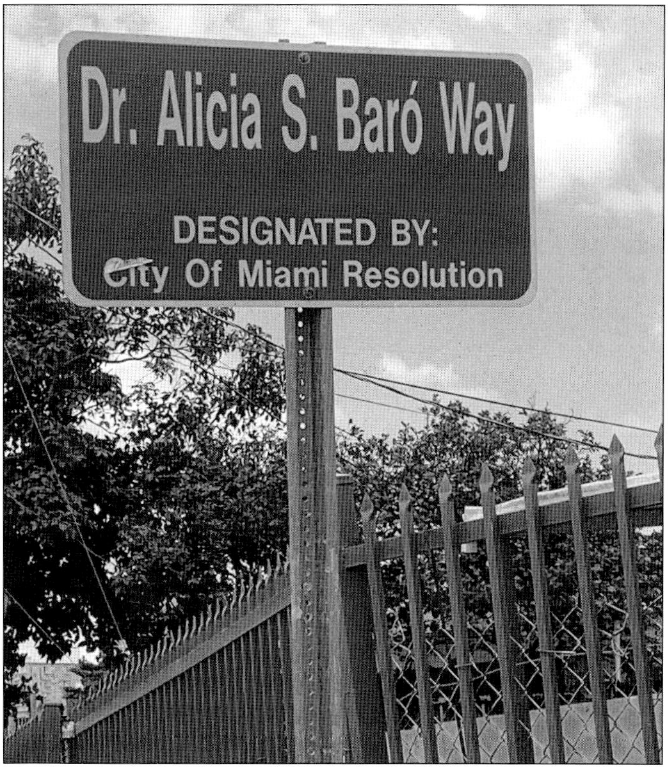

Dr. Alicia S. Baro Way was designated by the City of Miami in 2013 to recognize the amazing accomplishments of the Puerto Rican leader, including her more than 50 years of service empowering women and civil rights. She fought for better education and equality. The stretch of NW Thirty-Fourth Street runs between NW Second and North Miami Avenues. (Courtesy Luz Sofia Vazquez-Hernandez.)

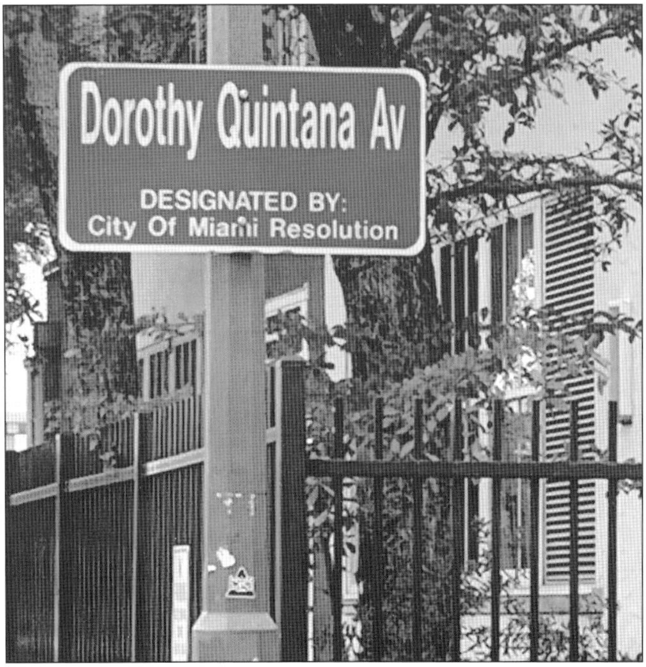

In 2011, Miami–Dade County and the City Commission of Miami renamed NW Second Avenue between NW Thirty-Sixth Street and NW Thirtieth Street in Wynwood as Dorothy Quintana Avenue. This was done recognizing her community work on behalf of not only Puerto Ricans, but Cuban and Haitian refugees as well. For more than 50 years, Quintana was a fixture in her community. (Courtesy Luz Sofia Vazquez-Hernandez.)

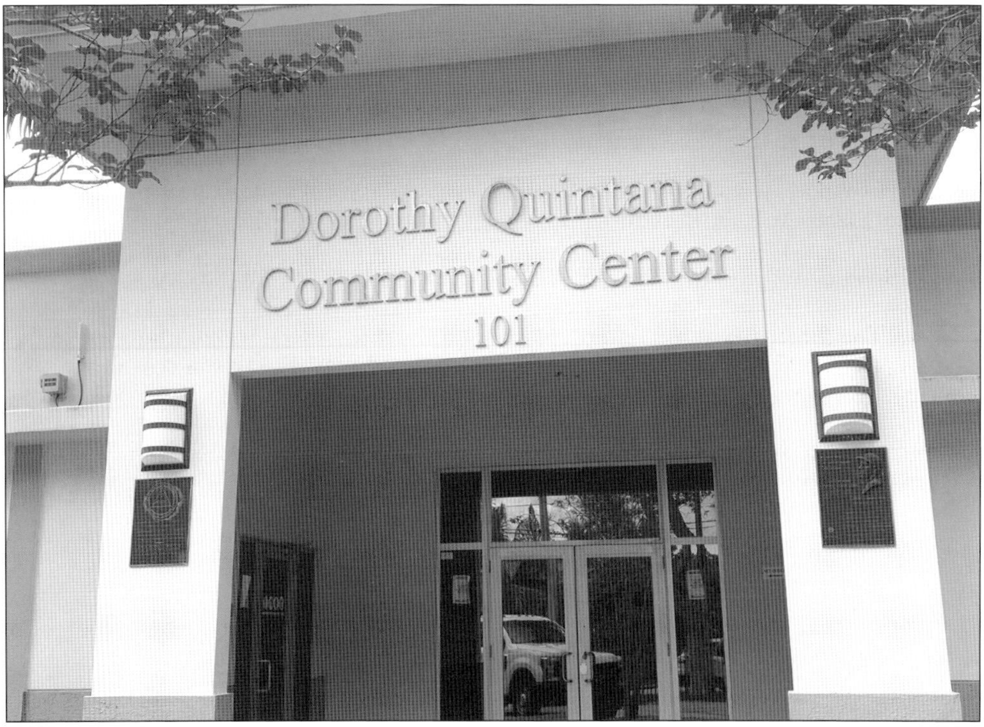

In 2011, Dorothy "Dottie" Quintana passed away at 101 years old. Even at that age, she could still be found at the Miami Commission meetings advocating for her Wynwood community. For 60 years, Quintana had been a devoted community leader and fighter. She was, until her death, an adamant block watcher. When the City of Miami refurbished the Community Center in the Roberto Clemente Sports Complex at a cost of $2 million, it was named after her. (Author photograph.)

Bibliography

Aranda, Elizabeth M. *Emotional Bridges to Puerto Rico: Migration, Return Migration, and the Struggles of Incorporation*. New York, NY: Rowman and Littlefield Publishers, 2007.

Cabrera Perez, Nydia M. "In their Own Voices: Evolution, Identity, and Contributions of the Puerto Rican Community to Miami-Dade, Florida, 1940–2010." PhD Dissertation. Centro de Estudios Avanzado de Puerto Rico y el Caribe, August 2011.

Feldman, Marcus. "The Role of Neighborhood Organizations in the Production of Gentrifiable Urban Space: The Case of Wynwood, Miami's Puerto Rican Barrio." PhD Dissertation. Florida International University, November 2011.

Silver, Patricia. *Sunbelt Diaspora: Race, Class, and Latino Politics in Puerto Rican Orlando*. Austin, TX: University of Texas Press, 2020.

Vazquez-Hernandez, Victor. "Puerto Ricans in Greater Miami, 1920–1960." *Tequesta: The Journal of HistoryMiami Museum* LXXIX (79), 2019: 126–152.

———. *Before the Wave: Puerto Ricans in Philadelphia, 1910–1945*. New York, NY: Centro Press, 2017.

———. "The Boricua Triangle: Tampa, Miami and Orlando—A Historical Overview of the Development of a Transnational Puerto Rican Diaspora in Florida." Florida Council of Historians *Annals: The Journal of the Florida Conference of Historians* Volume 22, June 2015: 155-170.

Whalen, Carmen Teresa and Victor Vazquez-Hernandez, editors. *The Puerto Rican Diaspora: Historical Persives*. Philadelphia, PA: Temple University Press, 2005.